PATENT PORTFOLIO DEPLOYMENT

Bridging the R&D, Patent and Product Markets

PATENT PORTFOLIO DEPLOYMENT

Bridging the R&D, Patent and Product Markets

LIU Shang-Jyh
FONG Hoi Yan Anna
LAN Yuhong Tony

World Scientific

EW JERSEY · LONDON · SINGAPORE · BEIJING · SHANGHAI · HONG KONG · TAIPEI · CHENNAI · TOKYO

Published by

World Scientific Publishing Co. Pte. Ltd.

5 Toh Tuck Link, Singapore 596224

USA office: 27 Warren Street, Suite 401-402, Hackensack, NJ 07601

UK office: 57 Shelton Street, Covent Garden, London WC2H 9HE

Library of Congress Cataloging-in-Publication Data

Names: Liu, Shang-Jyh, author. | Fong, Hoi Yan Anna, author. | Lan, Yuhong Tony, author.
Title: Patent portfolio deployment : bridging the R&D, patent and product markets /
Shang-Jyh Liu, Hoi Yan Anna Fong, Yuhong Tony Lan.
Description: [Hackensack?] New Jersey : World Scientific, [2017] |
Includes bibliographical references.
Identifiers: LCCN 2016026157 | ISBN 9789813142435 (hc : alk. paper)
Subjects: LCSH: Patents. | Patent laws and legislation.
Classification: LCC T211 .L58 2017 | DDC 608--dc23
LC record available at https://lccn.loc.gov/2016026157

British Library Cataloguing-in-Publication Data

A catalogue record for this book is available from the British Library.

Desk Editors: Dipasri Sardar/Dong Lixi

Typeset by Stallion Press
Email: enquiries@stallionpress.com

Printed in Singapore

Contents

About the Authors

LIU Shang-Jyh

LIU Shang-Jyh is a Professor of Law and Technology Management at National Chiao Tung University (NCTU), Taiwan. He has a Ph.D. in engineering (Texas A&M University) and a degree in law (National Taiwan University). This interdisciplinary background integrating technology, business and law strategically shaped his teaching, research and practice.

At NCTU, he is the Dean of the Law School, the Founding Chairperson of the Graduate Institute of Technology Law, as well as a former Dean of International Affairs of NCTU. In particular, he is a pioneer and a leader in Intellectual Property (IP) education and service. He has successfully established a new paradigm of legal education and empirical research in Taiwan. Ever since 1994, he has trained more than 7000 IP professionals in Taiwan and who in turn contributed to the competitiveness of Taiwan's industry. Internationally, he has lectured at the National University of Singapore, Tulane University (Asia Global MBA), Beijing University, Nanyang Technological University, the Hong Kong Polytechnic University, etc.

Professor Liu is active in both academia and industry. He is an international arbitrator and an advisor to many high-tech companies and public agencies. Professor Liu published widely in renowned international journals such as IEEE Transactions on Engineering Management & International Journal of Technology Management. He also authored a chapter in APEC's "Strategic Intellectual Asset Management for Emerging Enterprises" and a chapter in WIPO's "Leveraging Intellectual Property as a Strategic Business Asset: Making IP Assets the Core of Strategic Business Management". Furthermore, he serves as the Chief Editor of Technology Law Review.

FONG Hoi Yan Anna

Anna Fong has years of working experience in a few multinational companies. She has worked in various positions from R&D, design to testing. Anna graduated with a Bachelor and Master in Electrical and Computer Engineering. Her work as an engineer was focused in the Microwave Communications Technology, in particular Surface Acoustic Wave (SAW) components designs. She has published in scientific papers in SAW filter designs and is a named inventor in a US granted patent.

Anna has been working in the field of Patent Management since she graduated from her Ph.D. in IP Management & Strategy. She has a keen interest in Technology Planning to IP monetization. With her experience in Telecommunications industry, she has a thorough understanding of patent landscape analysis and patent licensing and litigation management in such fields and has been involved in various consulting projects on patent analysis and deployment.

LAN Yuhong Tony

Tony was educated in National University of Singapore on a scholarship of Singapore government, and graduated with a First-Class Honors degree in Biomedical Sciences. He later obtained a Graduate Certificate in Intellectual Property Law (GCIP) with Merit from NUS Law School and Singapore IP Academy, a Master in Intellectual Property Management and a Ph.D. in Technology Intelligence and IP strategy.

Tony is a qualified patent agent in China and has years of experiences working in Intellectual Property law firm, specializing in patent drafting, prosecution, and exploitation. He has also worked on various consulting projects in relation to patent analysis and deployment strategies covering various technical areas such as wind turbine, LED, stem cell, big data and cloud computing. Tony has also published on biomedical sciences & patent management in international journals, and presented on patent management and strategy at international conferences in countries such as US, Canada, Japan and India.

Chapter 1

The Rise of the Patent Industry

1.1 The Phenomena — The Surge of Patent Filings

A patent is an exclusive right granted by a sovereign state to an inventor or assignee for a limited period of time. This is granted in exchange for detailed public disclosure of an invention. This definition highlights two key functions of a patent: it is both a legal right, as well as a signal of technological invention.

With the advent of the knowledge economy, a patent, given its five exclusive rights of make, use, sell, offer to sell, and import, has evolved from an "infringement gatekeeper" to an effective instrument of industry power. In addition, the patent system has been institutionalized by legal statues worldwide to harmonize its protection and commercialization in all jurisdictions. Never before have any statutory rules been established globally on the scale enjoyed by patents (or other forms of intellectual properties). This further expands the industrial influence of patent rights.

As a signal of technological invention, patents worldwide have come together to form one of the largest technology databases, providing a great source of technological intelligence for analysis and exploitation. In addition, as patents include legal and commercial information, patent databases could also reveal valuable legal and commercial intelligence. Corporations and public agencies could employ such intelligence, including the technological, legal, and commercial aspects, to derive their business strategies.

Against the backdrop of patents becoming an instrument of industrial power and signal of technical invention, the media has reported that the patent-filing rate is growing exponentially on a global scale.[1] There are also numerous reports on a patent arms race (Chien, 2010; Chien & Lemley, 2012). The surge of patents has become an undeniable global phenomenon.

The driving force behind this patent surge is multidimensional. Research and development (R&D) activities today systematically generate inventions, increasing the number of potential candidates to be filed as patent applications. Moreover, technology products in the market are increasingly sophisticated, involving the integration of multiple features and functions, all of which require proper patent protection against infringers and competitors. Last but not least, patent laws across the world are undergoing rapid change, altering the patent practice and creating uncertainty. Thus, technology organizations need to file multiple patents for a single inventive concept to adapt to the changing legal regime.

However, the increasing number of patents worldwide does not promote the value of patents as a whole. Instead, "patent paradox" is found to depreciate the value of patents on average (Hall & Ziedonis, 2001). An individual patent scarcely stands firmly on its own, be it in terms of legal strength or economic returns, the causes of which have been discussed and speculated broadly (Guellec & de la Potterie, 2000; Parchomovsky & Wagner, 2005). Is there a failure of the valuation process of technology commercialization? Or is the poor performance an outcome of patent thickets being in a haphazard manner?

A careful interpretation of such a phenomenon shows that the key players in such a global trend are undergoing organizational restructuring to accumulate not only a huge number of individual patents, but also purposeful patent portfolios. In this chapter, we first review the advantages and disadvantages of the existing definitions of the patent portfolio and propose our own version of definition — without a proper definition that clearly addresses the characteristics and functions of the patent portfolio, it is impossible to master the art of deployment in modern knowledge-based economy.

---

[1] World Intellectual Property Indicators, 2015, World Intellectual Property Organization, pp. 23–32 (http://www.wipo.int/edocs/pubdocs/en/wipo_pub_941_2015.pdf).

1.2 What is a Patent Portfolio?

According to the European Patent Office, a patent portfolio is the list of patents owned by an individual or a company.[2] This definition, while widely adopted, focuses on the ownership aspect, but provides little information on the exact nature and functions of a patent portfolio. Extending this basic definition, Parchomovsky and Wagner (2005) further proposed that a patent portfolio is an aggregation of a number of related patents that generate a value greater than the sum of its parts. In this book, we will argue that it is not merely an aggregation of related patents, but a strategic aggregation of individual patents into purposeful assets. More importantly, we believe that the essence of a patent portfolio is in its deployment (i.e., the underlying structure and the strategies behind making use of the portfolio). The value of patent portfolios can multiply many folds if one can identify the links to products sold and master the strategies and tactics behind the use of the portfolio. This involves both the formation and the exploitation of patent portfolios.

1.3 Organizational Restructuring

The quality of human life has improved dramatically since the First Economic Revolution with the rise of property rights (North, 1990). The First Economic Revolution was a time when mankind switched from being hunters and gatherers to being farmers. Property rights arose during this time to facilitate trade. Organized trade helped to manage the transaction costs more efficiently. At that time, the legal system started to develop to protect physical property and spurred this Economic Revolution.

This continued for another 6,500 years or so until the Industrial Revolution kicked off in England in the mid-1700s. People started to leave the farms and began to work in factories. The new economy encouraged new knowledge accumulation and revolutionized property rights. Structured organizations and society started to take shape. These organizational structures helped society to run more efficiently. As the Second

---

[2] https://www.epo.org/service-support/faq/searching-patents/valuation.html#faq-131 (Last accessed 20th November 2016).

Economic Revolution continued and developed, the legal system also evolved and gave rise to patents. Its primary purpose at the time was to provide protection for industries.

The 21st century signaled the coming of the Third Economic Revolution, which was propelled by the same need to manage transaction costs efficiently. This era has seen knowledge generation rate grow to unprecedented levels. During the Second Economic Revolution, vertically integrated companies dominated the full value chain from R&D to manufacturing, then marketing and sales to the final product. This changed after the Third Economic Revolution when the economy encouraged further segmentation of the value chain. While there may still be companies that are vertically integrated, more and more companies only focus on one particular segment of the value chain. Entities such as universities, research institutes, and even some individual inventors and intellectual property (IP) providers dominate the R&D segment. They focus on knowledge creation, resulting in new inventions. There are some companies that only focus on patent drafting and maintenance. There are also companies that take the IP from the inventors and use the technology to manufacture products. In particular, the Third Economic Revolution demands an efficient way to perform R&D to meet the demand of new products.

This has pushed the organizational restructuring to a higher level to the extent that some companies have spun off their R&D arms into new business units focusing solely on R&D. The inventions from R&D need to be passed onto the manufacturers. This encouraged the appearance of brokers for patent sales and the rise of the licensing business for patents. In this Third Economic Revolution, patents no longer play a supportive role to protect the inventions. They have become business units in their own right. The rise of this patent business has given rise to various types of patent entities: patent management companies, patent holding companies, patent brokering companies, patent service companies, non-practicing entities (NPEs), and patent aggregators, alliances and pooling to further increase the transaction efficiency. It has been demonstrated in recent years that the grouping of patents into portfolios allow them to be deployed more strategically. There is also a need for technical service providers to develop these portfolios strategically (see Figure 1.1).

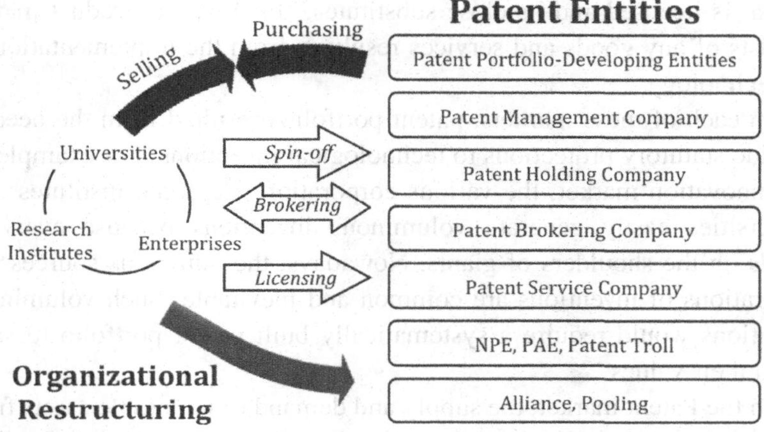

Figure 1.1 Organizational restructuring of patent entities

1.4 The Emergence of Patent Portfolios and Patent Market

Patent portfolios have emerged from macro and micro understandings of the changing knowledge-based economy. The organizational restructuring heralded the rise of a new industry. The Patent market is in effect, a response to the need to aggregate multiple patents to meet supply and demand in the value system.

1.4.1 An industrial perspective

At a macro level, the knowledge-based economy can be divided into three markets: Innovation, Patent, and Product. According to the Antitrust Guidelines for Collaborations Among Competitors issued by the Federal Trade Commission and the U.S. Department of Justice (2000),[3] the Innovation market "consists of the research and development directed to particular new or improved goods or processes and the close substitutes for that research and development." The Patent market "consist[s] of the

[3] https://www.ftc.gov/sites/default/files/documents/public_events/joint-venture-hearings-antitrust-guidelines-collaboration-among-competitors/ftcdojguidelines-2.pdf (Retrieved on 19 August 2015).

IP that is licensed and its close substitutes." Finally, the Product market consists of any goods and services resulting from the implementation of the technology.

In each of these markets, patent portfolios resulted from the need to provide statutory protections to technological inventions. For example, in the Innovation market, the various corporations, research institutes, and universities easily generate voluminous inventions because everyone stands on the shoulders of giants. Nowadays, the numerous sources and integrations of inventions are common and inevitable. Such voluminous inventions would require a systematically built patent portfolio to safeguard their values.

In the Patent market, the supply and demand of intangible assets from institutions and corporations doing R&D and those producing the final products have encouraged new business models to provide trading platforms and consortia. Many new entities have arisen up to contribute to the flourishing patent market. NPEs are one result of new business models arising to facilitate such transactions.

The Patent market has developed a higher level of sophistication in recent years due to the increasing complexity of modern high-tech industry and the evolution of patent law to cater to the changing Patent market landscape. Patents are seldom operated individually today. Instead, they are often managed, licensed, litigated, and transacted as portfolios. Working with a patent portfolio offers higher value because it has a higher chance of surviving invalidation challenges by competitors in response to demands for licensing fees (Lanjouw & Schankerman, 2001; Somaya, 2012). Patent portfolios also provide additional insurance to the fast-changing legal regime that constantly reviews and refines the validity of patents. It is, therefore, advisable to have a portfolio of patents to protect the various aspects of the technology in case some of the patents are invalidated due to changes to substantive law (Cahoy, 2013). Besides strengthening the legal aspects of patents, patent portfolios extend the protection of a technology by aggregating similar inventions. In such a way, the added value of the patents to the products would be greater. This may provide a better basis for higher damages awards and/or licensing fees.

In addition, the standardization of technologies and the subsequent formation of alliances as well as the evolution of standard-essential patents (SEPs) have further expanded the patent system to a new industrial dimension. As such, the Patent market has more exciting activities with the appearance of the evolving Patent market.

In the Product market, patents continue to provide a reasonable protection to the technical features of products. The various product features could each constitute a patent portfolio too. Moreover, the formation and diversification of patent portfolios will enhance the product competiveness and encourage cooperation among market players. Therefore, from an industrial perspective, patents need to be managed at a portfolio level (see Figure 1.2).

Patent portfolios, however, are not just the inevitable results of the modern economy; they are also the catalyst for a chain reaction of exponential growth of the industry. Patent portfolios play an important role in bridging the Innovation and Product markets. The effective use of patent portfolios would enhance and leverage the Innovation and Product markets. Patent portfolios serve to interlock the R&D (or Innovation) and Product markets to build up an industry.

1.4.2 A corporate perspective

At a micro level, which is in effect, analyzed from a corporation's perspective, patent portfolios arise as a result to mitigate the risks along the

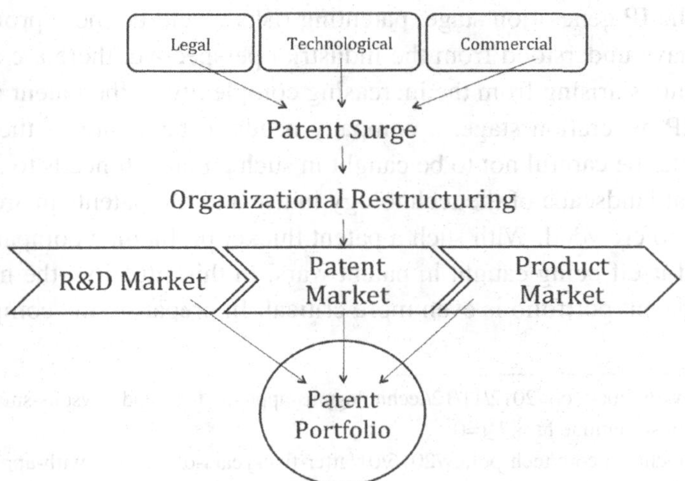

Figure 1.2 The emergence of patent portfolios from an industrial perspective

product development cycle of an enterprise. The product development cycle can be divided into the design stage, the IP generation stage, and the product commercialization stage. At each stage, the enterprise will encounter various types of risks. Some of these risks remain throughout the product development process. There are, however, some risks that are more prominent at specific stages of product development. For example, technology risks are higher at the design stage. A company will face market uncertainties especially when it wants to develop a completely new product that the market does not have at the moment. Smart phones is one such example. In order to mitigate such risks, a company may need to have a good combination of market, technology, and patent intelligence to build up a strong portfolio of intellectual assets even at the initial design stage. It may not be the first mover like Apple in the iPhone industry; nevertheless, it can be an intimidating fast follower to compete with it. Samsung and HTC are good examples.[4,5] Other more subtle risks in relation to the market may be the geographical uncertainties, such as the location where a product is launched. Considering risks like these early on would help a company plan an IP portfolio that is able to withstand challenges in various markets. There will also be technology uncertainties at the initial stage, because companies are not clear about the best technology to use in a new product. A company also needs to keep abreast of new inventions by other companies and ensure that they do not reinvent the wheel.

At the IP generation stage, patenting risks would be more prominent. As we have understood from the industrial perspective, there are a lot of uncertainties arising from the increasing complexity of the Patent market. At the IP generation stage, a company needs to be aware of the patent thicket and be careful not to be caught in such a maze. It needs to analyze the patent landscape of the technology in use and file patents in areas that are not too crowded. With such a patent thicket problem, a company may also find itself being caught in patent wars. In this situation, the need for a good patent portfolio is even more critical. In preparing the company to

[4] http://www.nytimes.com/2012/11/12/technology/as-apple-and-htc-end-lawsuits-smartphone-patent-battles-continue.html?_r=0.

[5] http://arstechnica.com/tech-policy/2016/01/after-five-years-of-conflict-with-apple-some-samsung-phone-features-are-banned/.

understand the patent landscape of the technology, a company may also find itself facing uncertainties related to the use of analytical tools and methods. This is the information extraction uncertainty. Besides these intrinsic risks of patent analysis, a company may also be subjected to risks in partnership. No single company would be able to amass sufficient patents to defend its products. The solution to this may lie in cooperating with others by patent pooling, cross-licensing, and even engaging in patent alliances.

At the commercialization stage, the related risks may involve valuation and infringement threats. Valuation is a complex topic. It involves technological, legal, and economic analyses. An efficient and agreed-upon method of patent portfolio valuation has yet to be found. Patent infringement is a key threat for many practicing companies. It means that their products may be subjected to injunction threats, which would directly affect their sales.

An effective mitigation system for such risks relies on the strategic formation and enforcement of multiple patent portfolios. These multiple patent portfolios are the bolts and nuts of a system that helps enterprises develop their products from R&D to profitable products (see Figure 1.3).

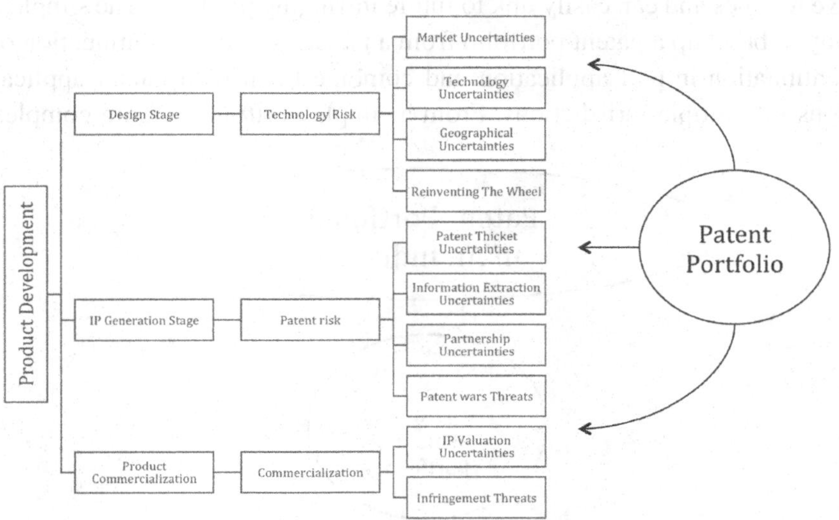

Figure 1.3 The emergence of patent portfolios from the corporate perspective

1.4.3 Interaction between industry and corporation

The success of an industry at a macro level and that of an enterprise at a micro level requires a good understanding of the dynamic relationship between the Innovation, Patent, and Product markets. At the same time, it also requires the establishment of an effective risk mitigation mechanism to ensure the smooth transition between the R&D ideas in the design stage, the IP generation stage, and finally the product commercialization stage within an enterprise. In fact, the overall success hinges upon the dynamic interaction between the enterprise and the industry. The enterprise on the one hand will contribute inventions and hence patent portfolios to build up and influence the patent portfolios in the industry. On the other hand, the industry will influence the relevance and usage of patent portfolios to be formed within an enterprise. This builds up an ecosystem for the growth and application of patent portfolios (see Figure 1.4).

The secret to forming a patent portfolio as illustrated in Figure 1.4 lies in a thorough understanding of the nature and usage of patents and patent portfolios. For individual patents, the details to master include deciding the type of patents to be filed (such as product or process patents) and drafting the patents such that the claims will properly disclose the protective regimes and can easily link to future infringing products. The simplest way to build up a patent portfolio from a patent is to file a continuation or continuation-in-part application and combine them with patent applications in multiple jurisdictions. From a simple portfolio, a more complex

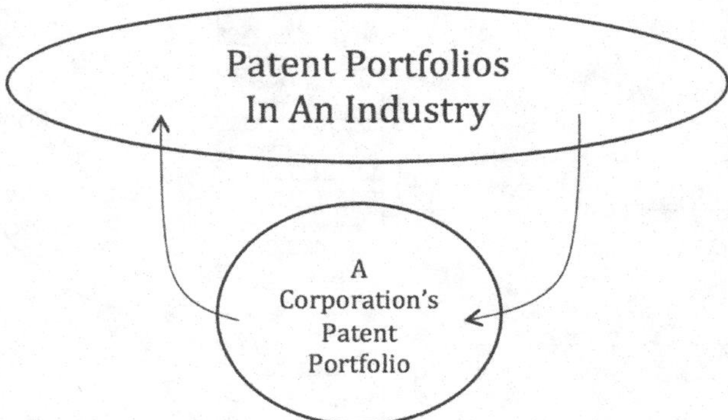

Figure 1.4 The dynamic interaction between corporation and industry

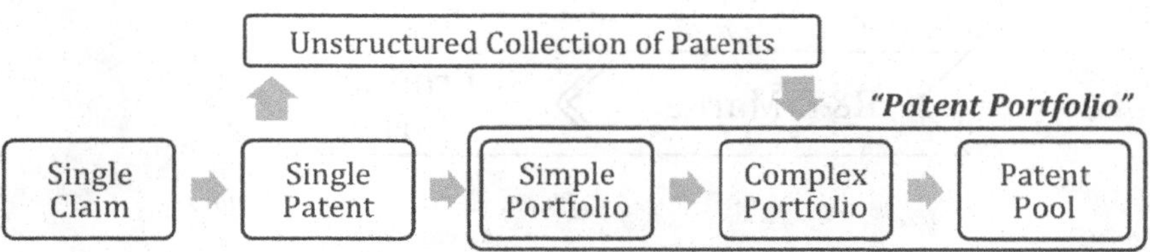

Figure 1.5 The formation of patent portfolio

patent portfolio requires the protection of the invention using hardware and/or software. It may also entail a portfolio with patents that protect the core product and associated products. For a more sophisticated technology, a patent portfolio would comprise patents linking directly to the core technology, and enabling and enhancing technologies of the whole platform. A further expansion of the patent portfolio would require collaboration between multiple enterprises to form alliances and standards to best protect the interests of everyone (see Figure 1.5). Only with such an understanding and treatment of patents can there be a flourishing patent industry.

1.5 The Emergence of Intermediaries

The emergence of patent portfolios and the rise of the Patent market indicate that the Patent market is a crucial connector for innovation flowing from the Innovation market to the Product market. Patents are no longer just bystanders standing on the sidelines at the success of the economy (see Figure 1.6). In fact, patents have their own market. The operation to fulfil the supply and demand of technology is being implemented through patents.

While the three markets are distinct in their core competence; they are interconnected for the well-being of one another. The R&D market needs to translate the inventions accurately into patents. The patents need to be aggregated constructively to form a portfolio that has a strong link with products. If this mechanism is not operating efficiently, there will be two valleys of death in the ecosystem, and the economy will stagnate (see Figure 1.7).

To support the rise of the Patent market, more companies are specializing as intermediaries to ensure effective and efficient collaborations between the operations of the various markets. To bridge the chasm

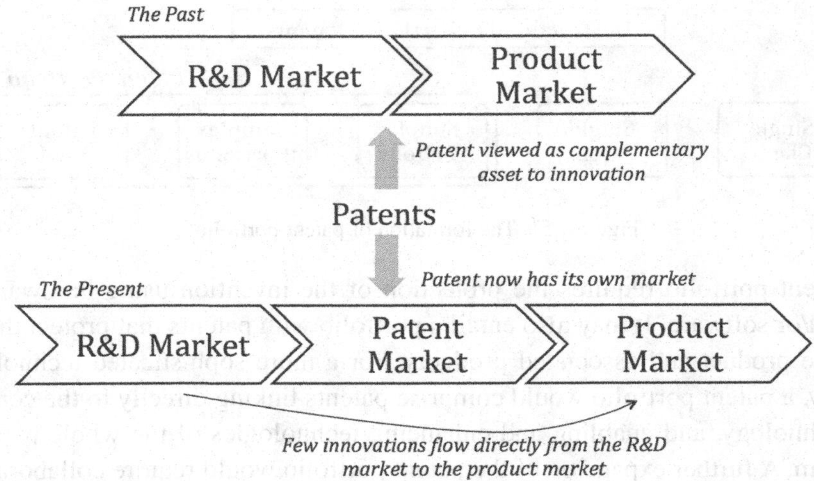

Figure 1.6 The Patent market has become a crucial connection between R&D market and Product market because of organizational restructuring

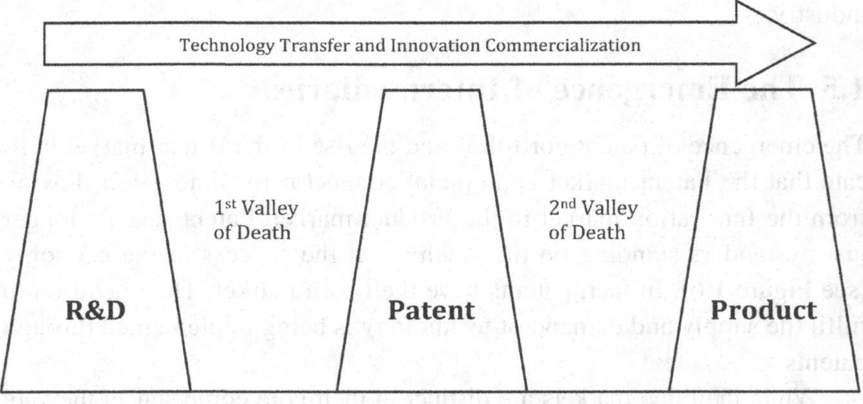

Figure 1.7 Death valleys (chasms) through the three markets

between the Innovation market and the Patent market, qualified patent agents/attorneys are needed to translate the ideas from the inventors to legal documents. In addition, the communication between the patent agents/ attorneys and the inventors has to be effective so that the essence of the inventions can be translated correctly in the patent documents. For example, a firm may consider opening up the patent drafting service to a few patent firms and allow them direct access to their inventors under signed non-disclosure agreements. In this case, the patent agents/attorneys can have a better understanding of the inventions through direct interactions with the inventors, instead of acting through the IP managers. Furthermore, the inventors, through such interactions, can also understand the capabilities and advantages of the different agents/attorneys, and can accordingly, select the more suitable ones for their future work. A company may also consider extending the operations with the patent firm by allowing them to review the patents of the company and identify those that have a higher potential for commercialization (Cheng *et al.*, 2012; Li, Lan, & Liu, 2015). The patent firm may also share in the profits of successful commercialization. In this case, the patent firm will have a vested interest in drafting good patents that can be commercialized in the future. Other higher levels of services also start to emerge to assist the R&D entities to identify trends for R&D investment and development and to design patent portfolios that can be eventually monetized (Hagiu & Yoffie, 2011).

Technology transfer intermediaries which ensure that patents can be licensed or sold and be used in the Product market can be used to bridge the Patent and Product markets. Vertically integrated companies integrate the inventions directly into the products. In this case, a dedicated patent manager may be needed to keep track of potential infringers. With a more streamlined economy, however, more companies are involved in various segments in the product production value chain. New inventions from the technology provider may be licensed to third party manufacturers, who in turn produce for other end-product providers. In order to facilitate the licensing of inventions to these players, specialized licensing agents are needed to match the supply and demand between the technology providers and implementers (Wang, 2010). They are the ones who bridge the chasms between the Patent market and the Product market. These licensing professionals have a good knowledge of the use of the inventions. In addition, they are highly skilled in negotiations and communications. They also have experience in patent prosecution and litigation. As not many practicing entities (operating companies) have these skilled professionals in-house, licensing agents have a critical role in ensuring good collaboration in commercializing the technology. NPEs can also facilitate such activities,

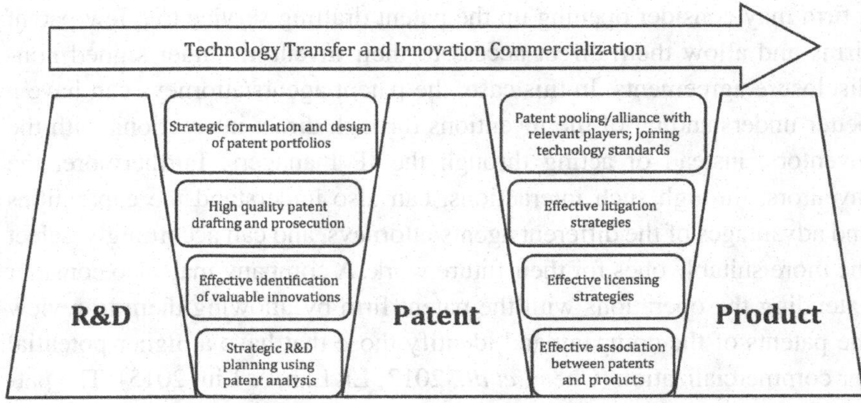

Figure 1.8 Crossing the death valleys through the three markets

sometimes by initiating patent litigations. However, their primary objective is to promote patent licensing. This is especially helpful to practicing entities when it is inconvenient for them to pursue potential licensees through patent litigation. They need a third party to coordinate all these activities for them. "Strategic Tools" such as patent pools, alliances, and standard setting organizations are frequently employed in today's society. Other IP consultant firms are also flourishing by providing licensing and litigation support.

In this way, these intermediaries can bridge the valleys of death to ensure a sustainable ecosystem (see Figure 1.8).

As the demand for such IP intermediaries increases, newer business models evolve. Patent aggregators emerge to gather more patents and mass-license them to manufacturing companies to commercialize inventions (Hagiu & Yoffie, 2013). This helps lower the transaction costs and allows more companies to participate in the patent market.

Other important IP intermediaries in this value chain are brokers for the sale of patents, patent analytics, patent monetization consultants, and even patent-based financing intermediaries (see Figure 1.9).

In sum, Figure 1.9 summarizes how intermediaries function and operate across the three markets by leveraging patent portfolios. As earlier discussed, patent agents bridge the Innovation and Patent markets, while

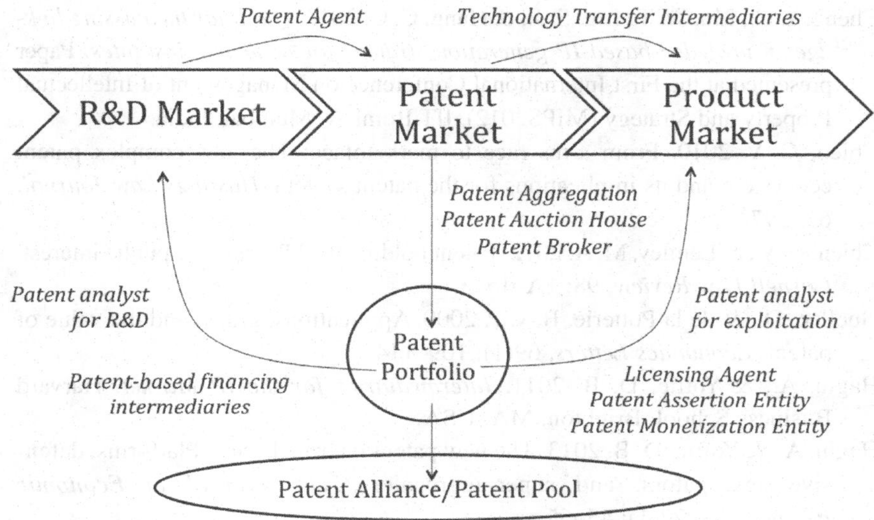

Figure 1.9 Intermediaries operate throughout the three markets

the technology transfer office bridges the Patent and Product markets. Emerging business models such as patent aggregation entities, patent auction houses, and patent brokers facilitate the trade and exchange of patents, and encourage the formation of patent portfolios. Patent-based financing intermediaries could leverage on well-constructed patent portfolios to get funding for future R&D. Patent licensing agents and many other forms of patent monetization agents focus on using patent portfolios to generate revenue. Patent analysts who specialize in analyzing patent data could influence both the Innovation and the Product markets by supplying valuable intelligence, such as making suggestions on R&D and licensing opportunities. Furthermore, patent alliance and patent pool organizations bring related patent portfolios from different proprietors together to exploit the monetary and strategic value of the portfolios.

Bibliography

Cahoy, D. R. 2013. *The Changing Face of US Patent Law and Its Impact on Business Strategy*. Edward Elgar Publishing, Cheltenham UK and Northampton, Massachusetts, USA.

Cheng, Y. C., Liu, W. T., Liu, S. J., & Hang, C. C. 2012. *Quest for the missing linkage: Knowledge-based IP generation strategy for academic institutes*. Paper presented at the First International Conference on Management of Intellectual Property and Strategy (MIPS2012), IIT Bombay, Mumbai, India.

Chien, C. V. 2010. From arms race to marketplace: The new complex patent ecosystem and its implications for the patent system. *Hastings Law Journal*, 62: 297.

Chien, C. V., & Lemley, M. A. 2012. Patent holdup, the ITC, and the public interest. *Cornell Law Review*, 98: 1A–1573.

Guellec, D., & de la Potterie, B. v. P. 2000. Applications, grants and the value of patent. *Economics Letters*, 69(1): 109–114.

Hagiu, A., & Yoffie, D. B. 2011. *Intermediaries for the IP Market*. Harvard Business School, Brighton, MA, USA.

Hagiu, A., & Yoffie, D. B. 2013. The new patent intermediaries: Platforms, defensive aggregators, and super-aggregators. *The Journal of Economic Perspectives*, 27(1): 45–65.

Hall, B. H., & Ziedonis, R. H. 2001. The patent paradox revisited: An empirical study of patenting in the US semiconductor industry, 1979–1995. *RAND Journal of Economics*, 32(1): 101–128.

Lanjouw, J. O., & Schankerman, M. 2001. Characteristics of patent litigation: A window on competition. *RAND Journal of Economics*, 32(1): 129–151.

Li, C., Lan, T., & Liu, S.-J. 2015. Patent attorney as technology intermediary: A patent attorney-facilitated model of technology transfer in developing countries. *World Patent Information*, 43: 62–73.

North, D. C. 1990. *Institutions, Institutional Change and Economic Performance*. Cambridge University Press, Cambridge, UK.

Parchomovsky, G., & Wagner, R. P. 2005. Patent portfolios. *University of Pennsylvania Law Review*, 154(1): 1–77.

Somaya, D. 2012. Patent strategy and management an integrative review and research agenda. *Journal of Management*, 38(4): 1084–1114.

Wang, A. W. 2010. Rise of the patent intermediaries. *Berkeley Technology Law Journal*, 25(1): 159–200.

Chapter 2

Patent Portfolio Deployment in Modern Economy

2.1 Patent Rights: Evolution of Their Industrial Power

Patent rights started off with the simple statutory rights of "making, using, selling, offering for sale, and importing" granted to each patent. These five rights actually provide a comprehensive protection to exclude others from manufacturing (making) to integrating with other components to form the final products (using). In addition, they provide protection for the after-production operations, such as sales (selling and offering for sale) and logistics in commercializing the technology (importing). These are a set of negative rights to prevent others from executing any operation based on these granted rights to the patented invention. Inherent to these five rights are the rights to sue for either direct or indirect infringement. Direct infringement occurs when all elements of a patented claim can be linked to an accused product or process. Indirect infringement, on the other hand, extends a patent owner's right to the material components that contribute to the entire product being claimed of infringing. In addition, the promotion or encouragement of using infringing products may also constitute unlawful inducement. It is highly likely that all the players in a production supply chain may be liable for the violation of patent rights, so long as the infringement is claimed for one segment of the supply chain.

Therefore, patents provide statutory rights to the patent owners with monopoly for a period of time so that they can sue for infringement or license the patents. In addition, like property rights, patent rights may be sold, mortgaged, assigned, transferred, given away, or simply abandoned. The most common use of these rights is to serve as infringement gatekeepers to defend the company that owns the patents. As the influence of patents increases, companies are devising more sophisticated strategies to bundle more rights with patents.

As early as the eighteenth century, companies have been using patents to gain industrial control (Figure 2.1). An interesting case is the Motion Picture Patents Company (Thomas, 1971). It was a trust initiated by Thomas Edison against his domestic competitors to gain complete control of the American motion-picture industry between 1908 and 1912. Since the 1890s, Edison owned most of the American patents relating to motion picture cameras. In 1902, Edison started to notify distributors and exhibitors that if they did not use the machines and films made by Edison exclusively, they would be subject to litigation for supporting filmmakers who infringed Edison's patents. In view of this threat, most of Edison's competitors approached him and sought to obtain a license for his patents. This evolved into a trust agreement for motion picture patents. However, eventually the Supreme Court cancelled all the related patents owned by Motion Picture Patents Company, and in 1917, found the company to be in violation of the Sherman Antitrust Act.

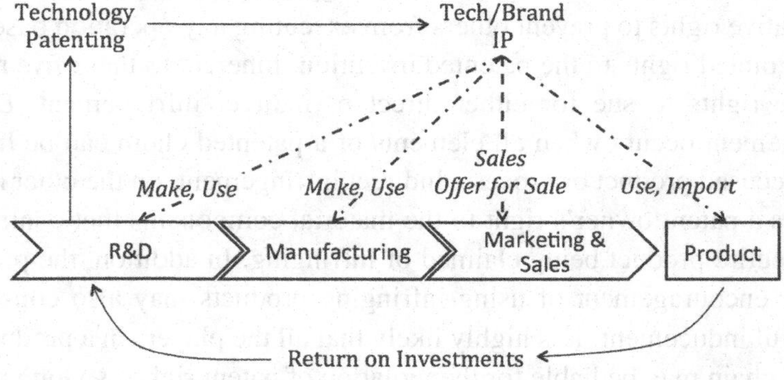

Figure 2.1 Combinative use of the five statutory rights equip patents with industrial power

A similar strategy was used by Qualcomm. It is alleged that Qualcomm discouraged phone makers from buying chips from its rivals through its licensing agreements. For example, Qualcomm demanded higher royalties from vendors who bought their modems elsewhere. This, however, has created some antitrust issues. The South Korean Federal Trade Commission (FTC) accused Qualcomm of antitrust violations and as a result, fined Qualcomm US$235M in 2009.[1] There were also antitrust litigations brought against Qualcomm in China, the European Union, and the USA.[2] In 2015, the Chinese National Development and Reform Commission (NDRC) fined Qualcomm US$975M and required it to cut its royalty rates for Chinese vendors.[3] The outcomes of the other lawsuits are pending. The Qualcomm case shows that it is possible to extend the patent rights beyond the five granted rights to secure extensive industrial power.

There are also cases where companies from one segment of the industrial chain use patents to exert their influence on other segments of the value chain. For example, a company may carefully design the licensing agreement so that each segment of the value chain will be granted with only a portion of the five patent rights. In this way, there will be more potential licensees, and the patent owners can extend their power down the value chain. A good understanding of patent law, however, is required to avoid exhausting the rights. Some semi-conductor companies in the telecommunications and lighting industries may employ such a strategy of segregating the value chain and granting limited rights. In the subsequent chapters, we will analyze such licensing models in greater detail and discuss their effect on other smaller players in the industry.

Further extensions of patent rights, resulting from industrial power evolution, include the formation of a patent alliance and patent aggregators. A patent alliance is a variation of the Motion Picture Patents Company. The main difference between the two is that patent power is shared among more entities in the modern world. Usually, two or more companies cross license their related patent portfolios to avoid malicious patent litigations

---

[1] http://www.theregister.co.uk/2016/01/11/qualcomm_sues_customers_antitrust_probe/

[2] http://www.ft.com/intl/cms/s/0/fa223b00-6543-11e4-91b1-00144feabdc0.html#axzz44OxADgNV

[3] http://www.chinadailyasia.com/business/2015-02/10/content_15225830.html

that can disrupt their businesses. An example is the cooperation between Samsung and Google. In January 2014, the two giants announced a 10-year patent alliance for all of their existing and future patents the next decade.[4] This alliance enhances the dominance of the Android operating system. Another example of a patent alliance is companies joining together to form a consortium, which manages a portfolio of patents purchased from other parties. A prominent case is Rockstar Consortium formed to negotiate licenses for patents acquired from bankrupt telecommunications and data networking equipment manufacturer Nortel in a US$4.5 billion deal. Members of the consortium include Apple, Blackberry, Ericsson, Microsoft, and Sony.[5] Rockstar later initiated lawsuits against Google, Huawei, Samsung, and other Android manufacturers for infringement of patents in the Nortel patent portfolio.[6]

In 2014, Rockstar sold 4000 patents to RPX Corporation, a patent aggregator.[7] Patent aggregation is a new business model that arose to be a middleman to support the flourishing Patent market by reducing transaction costs. There are two types of patent aggregators. One is an offensive aggregator operated by non-practicing entities or operating companies, which purchase patents to assert them against companies in return for licensing fees. The other type is the defensive patent aggregator. They purchase patents to keep them out of the hands of entities that would assert them against operating companies. An example of such a defensive patent aggregator is Allied Security Trust (AST). RPX is also a defensive patent aggregator. Its business model is slightly different from AST's. RPX charges its members a fixed annual membership fee which equates to their licensing fee, to help companies mitigate patent litigation risks from non-practicing entities.

The use of patent rights has grown complicated with the rise of various standards to facilitate cross platforms for product development. This is

[4] http://www.techradar.com/news/phone-and-communications/mobile-phones/google-and-samsung-form-landmark-patent-alliance-to-aid-fight-against-ios-1218831

[5] https://en.wikipedia.org/wiki/Rockstar_Consortium

[6] http://www.reuters.com/article/us-google-rockstar-lawsuit-idUSBRE99U1EN20131031

[7] http://www.wsj.com/articles/rockstar-consortium-to-sell-4-000-patents-to-rpx-corp-for-900-million-1419345685

especially the case for telecommunications technology, such as the Global System for Mobile Communications (GSM), 3rd Generation Partnership Project (3GPP), and the 4G Long Term Evolution standard. The rise of standards, on the one hand, proliferate technology development and ensure that such patents are essential. On the other hand, the standards may in some ways curtail the amount of royalty rates that can be collected. This is because the patent owners of such standards are usually restricted by the Standard Setting Organizations to license their patents to potential licensees under the Fair, Reasonable and Non-Discriminatory (FRAND) terms, thus limiting the royalty rate that can be charged.

From the above overview, patent rights provide a set of assets that can perform far more wonders than any other tangible assets (Figure 2.2). The magic wand here is the skill of the patent owners to come up with innovative business models in the form of licensing and litigation strategies to extract those values.

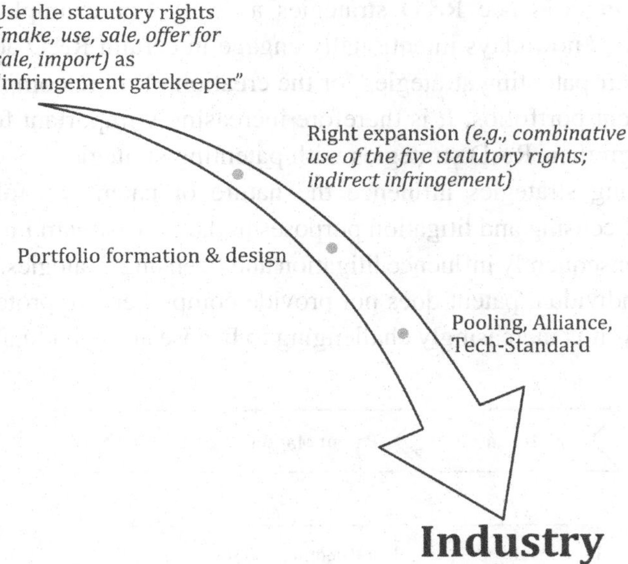

Figure 2.2 The expansion of patent's power in technology industries

2.2 Patent Portfolio Deployment: A Holistic Approach of R&D, Patenting, Licensing, and Litigation

2.2.1 A holistic approach

To extend their industrial power, patents, should be deployed holistically through the integration of R&D, patenting, licensing, and litigation strategies (Figure 2.3).

One central issue in R&D strategy is direction: what should be invented? Which direction needs to be pursued? Which path of the technology roadmap should be followed? The output from R&D provides the basis for patenting (i.e. patent generation), and could greatly affect the patenting strategies that a company adopts. The traditional practice considers patents a complementary asset for R&D output, and the corresponding patenting strategy is hence unsurprisingly passive. With the rise of the Patent market, however, patents are no longer just a complement. Patenting strategy can influence R&D strategies as well. For example, research organizations nowadays intentionally engage in certain R&D activities to support their patenting strategies for the creation of more comprehensive/ strong patent portfolios. It is therefore increasingly important for companies to align their R&D strategies with patenting strategies.

Patenting strategies influence the nature of patent portfolios to be suited for licensing and litigation purposes in the downstream Product market, and consequently influence litigation and licensing strategies. However, since an individual patent does not provide comprehensive protection of a technology, it is increasingly challenging to license an individual patent (or

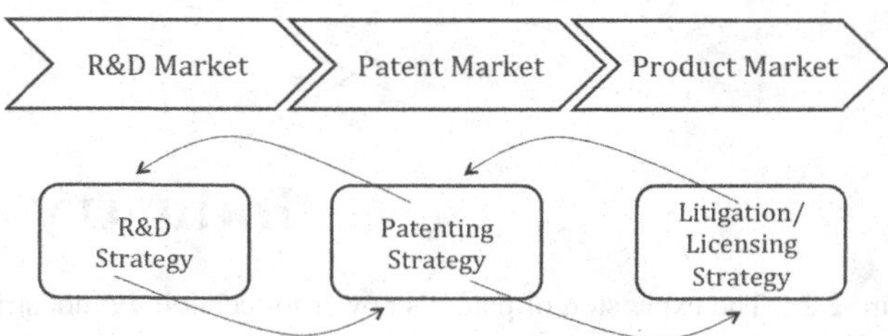

Figure 2.3 A holistic perspective of R&D, patenting and litigation/licensing strategies

a group of unstructured patents) effectively. Companies are also pressured to generate or acquire additional patents to strengthen their existing patent portfolios, or join patent pools to maximize their returns either monetarily or strategically from patent licensing and litigation. Thus, it is no longer a one-way relationship between patenting strategy and litigation/licensing strategies — companies must take licensing and litigation strategies into consideration when devising their patenting strategies.

Therefore, in this book, we emphasize the need to adopt a holistic approach to patent portfolio deployment with regards to R&D, patenting and exploitation (licensing/litigation).

2.2.2 R&D and patenting

Preliminary work before crystallizing licensing and litigation strategies needs to be performed. Very often, companies neglect the inclusion of IP considerations at the R&D and patenting stages. This deprives the company of their ability to maximize their profits from their patent portfolio. A patent portfolio needs to be carefully constructed to meet the needs of the market before they can fetch substantial value. With patent portfolios analytics, companies can use a patent as an indicator to direct their R&D focus to contribute to the innovation market. At the same time, they can derive marketable products.

A patent is a very good guide for R&D direction because it is a systematic collection of inventions that have been examined and conferred with legal rights. In addition, it costs money to file these patents and keep them alive. The patent database, thus, gives an indication of whether companies are still investing in that technology. Therefore, patent analysis may be used for R&D technology road mapping. To effectively achieve this result, there must be a systematic approach to extract patent information from these patent databases. There are many existing tools and maps used by IP consulting companies to provide patent landscape analysis. Not many of them, however, can successfully provide insights for R&D direction. One must integrate technology patent and market information in order to propose useful strategies for R&D. As understood from the previous chapter, the R&D market and the Product market must connect in order to proliferate the ecosystem in the industry. Analyzing patent databases would help make this connection. In the next section of this book, we will unveil how this mechanism works.

Besides R&D strategies, the operation of an effective ecosystem needs to have proper patenting strategies. Patenting strategies are the means to achieve successful exploitation in the later stage of the patent life cycle. Patent strategies are important at a passive level to protect the company from infringers and thus providing necessary remedy or defend itself against potential patent infringement lawsuits. They are also important at a proactive level in the event that a company would like to assert its patents against potential infringers or to license its patent portfolios as an extra revenue stream. In either scenario, the patent portfolio that the company has must be useful to read on the final infringing products. Therefore, it is important to carefully plan the technology to be protected, and what the applications to be filed to provide optimum protection and maximum monetization potential. In this book, we will analyze ways to structure patent portfolios, and suggest when and how they can be employed under different scenarios.

2.2.3 Litigation and licensing strategies

With an understanding of the rise of the patent industry and the rights inherent in patents, the following sections elaborate the deployment of the resulting patent portfolios from the growth of the knowledge-based economy. Traditionally, licensing and litigation are the two fundamental exploitation strategies to realize the values in patents. Licensing operates under a cooperative environment where the technology contributor offers a combination of legal rights such as making, using, selling, offering for sale, and importing the protected technology. In return, the potential licensee negotiates a price in exchange for those rights associated with this technology. The two parties will eventually negotiate a set of terms and price acceptable to both parties.

On the other hand, litigation operates under a competitive and more hostile environment. Litigation is a right conferred by the legislation to enforce rights granted by the patents against anyone violating such rights. While the success of licensing hinges on the ability of two parties to reach an agreement, the success of litigation relies on the effectiveness of legal institutions to properly execute such enforcement of rights. Many countries have well-structured substantive and procedural rules for patent rights. However, that does not equate to having an effective enforcement system. Many multinational companies hesitate to expand to large markets because they fear that they may not be able to enforce their legal rights in certain countries. For example, companies imitating products from multi-national companies often close down when they are being sued, making it difficult for multi-national companies to seek damages. Therefore, even if they eventually decide to invest in these countries, they will do so with extra precautions to safeguard their technologies and intellectual properties.

This is the case for the traditional Product market. It is even more so for the Patent market. The value of patents lies entirely in the legal rights conferred. If these rights cannot be enforced, it makes no sense to license or initiate patent infringement lawsuits. Companies would be free to use protected technologies and deprive the patent owners of their ability to profit from their inventions. Such a situation would threaten new players with new business models. For example, ARM is known to license its CPU and memory architecture patents to chip makers. If ARM's intellectual property rights cannot be effectively enforced, its business model would collapse. Thus a strong legal regime in both rules and enforcement is needed for the survival of the Patent market. It also follows that litigation is highly jurisdictional. In this book, we will focus on litigation in the USA as most companies would encounter patent litigation in the USA due to the size of the market and the maturity of the patent enforcement system.

Licensing and litigation, however, cannot be considered entirely separate. There is an intricate dynamic relationship between them (Figure 2.4). On the one hand, licensing negotiations are always under the shadow of litigation because if negotiation fails, the technology contributors may resort to litigation to assert the values of their patent portfolios (Michel, 2011). On the other hand, the reaction of most industry players toward technology licensing is almost always passive. In such situations, technology contributors may use litigation as a strategy to force the potential licensees to respond to the licensing request more urgently. The ultimate aim is to reach a settlement with the potential licensees. In reality, many lawsuits are filed for the purpose of licensing.

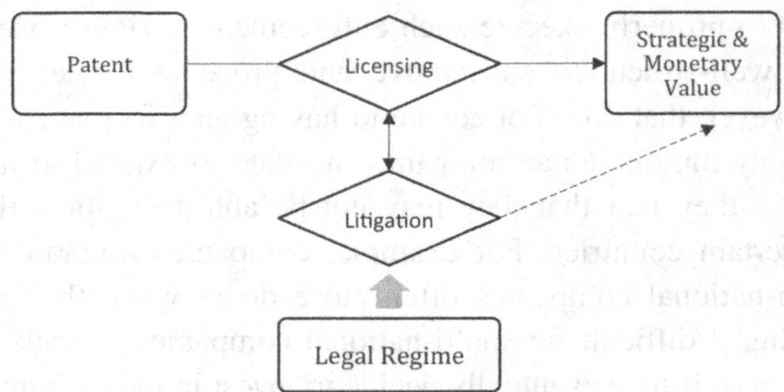

Figure 2.4 The dynamics between licensing, litigation, and legal regime

2.3 Structuring the Valuation of Patent Portfolios

Valuation is important as the process of concluding licensing and litigation deals is long, expensive, and risky. One needs to consider the potential returns from such risky enforcement before deciding on the appropriate strategies and tactics to deploy. There are many occasions when the valuation of patents is required. Some examples include using patent portfolios for the purpose of financing, equity sharing, and taxation.

2.3.1 Financial valuation of patents

We have unfolded the value of patents as an asset under the backdrop of industrial environment from the legal, economical, and business perspectives. In the German patent valuation standard DIN77100,[8] developed by the German Institute for Standardization (DIN), the values of patents are determined by a set of legal, technical, and economic factors (Figure 2.5). In this book, we will extend the understanding of these factors by looking into the relationships among them. We believe that the fundamental values of patents are determined by legal factors, which determine the strength, validity, and likelihood of success of patent portfolios. The legal factors are also less debatable and more objective. The technical factors are more specific and may be linked to the actual usage of the patents with the final implementation of the products.

[8] Available at: http://www.beuth.de/en/article/din77100

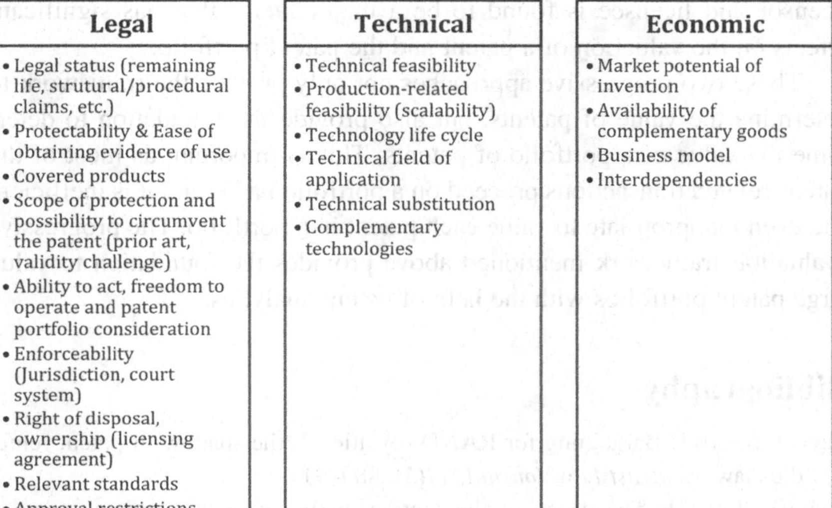

Legal
• Legal status (remaining life, strutural/procedural claims, etc.)
• Protectability & Ease of obtaining evidence of use
• Covered products
• Scope of protection and possibility to circumvent the patent (prior art, validity challenge)
• Ability to act, freedom to operate and patent portfolio consideration
• Enforceability (Jurisdiction, court system)
• Right of disposal, ownership (licensing agreement)
• Relevant standards
• Approval restrictions
Technical
• Technical feasibility
• Production-related feasibility (scalability)
• Technology life cycle
• Technical field of application
• Technical substitution
• Complementary technologies
Economic
• Market potential of invention
• Availability of complementary goods
• Business model
• Interdependencies

Figure 2.5 Factors relevant to patent valuation

The economic factors are more unpredictable and subjective. The values of patents may also be affected by external factors that may not be related to the intrinsic nature of the invention. For example, the design of a product may affect market acceptance, thus, its economic values.

2.3.2 Patent valuation in patent disputes

With a broad understanding of the industrial environment that affects the values of patents, a more refined set of 15 factors has been adopted by USA courts to determine reasonable royalties. This can be viewed as compensation to patent owners when infringing products or processes have violated their legal rights conferred by patents. These factors are well documented in *Georgia-Pacific Corp. v. U.S. Plywood Corp.*, 318 F.Supp 1116 (S.D.N.Y. May 28, 1970). Categorically, these 15 factors are related to the historical information of patents, the intrinsic patent values, the licensing environment, and holistic considerations such as expert opinions. Each of these factors, if applicable, may affect the valuation of a patent and the patent portfolio. Some factors may have more influence than others. For example, the commercial relationship between the licensor and licensee is found to be a major factor that has significant effects on the valuation of a patent and the patent portfolio.

These two progressive approaches not only provide the framework to determine the value of patents, but also provide the foundation to determine the value of a portfolio of patents. This is important as most of the patent-related transactions proceed on a portfolio basis, and it is inefficient and even inappropriate to value each patent in a portfolio. The progressive evaluation framework mentioned above provides the foundation to value large patent portfolios with the help of patent analytics.

Bibliography

Michel, S. 2011. Bargaining for RAND royalties in the shadow of patent remedies law. *Antitrust Law Journal*, 77(3), 889–911.

Thomas, J. 1971. The decay of the motion picture patents company. *Cinema Journal*, 10(2), 34–40.

Chapter 3

Deployment with Patent Analytics: Theory and Practice

Patent Analytics

This is the beginning of Part II — Exploration — of this book. It is divided into two portions: gathering intelligence from both patent and non-patent literature, and deriving R&D and patenting strategies from that intelligence. Part II lays the foundations for understanding one's patent portfolio and using it as an asset to make profits for the company. In addition, we pay special attention to the construction of a patent portfolio, and offer the reader a pragmatic guide to constructing patent portfolios.

3.1 Objectives of Patent Analytics

Patent data is a valuable source of information. It is free for anyone to use, and anyone may make his inventions available through it. Patent analytics exploit the patent system by transforming the publicly available information into insightful strategies and tactics (Liu & Shyu, 1997). This becomes Patent Intelligence. When properly conducted and applied, intelligence from patent analytics can provide valuable insights into not just the Patent market, but the innovation and Product markets as well (Figure 3.1).

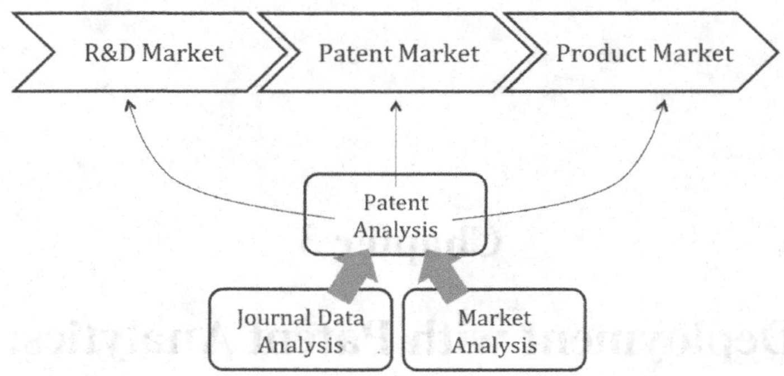

Figure 3.1 The objectives of patent analytics

However, many companies remain skeptical about the role of patent analytics. Many take the view that patent analytics only provides an industry-wide or macroscopic overview and does not serve the specific needs of operating companies that just want to monetize their existing patent portfolios.

Patent analytics, however, can provide micro analysis for specific entities. At the lowest level, patent analytics helps a company understand its own patent portfolio by analyzing the claim construction and strength of each individual patent via comparisons with similar patents. If there is a need to amend or acquire additional patents to strengthen the scope of protection, patent analytics provides the means to scout these necessary patents to construct a stronger patent portfolio.

At a higher level, patent analytics helps a company map out all the relevant patents that may be used when producing a new product. In this case, a company can reduce the risk of being sued for infringement by engaging in licensing negotiations with the patent owners. A technology that falls in a less researched area may warrant more investment in R&D and patent applications. On the other hand, if the technology has already been well researched, or falls outside the company's core competency, obtaining a license for the technology may be more economical.

With the rise of the patent market and the fierce competition between companies for patent filings and litigation, patent analytics provides an additional source of information for company analysis, and an additional tool to fight competitors. A company can use patent analytics to compare competitors' patent portfolios with its own. When competitors' patents are very similar to its own, there is a high chance that the competitors are employing similar technology. In this case, the company may consider filling a patent infringement lawsuit against these competitors. On the other hand, should there be threatening patents identified in the competitors' patent portfolios, and a high likelihood that the competitors would use such patents to sue for infringement, the company can attempt to invalidate such patents first, before its competitors use these patents against it. As such, patent analytics is essential for companies if they want to monetize their patent portfolios effectively.

At the macro level, patent analytics is also important to companies. There is misunderstanding in the industry about the value of macro-level patent analytics such as the patent landscape report. Many companies lament that they cannot get any useful insights or derive any "action plan" from such macroscopic patent-analysis reports. They do not realize that patent analytics, if properly prepared and interpreted, can provide valuable information about the technology direction. For example, understanding the mega trends of patent filing can provide insights into the technology that is more likely to facilitate the implementation of certain functions in products. By analyzing the density of the patent filings of various alternative technologies, a company can decide whether to invest in R&D resources or patent acquisition.

At an even higher level, patent analytics helps a company identify the segment of the industry that can be the potential target for patent licensing. This is especially the case for the semiconductor industry, where chip architecture providers such as ARM provide the CPU architecture, and chip-design companies like Mediatek that license CPU architecture from ARM. Mediatek then engages original equipment manufacturers (OEMs) such as Amkor to produce the chips for them. These chips are then assembled by contract manufacturers like Foxconn to form the end product. However, the end-product design is produced by end-product providers such as Samsung, which decides the chips to be used and the functions in the final products. Understanding the patent strength of these companies in the context of the entire eco-system of the industry is important to best

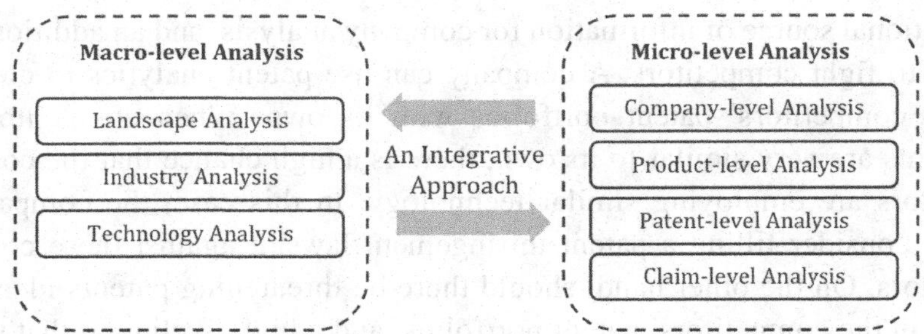

Figure 3.2 An integrative approach that links the macro-level and micro-level patent analytics

leverage one's own patent portfolio, and identify areas of risk at the same time.

Sometimes, an even higher level of patent analysis is essential for developing effective policies. Government agencies need to understand these macroscopic trends to provide necessary funding and other resources to promote economy. Investors also need to understand these mega trends to identify potential areas of investment. For companies, the macroscopic analysis may provide an indication that a company should look at non-core areas for investment, to diversify the business.

To shape the industry, it is important for companies to be aware of the viable business models to adapt to changes in the industry. Patent analytics is the tool to help companies to shape their business models. Unfortunately, patent analytics is not effective for many companies because the patent-analytics providers do not communicate sufficiently with the company to understand the reasons for the analysis. On the other hand, the companies do not make an effort to allow the patent analytics to guide their R&D and patenting directions. A company needs to adopt an integrative approach in order to use patent analytics purposefully (Figure 3.2).

3.2 Visualization of Patent Analytics: Patent Maps

A "Patent Map" is defined as "Patent information collected for a specific purpose of use, and assembled, analyzed and depicted in a visual form of presentation such as a chart, graph or table."[1] In short, a patent map is the visual representation (e.g., charts, figures, tables, and diagrams) of related patent information. It is not only a tool to represent the patent information in a neat and easily understandable manner, but also a means to discover patterns and derive insights.

A patent map is produced by gathering related patent information about a targeted technology field, and grouping and analyzing it. Examples of simple patent maps are the *Element-Based Map*, *Diagram of Technological Development*, *Inter-patent Relations Map*, *Matrix Map*, *Systematized Art Diagram*, *Time Series Map*, *Twin Peaks Analysis Map*, *Maturation Map*, *Ranking Map*, *Share Map*, *Skeleton Map*, and *Radar Map*, as well as many other maps that mix and match different patent data to form charts. More complex patent maps are the *Technology-function-application-product feature matrix*, *Themescape map*, *Neuron network map*, *Cluster map*, and *Hierarchical map*, as well as other fanciful maps that require patent-analytic software to generate. Examples and objectives of these maps are well documented and will not be repeated in this book.[1] However, the emphasis of this book is on using these maps or modifying them to draw insights from patent data.

The basic components for the construction of these maps are bibliographic data, text data, citation data, and more privileged data such as information about assignment, licensing, and litigation. Such data is usually not available free of charge. It is provided by patent-analytic software as additional and optional modules for customers who need this extra information. It is not essential to have this information to derive useful patent intelligence. This data, however, usually gives extra dimensions to derive extensive and concrete strategies.

In order to derive patent intelligence from patent analytics, one needs to identify the purpose of analysis as specifically as possible, choose the relevant patent map to depict the results, collect the required patent information, including determining what patents should be included in the analysis and what components need to be analyzed. Then the patent map can be drawn and be used to define patent intelligence (Figure 3.3).

[1] "Introduction to Patent Map Analysis", Japan Patent Office, Asia-Pacific Industrial Property Centre (2011).

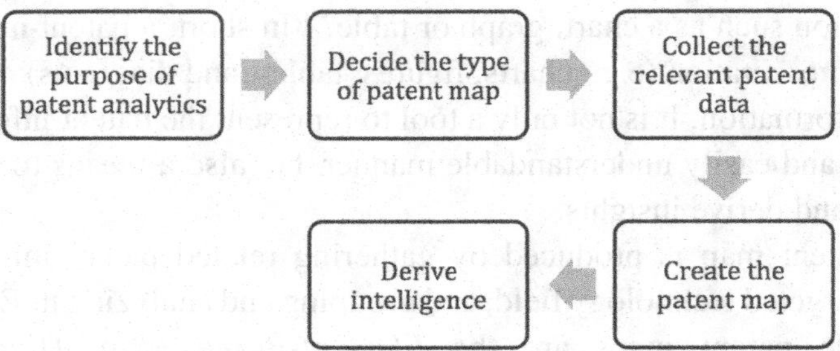

Figure 3.3 Deriving patent intelligence from patent analytics

3.3 Limitations and Problems in Patent Analytics

Patent analytics does have its shortfalls. As mentioned earlier, there are macroscopic and microscopic objectives to patent analytics. Sometimes, patent analysts who perform the patent analytics tend to focus too much on the macroscopic aspects and neglect the vital needs of companies to address their immediate problems. On the other hand, some companies do not understand the need for a macroscopic view to derive more meaningful microscopic strategies. A more balanced approach is to integrate both the macroscopic and microscopic aspects of analysis in order to best serve the company's interests.

Macroscopic analysis should be conducted in consideration of its relevancy at the microscopic level. For example, patents from its direct and indirect competitors should be identified and considered. At the microscopic level, companies should look beyond their own patent portfolios at the macroscopic level to leverage on others' patents for advancing their interests.

Besides this controversy on the usefulness of patent analytics, there are other limitations inherent in the patent database. One limitation is the subjectivity of patent evaluation. A reliable evaluation requires contextual interpretation such as comparing the patented invention with other similar technologies. Another limitation is the usefulness of the numerical patent indicators, which are usually not directly useful for licensing and litigation opportunity analysis. The indicators are usually interpreted with assumptions that may not be true for all analysis. An example is the assumption that higher citation counts mean stronger patents. This may not necessarily be true, as the strength of patents is also related to how well they are drafted. Patents may not be enforceable simply because they may be easily invalidated. Patent data also suffers from being unidimensional and may not be able to provide a holistic understanding for deriving strategies. A better approach should corroborate patent data with other information such as non-patent literature, market reports, and industry reports for a wholesome analysis.

3.4 Patent Analytic Scheme

Our unique approach towards patent analytics is an integrative set of theories combined with an understanding of the pragmatic requirements in industries to allow the readers to derive patent intelligence from patent analytics. The flowchart in Figure 3.3 provides an overview of deriving patent intelligence from patent analytics; in the subsequent sections, we will describe our approach on an operational level so that readers can consider using them as their standard operating procedures when performing patent analytics.

The first step in the patent analytic scheme is to define the right terms for searching related prior art of the patent. The resulting search terms can be extended and modified for the filing and acquisition of patents that are beneficial to the companies. The resulting patent portfolios are key to further effective patent strategies to be derived. Therefore, having a comprehensive and systematic methodology of patent search is the fundamental building block to further patent management activities.

There is a myriad of ways to describe a technology. This makes a full-proof search impossible. Good patent search scheme relies on the experience that a company has accumulated over the years. In addition, such a search scheme might overlook the peripheral technology that might be related to the invention. Therefore, a scheme with a wide scope and highly relevant to the invention is needed. We propose that the search scheme makes use of the technology life cycle, value chain, and the latest cooperative patent classification (CPC) as the fundamental clues to define the search string.

Considering the technology life cycle in the keywords search scheme is like tracing the historical development of the technology. This is especially useful when searching for prior art of the patent. Very often, the naming convention of the technology changes over time. However, the technology might have the same root and might be highly related. Therefore, considering the technology life cycle will provide additional ways of pinpointing prior art.

Considering the value chain in the keywords search scheme allows one to identify the key players, potential partners, or competitors that have similar technology. In particular, when considering the potential infringement either from or by the company, it is necessary to relate the technology with the products. Listing out all the related components and technology involved in the production of the final product will facilitate the trace from technology to product and enable the company to identify the end users of the final product. This will in turn help to identify the potential infringer or the potential patent owners whose patents the company is infringing on.

In addition to the technology life cycle and value chain, the usual information such as the companies, inventors, and the corresponding CPC of concern are used for further narrowing down the scope of the search. The specific steps and information used for the patent search scheme may vary depending on the purpose of the patent portfolio. However, the general direction is summarized in Figures 3.4 and 3.5.

3.5 Benefits Over Past Practices

Defining search keywords based on the technology life cycle and value chain will help to break down the search process into modules. Depending on the objectives of the search, the modules that need to be applied in the search can be included or omitted accordingly. For example, if a company wants to search for prior arts for a specific patent portfolio, it can identify which stage of the technology life cycle that portfolio is in. The company can also identify which segment of the value chain the portfolio is in. Once the status of the patent portfolio is defined, the corresponding players and/or components can be identified for a targeted search.

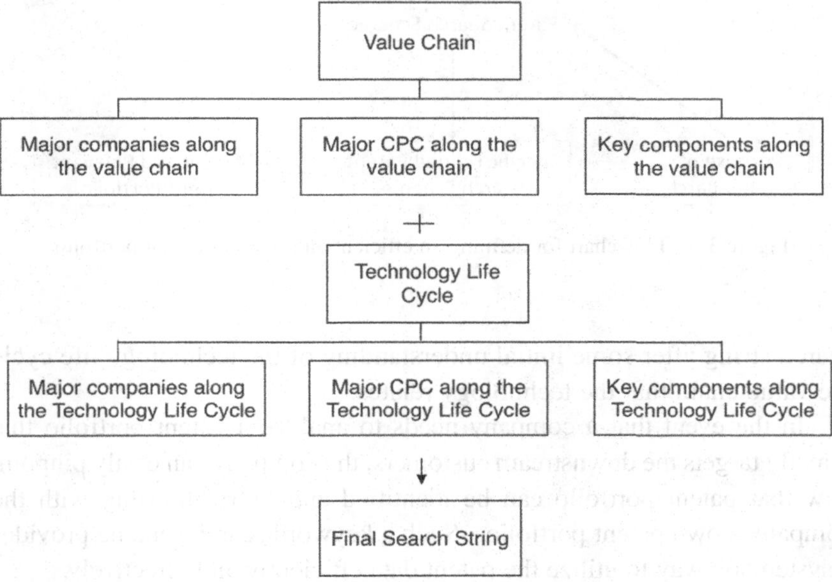

Figure 3.4 Keywords search scheme flowchart

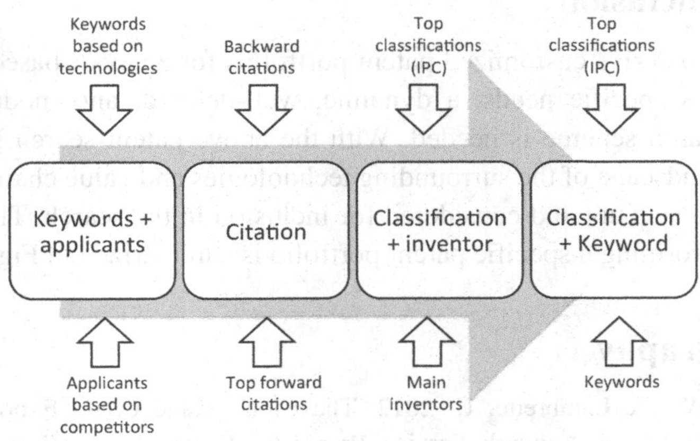

Figure 3.5 Patent search scheme

This framework has been found to be efficient. Traditionally, it took many rounds of discussion with the experts and refinement for the final, acceptable and agreeable search string to be formulated. With this modular approach, a non-expert can come up with a reasonably comprehensive

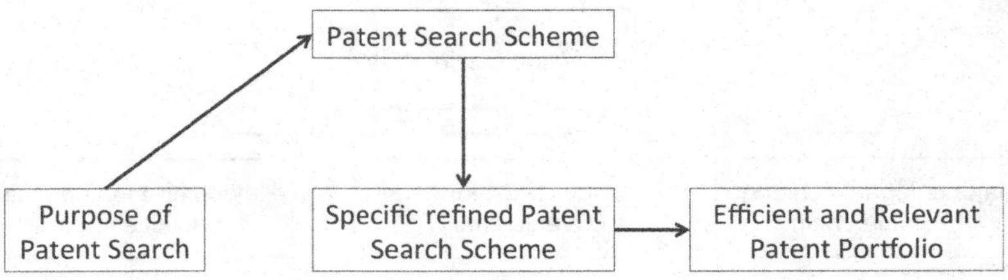

Figure 3.6 Flowchart for defining an efficient and relevant patent portfolio

search string after some initial understanding of the technology life cycle the value chain that the technology relates.

In the event that a company needs to analyze a patent portfolio that directly targets the downstream customers, the company can easily pinpoint how that patent portfolio can be identified and its relationship with the company's own patent portfolios. Such a keyword search scheme provides a systematic way to utilize the patent data efficiently and effectively.

3.6 Conclusion

In order to derive customized patent portfolios for analysis based on the company's specific needs, a dynamic, well-defined, and modularized patent search scheme is needed. With the above patent search scheme, the full landscape of the surrounding technologies and value chain can be taken into account and considered for inclusion in the search. The flowchart for forming a specific patent portfolio is summarized in Figure 3.6.

Bibliography

Belmans, W., & Lambrette, U. 2012. The Cloud Value Chain Exposed Key Takeaways for Network Service Providers. *White Paper, Cisco Internet Business Solutions Group (IBSG)*. Available at: http://www.cisco.com/c/dam/en_us/about/ac79/docs/sp/Cloud-Value-Chain-Exposed_030512 FINAL.pdf. Last retrieved on 6th Sept 2016.

Jaekel, M., & Luhn, A. 2009. Cloud computing — business models, value creation dynamics and advantages for customers. *Siemens IT Solutions and*

Services. Available at: http://www.cloud-finder.ch/uploads/media/Siemens_Cloud_Computing_Whitepaper_PDF_e.pdf. Retrieved on 6th Sept 2016

Liu, S.-J., & Shyu, J. 1997. Strategic planning for technology development with patent analysis. *International Journal of Technology Management*, 13(5–6): 661–680.

Mohammed, A. B., Altmann, J., & Hwang, J. 2009. Cloud computing value chains: Understanding businesses and value creation in the cloud. In *Economic Models and Algorithms for Distributed Systems*, D. Neumann, M. Baker, J. Rana & O.F. Rana (eds.). Springer, pp. 187–208. http://www.springer.com/gp/book/9783764388966.

Schultz, B. 1988. The evolution of ARPANET. *Datamation*, 34(15): 71.

Strawn, G. 2014. Masterminds of the Arpanet. *IT Professional*, 16(3): 66–68.

Su, Y.-S. 2014. Competing in the global LED industry: The case of Taiwan. *International Journal of Photoenergy*, 2014: 11. Article ID 735983. doi:10.1155/2014/735983. Available at: https://www.hindawi.com/journals/ijp/2014/735983/cta/.

Walden, D. 2014. The arpanet IMP program: Retrospective and resurrection. *Annals of the History of Computing IEEE*, 36(2): 28–39.

Chapter 4

Non-Patent Literature and Journal Intelligence

4.1 Introduction

Patent data provides a broad understanding of current technology based on past and present information. Such information, however, cannot be used to predict or project future technology trends. In this chapter, the information from journal database will be used to project or make an informed prediction of the next key technology areas to file patents in. The journal information is especially important for early stage technologies and when one wants to know the latest development of a technology, given that patent data has a 18-month time lag.

Commercial software such as "Web of Science" provides literature searches across a large database and fundamental analytic tools for refining the searches. This is similar to patent searches. By understanding the relationship between the technology life cycle, journal, and patent data, it is possible to derive patenting strategies to build up patent portfolios strategically. This chapter will provide an example of how the journal information and patent data are correlated and can thus be used in cooperation to derive technology direction.

4.2 Theoretical Background

With the boom of big data and many other analytical tools, using bibliometric studies for technology forecasting has become more promising. Journal articles and patent documents are often used as the measures of innovation. However, many studies have suggested that multiple sources of databases are necessary to eliminate biasness (Kleinknecht, Van Montfort, & Brouwer, 2002; Nelson, 2009). In addition, different sources have their own timeliness in a technology life cycle. Studies have proposed a list of technology life cycle (TLC) indicators to depict a comprehensive picture of the various stages in research and development (R&D) (Martino, 2003; Watts & Porter, 1997). For basic research, the Science Citation Index is used as an indicator; for applied research, the engineering index is used; for development stage, patent information is used; for application, newspapers are used and finally for social impact, business and popular press are used as indicators. Such bibliometric analysis can yield the TLC that the technology is in (Daim *et al.*, 2006). These studies, however, only pointed out that there are different indicators at the various stages of technology life cycle. They did not provide the linkage between these indicators, especially how one indicator can connect to another for technology forecasting as shown in Figure 4.1. It is the aim of this chapter

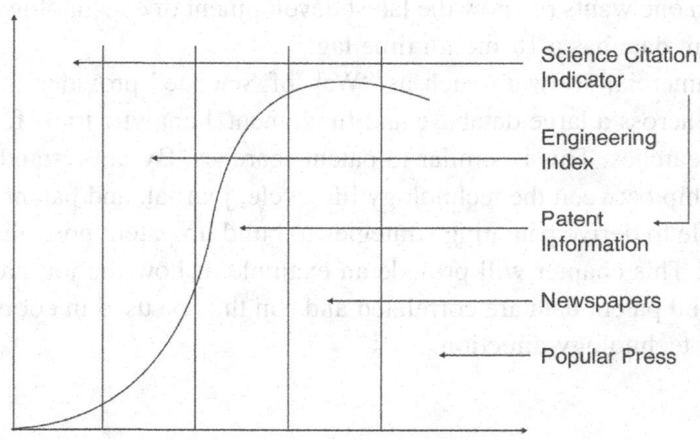

Figure 4.1 Linking the stages from science citation indicator to patent information

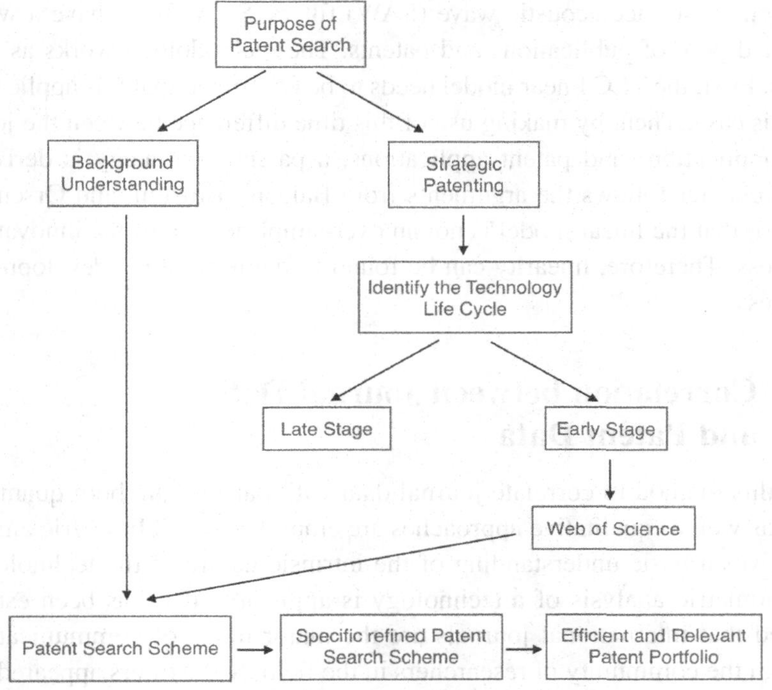

Figure 4.2 Flowchart for formulating the patent portfolio search for strategic patenting

to achieve this. Some critics have said that this model was only useful for the linear model of technology innovation and was in fact not applicable to real industrial cases (Rosenberg, 1994). Another criticism is that the sequence of occurrence of these indicators depends on industry and does not necessarily follow the stages in the R&D (Järvenpää *et al.*, 2011). However this book believes that if the technology in research is defined specific enough, the model can be used for technology forecasting.

Such technology forecasting can be used to answer the specific question of "what" kind of technologies or patents are needed moving forward, thus providing technology strategies. It can also provide direction for patent filing. Therefore, such a linkage is used to further expand the search scheme beyond patent database in order to derive patenting strategies as shown in Figure 4.2. To illustrate this methodology, a niche technology was chosen — surface acoustic wave (SAW) filters. SAW filters have a well-defined pool of publications and patents. The methodology works as follows. First, the TLC linear model needs to be confirmed that it is applicable in this case. Then, by making use of this time difference between the journal applications and patent applications, a patenting strategy is derived. This chapter follows the arguments from Balconi, Brusoni, and Orsenigo (2010) that the linear model is not an over-simplification of the innovation process. Therefore, linearity can be found in the technology development process.

4.3 Correlation between Journal Data and Patent Data

For this method to correlate journal data with patent data, both quantitative as well as qualitative approaches are employed. A bibliometric analysis gives a basic understanding of the intrinsic nature of the technology. Bibliometric analysis of a technology is applicable if it has been established that international journals are the major mode of communication within the community of researchers in the field. SAW filters appeared on the scene in the early 1970s with the discovery of the Rayleigh-wave or SAW. In the 1980s, there was a new call for low-loss filters. The properties of SAW met this need and there was a lot of development from that time (Morgan, 2000). By the 1990s, there were many journal articles on this technology. Therefore, bibliometric analysis is a justifiable measure for this technology.

In patent analysis, on top of the patent counts, there are various classifications, such as International Patent Classifications (IPC) defined by the World Intellectual Property Office (WIPO), European Patent Classification (ELCA) from the European Patent Office (EPO) and the newly joint development of Cooperative Patent Classifications (CPC) from US Patent Office (USPTO), and EPO. Examiners classify each patent document into the various relevant technology classifications. In this way, it is possible to have a finer categorization of the patent documents. For journal publications, there is no such classification. Therefore, the first step is to establish such a categorization for the journal articles and compare that with patent

Table 4.1 Profiles of experts in discussion

	Country based	Years of experience in SAW filters	Locations of SAW-related organizations worked for	Current position held
Expert 1	Germany	~20 years	Germany	Retired
Expert 2	Singapore	~13 years	France, Singapore	R&D Manager
Expert 3	US	~7 years	Singapore, US	Design Engineer

documents. First, a database that has a collection of the major journals encompassing the technology field was chosen. In the case of SAW, Web of Science is applicable as it provides a Science Citation Index that covers 250 disciplines and 120,000 journals with data ranging from 1900. It also provides Conference Proceeding Citation Index in Science and covers 5.2 billion papers published in books and journals from 1990 onwards. There are over 148,000 conferences covered yearly.[1] This database is also a convenient source of pattern and trend analysis as well as citation visualization.

Second, the document counts were analyzed. For SAW, five years of journal publications among the top journals for SAW filters were selected. The selection of these journals was based on interviews with experts in this field. One of the authors has worked in R&D in this field for six years in a multinational company that specializes in SAW filters and thus had a good overview of the technology. We have also discussed with ex-colleagues from France, Germany, and the United States — who have been working in this field for durations ranging from six to thirty years to ensure that this study includes all the major journals for this technology. The profiles of these experts are tabulated in Table 4.1.

In addition, journals relating to SAW filters were reviewed. It was found that all the top ten conference titles contributing to the pool of

[1] Available at http://thomsonreuters.com/products/ip-science/04_062/wos-next-gen-brochure.pdf (Last accessed 4th March 2014).

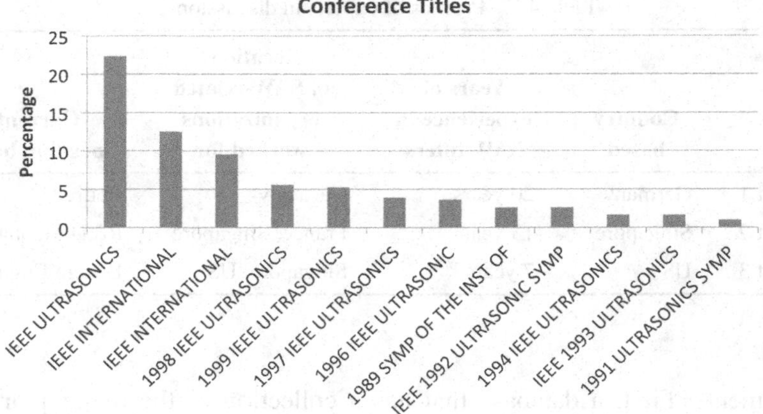

Figure 4.3 Spread of conference proceedings on SAW filters

articles stem from Ultrasonic Symposium as shown in Figure 4.3. There are no major journals specific for SAW filters.

Third, with this pool of major journals as one of the criteria and using Web of Science categorization to filter out articles that are directly related to SAW filters, 304 articles from 1979 to 2011 were collected and five years of documents from 1995 to 1999 were analyzed. Before 1995, the full journal articles were not available. The period between 1995 and 1999 appeared to be the prime period with major breakthroughs in SAW filters.

Fourth, a pool of US patent documents that ranging from 1995 to 2004 was searched. The database included the first year of analysis of the journal articles and extended another five years because, in a TLC linear model, the patent publications come after the journal publications. Patents that are published much later than the publication of the journal papers were not included because, in the SAW filter fields, the research cycle of most projects is around two to four years. The search strategy was discussed with the experts to confirm the comprehensiveness. From this pool of patent documents, the major IPC among them were identified and those categories were used as the basis for the classifications of journal documents.

Finally, these two measures for technology forecasting were compared. The steps involved and the relationship between the journal

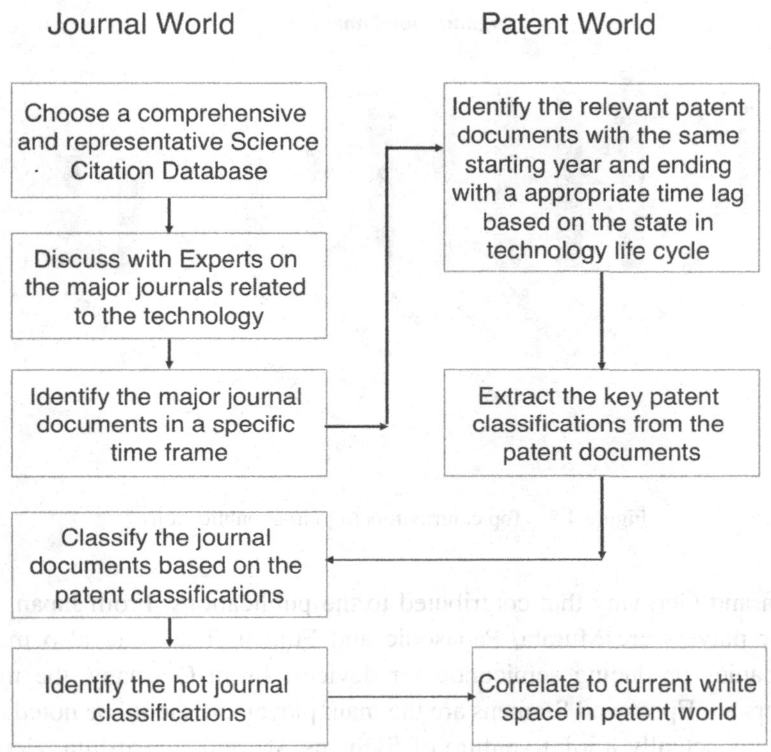

Figure 4.4 Overall scheme for journal search to achieve technology intelligence

documents and patent documents are depicted in Figure 4.4. It can be concluded that future directions for patenting can be derived from analyzing the trends of other sources of scientific publications.

4.4 Implementation of Scheme using Saw Filters

4.4.1 Profiles of SAW journal articles and patents

The publication trend of the organizations that contributed to the publications was investigated. Figure 4.5 shows the top organizations among the pool of publications analyzed. From the figures, most of the organizations that contributed to the journal articles were universities. They were from Japan, US, Finland, and Russia. There were also companies, mainly from

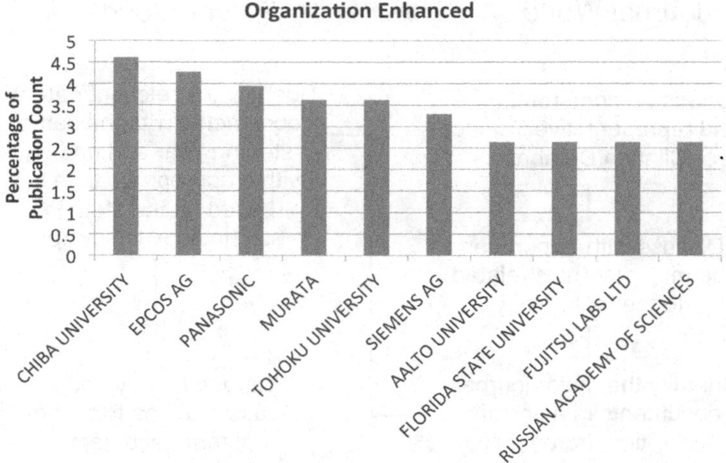

Figure 4.5 Top contributors to journal publications

Japan and Germany that contributed to the publications. From Japan, the major players are Murata, Panasonic and Fujitsu. These are also major companies producing semiconductor devices. From Germany, the main players are Epcos and Siemens are the main players. It should be noted that Epcos is actually a joint venture of Siemens AG and Matsushita. Hence, their publications are linked. This figure provides a background to the main players in SAW filters research.

Among the major patent contributors, Figure 4.6 shows that Murata is the top patent owners in SAW filters, followed by Matsushita, and Kyocera. Matsushita had collaborations with other SAW players in the industry and formed the joint venture, EPCOS AG with Siemens, in 1989, as previously discussed. Kyocera is a major supplier of piezoelectric crystal used to produce SAW in SAW filters. Universities do not top the list in patent ownership. This may either be because of the high costs of patent applications or the type of research published at journal publications was still at a stage when it was best communicated through major journals. Universities may contribute to fundamental research whereas the applied research is performed at the industrial level (Balconi & Laboranti, 2006; Bonaccorsi & Thoma, 2007). However, from Figures 4.5 and 4.6, companies have both journal publications and patent applications. And

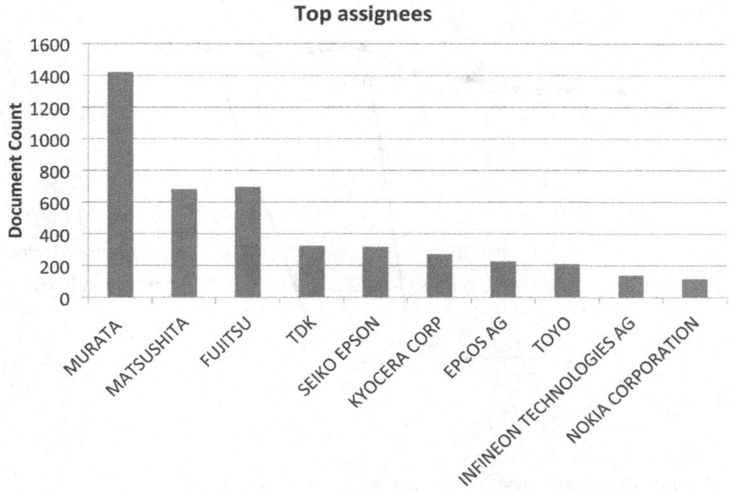

Figure 4.6 Top contributors to patent documents

some publications were joint efforts between universities and companies. Examples of collaborations between universities and companies are Russian Academy of Science and Taisaw from Taiwan, the Institute of Solid State & Material Research Dresden and Vectron International TELEFILTER as well as. Murata and Tohoku University.

4.4.2 TLC indicators

According to the linear model of TLC, there should be time differences between the journal publications and patent applications. Figure 4.7 shows the comparisons between the two indicators in original document numbers. The amount of patent documents related to SAW filters is about 50 times more than that of journal articles. This may be because of the explosion of patent applications after 1990s (Henderson, Jaffe, & Trajtenberg, 1998). It is also because not all journal articles were chosen for this study. In order to compare these two types of documents in one graph, the logarithm to base 10 of the patent publication numbers was compared to the logarithm to base 2 of the percentage of journal publications over the period 1995–2004. There are two peaks in each of the graphs of journal

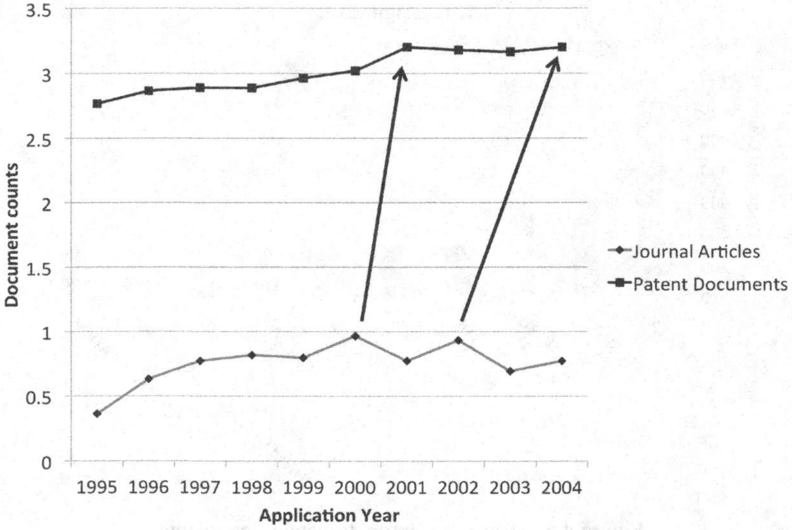

Figure 4.7 Correlations between journal articles and patent documents

articles and patent documents. The peaks in the journal article trend come around two years earlier than that from patent documents.

4.4.3 Major IPC of patent portfolio

In order to relate the document types of journal data to patent data, the IPC trends of patent applications from 1995 to 2004 was first analyzed. Figure 4.8 shows the trend. In early years, patents were mainly filed for structural designs of SAW filters: "network using surface acoustic waves", "constructional features of resonators using surface acoustic waves," SAW filters and "networks with electro-acoustic elements." They belong to the IPC H03H categories. It is only from 2000 that patent applications in "selection of materials for piezo-electric or electrostrictive elements" and "Processes or apparatus specially adapted for the manufacture or treatment of these elements or of parts" appeared. These belong to H01L and are more related to material research.

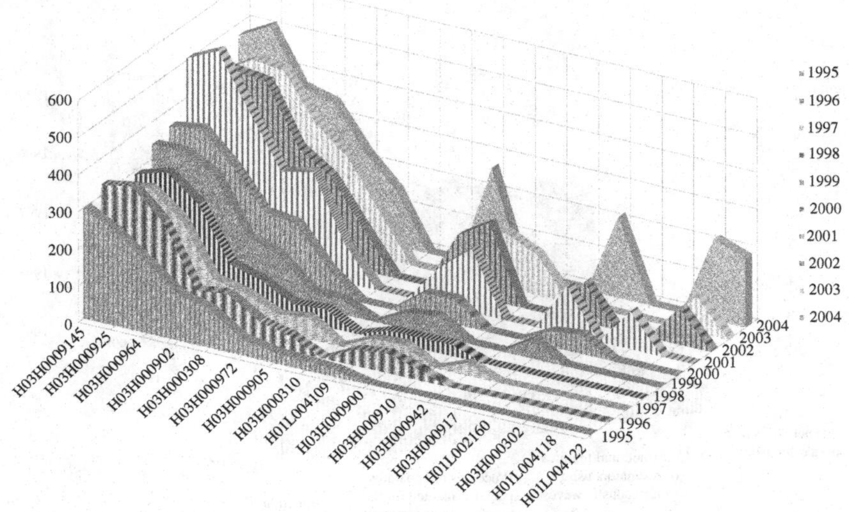

Figure 4.8 Technology trend from patent documents

4.4.4 Corresponding classifications for journal articles

The classification system of patent documents was applied to journal articles with the following results. Figure 4.9 shows that "selection of materials for piezo-electric or electrostrictive elements" and "processes or apparatus specially adapted for the manufacture or treatment of these elements or of parts" were the major topics of the publications since 1995. These two categories continued to dominate the research areas described in the journal papers through 1999. The number of publications also increased from 1995 to 1999.

4.4.5 Characteristics of the journal articles

In order to further analyze the relationship between the journal articles and patents, a company that has consistently been publishing journal

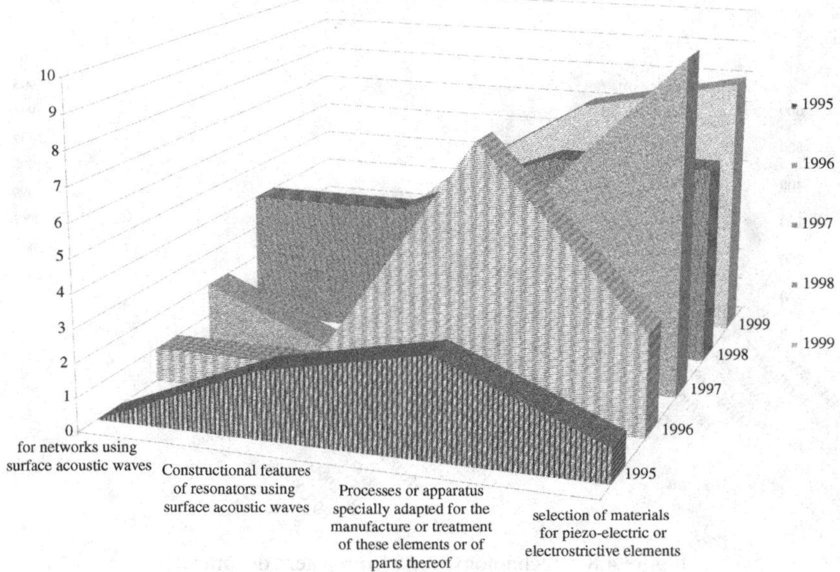

Figure 4.9 Technology trend from journal articles

articles and patenting was chosen — Murata. Table 4.2 shows the titles of the five top-journal-articles published by Murata between 1995 and 1999.

All these articles fall under the categories of the dominant research area identified in the previous session, i.e. materials related. In addition, all these articles were originated from the inventor Michio Kadota. The application trends of Murata's patents from 1995 to 2004 were then analyzed and shown in Figure 4.10. From the comparison, in the years between 1995 and 1999, Murata's patent counts were at the infant stage. The majority of the patents were filed in the direction of designs of the SAW filters, as reflected in H03H. It was from 2000 that patent applications started to climb rapidly. The rate of increase of patents related to materials (H01L) is more than 4 times from 1999 to 2000 (from 6 to 28 documents). The rate of increase of the patent applications for design increased slightly, by more than 2 times.

The patent application trends of the inventor Kadota (Figure 4.11) were to understand whether the time lag between patent applications and journal publication in the field of material research is due to the various

Table 4.2 Publications by Murata between 1995 and 1999

Title	Author	Year	Classifications
Piezoelectric properties of zinc-oxide films on glass substrates deposited by rf-magnetron-mode electron-cyclotron-resonance sputtering system	Kadota, M; Minakata, M	1995	Processes or apparatus adapted for the manufacture or treatments of these elements or of parts thereof
Influence of step-like portions on the surface of ZnO/glass SAW filters on their frequency characteristics	Kadota, M; Kondoh, C	1997	Selection of materials for piezo-electrostrictive elements
Surface acoustic wave properties on various rotated Y-cut Langasite crystal substrates grown by Czockralski method	Kadota, M; Nakanishi, J; Kitamura, T; *et al.*	1998	Selection of materials for piezo-electrostrictive elements
ZnO thin films for high frequency SAW devices	Ieki, H; Kadota, M	1999	Selection of materials for piezo-electrostrictive elements
Influence of leaky surface acoustic wave velocity of glass substrates on frequency variation of ZnO glass SAW filters	Kadota, M; Kitamura, T	1999	Selection of materials for piezo-electrostrictive elements

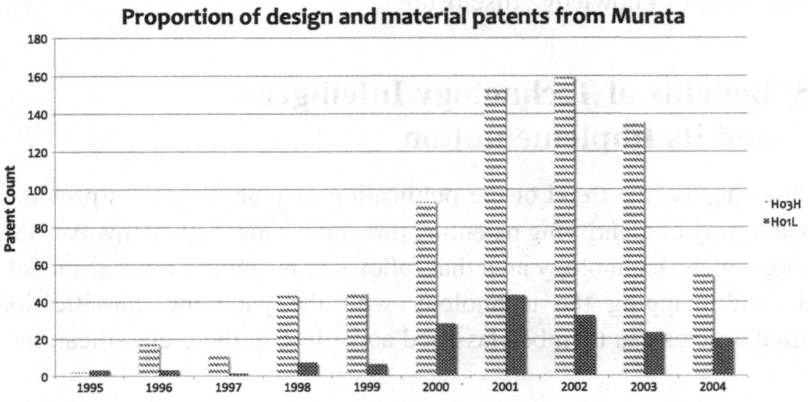

Figure 4.10 Proportion of material and design patents from Murata

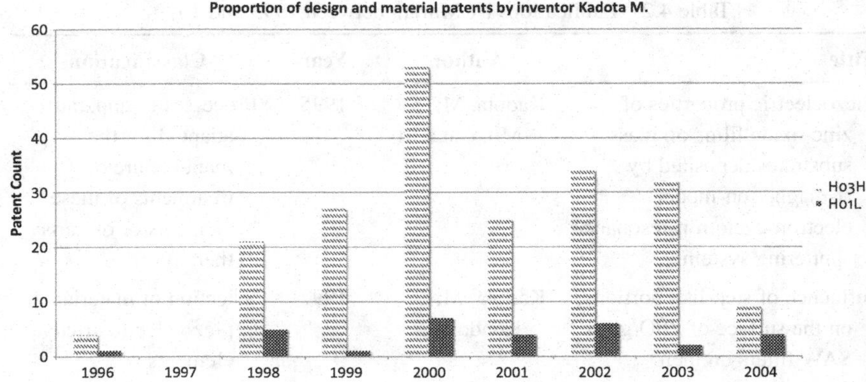

Figure 4.11 Proportion of design and material patents by inventor Kadota

research groups of the company researching in different research directions and each research group chooses a different mode of communication. More specifically, the patent applications of Kadota who authored the journal articles on Zinc-oxide from 1995 to 2004 were tracked. The results showed that while Kadota was doing research on Zinc-oxide and published articles in academic journals, he also did have patent applications in those years. But those patent applications were related to the design of SAW filters instead of material selection. His patents on materials (H01L) came about 3–5 years later. This seems to suggest that research in the Zinc-oxide material was not ripe for patent application in the period between 1995 and 2004. Journal publication seems to be a better mode of knowledge disclosure.

4.5 Benefits of Technology Intelligence and its Implementation

In this chapter, the trend of the publication of journal articles provides a possible way of identifying patenting direction. This method involves identifying a niche technology area that follows or resembles a linear model of TLC and mapping the technology with the patenting classifications. Journal articles can then be classified according to these classifications to deduce the future trend of patent applications. The "white space" where there are currently not many patent applications can be crowded after a few years. The technologies that are in these "white spaces" can be inferred from the "hot zones" in the journal articles landscape.

This method utilizes the combination of qualitative and quantitative methods to analyze a group of journal articles and patents. This not only provides an extra source of information for patenting directions; it also serves as a forecast. This method is applicable to well-defined technologies, such as SAW filters. Another similar technology is LED. An example of a niche LED technology that may follow linear model of development is blue LED and its similar upstream technologies. In this way, the patent classifications are precise, small, and analyzable. This method can also be extended to other semiconductor industries, such as touch screens and electric cars.

This chapter provided a way to identify future technology and patenting directions. This is especially useful in industries where time to market is very important.

In addition, there is a stream of research by Murray and team (Huang & Murray, 2009, 2010; Murray, 2002) on the relationship between scientific publications and patent filings. Murray looked at the co-evolution of science (reflected in journal publication) and technology (reflected in patents) and explored the intricate networks between these two realms (Murray, 2002). We find that the highly paper- published and patents filed inventor, Kadota, has in fact a lot of co-publication and co-filing on both the material and design technology areas in journal publications and patents filings. Some of the journal publications were co-published with the Japanese University. In this case, the knowledge has spilled over from the scientific to the technology networks. This study further introduced a time domain to suggest that since scientific publications in the same technology appears first; companies can use the information directly from the journal publication trends. This is especially beneficial in this big data domain where journal databases are massive and easily assessable provided the organization subscribes to these key journals. Therefore, companies can indirectly leverage on the journal publication trends to commercialize their products through understanding the maturity of the technology.

However, special attention is needed, as suggested by Huang and Murray (2009). They examined the paper-patent pair and found that patent publication had a negative effect on the amount of later paper publication. This chapter provided an explanation of such negative effects by introducing the time domain. The scientific publications normally describe fundamental research, which is at a stage that is far from commercializable products. Patents appear several years later when the science has matured to a stage where the technology can be developed into products. This is the time when it makes financial sense to protect the invention through legal means. From there the company can undertake further research on their invention simply because the company produces or uses such invention, it knows best what the problems are that need to be solved further.

To ensure that the patents do not impair scientific contribution, it is important to make sure that the fundamental science should not be patented. The government has a role to play to implement policies, either through legislation or through court judgments to ensure that the science can be freely explored by the public. This has partly been taken care of in many current national Patent Acts. Many governments are also in the process of refining the patentable subject matter, such as software and business patents. Once this segmentation of technology development stages is clear, the eco-system for product commercialization becomes more harmonized. More entrepreneurs can come into the ecosystem. In effect, all roads lead to Rome. Companies can have various manufacturing processes to implement the science. Entrepreneurs can contribute to the building of roads through good patenting strategies. But access to Rome should not be blocked.

4.6 Conclusion

From the above analysis of the relationship between journal publications and patent applications, it can be concluded that Universities tend to publish rather than patent and Universities and companies collaborate to publish journal articles together; Companies file more patents that are closer to the products. In addition, if the TLC follows the linear model, the journal publications are completed ahead of the patent publications. Hence a company can formulate their patenting strategies through understanding the publication trends of both academic papers and patents.

Through the case study of Murata's patent portfolio relating to SAW filters, it can be seen that companies choose the channel of communication of their research results according to the maturity and nature of the technology. Even though Kadota who published papers focuses only on one research field, he also filed patent applications at the same time and the nature of these inventions in patent applications was different from that in the journal papers.

Based on the above relationship, the following mechanism in Figure 4.12 is derived to predict the patenting trend:

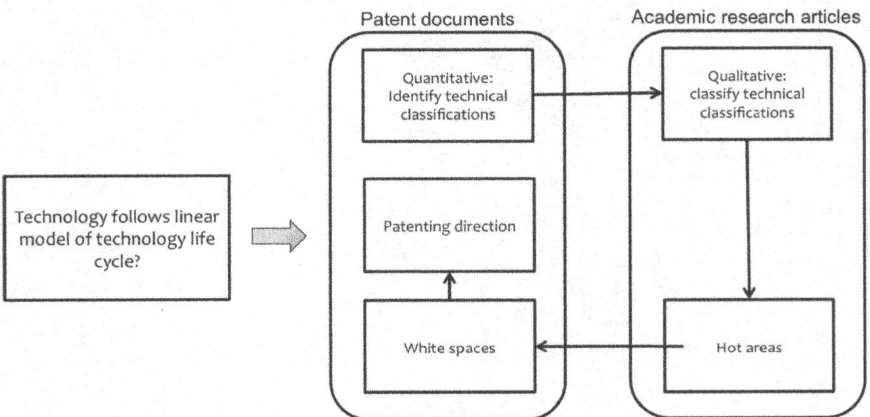

Figure 4.12 Methodology to predict patenting trend

Chapter 5
Patenting Strategies

5.1 Patenting Strategies for the Creation of Patent Portfolio

With the increasing complexities of research and development (R&D) and the fast changing patent law regime, as explained in the previous chapters the filing of a single patent is inadequate. The goal of patent filing cannot be just to pursue a single full-proof patent. The goal may be a strong patent portfolio. Unfortunately, the current understanding of the patent portfolio is too simplistic and uni-dimensional to be effective.

EPO defines a patent portfolio as "a list of patents owned by an individual or a company." This focuses largely on the ownership of a patent portfolio. However, this is insufficient because the strategic value of a list of patents randomly put together is limited and ambiguous unless there is an inherent structure that binds the individual patents together. Parchomovsky and Wagner (2005) advanced the understanding of a patent portfolio by highlighting that the individual patents inside a patent portfolio must be distinct-but-related.[1] However, both "distinct" and "related" are overarching terms that do not sufficiently explain how patent portfolios can be constructed.

Granstrand (1999) did establish some structures for patent portfolios along the line of patenting strategies although he did not use the

[1] Parchomovsky, G., & Wagner, R.P. 2005. Patent portfolios. *University of Pennsylvania Law Review*, 154(1): 1–77.

concept of patent portfolios. He suggested that there are six patenting strategies: *ad-hoc blocking and inventing around, blanketing or flooding, strategic patent searching, fencing, surrounding, and combination*.

The strategy of *ad-hoc blocking* and *inventing around* is the result of limited funds and manpower; *strategic patent searching* can be used when a single patent has a large blocking power for doing business within a specific product area. The *blanketing* and *flooding* strategy involves the systematic mining of the patent landscape to wipe out minor-competing inventions. The *fencing* strategy blocks a specific line of R&D using a series of patents whereas the surrounding strategy uses a group of patents that may be unimportant individually but may be capable of blocking the commercial implementation of the key patents owned by others. Finally, the *combination* strategy refers to the thoughtful planning and building up of patent portfolio to strengthen the overall protection and increase the bargaining power of the company. All these strategies provide insights to the structures of patent portfolios, but it is ambiguous how and when these strategies should be applied. In fact, certain strategies are more appropriate for particular stages along the technology cycle, and not all strategies are feasible for all types of technologies. In addition, depending on the company's size and its market status, particular strategies may be more applicable than others. Therefore, there is a need to make the strategies contextual and provide a framework for patent owners to devise their patenting strategies. There is also a need to provide guidance in analyzing and visualizing a patent portfolio systematically. This chapter attempts to fill this gap by providing some indicators for analyzing a patent portfolio.

5.2 A Multi-Dimensional Approach of Patenting Strategies

It is important to adopt a multi-dimensional approach to shaping patenting strategies. Patenting strategies consist of both intrinsic structure and extrinsic factors. The intrinsic factors aim to build up connectivity between patents in a portfolio. As we have explained in detail in the last chapter, patents and patent portfolios can be evaluated based on three broad criteria: legal, technological, and commercial values. In the same

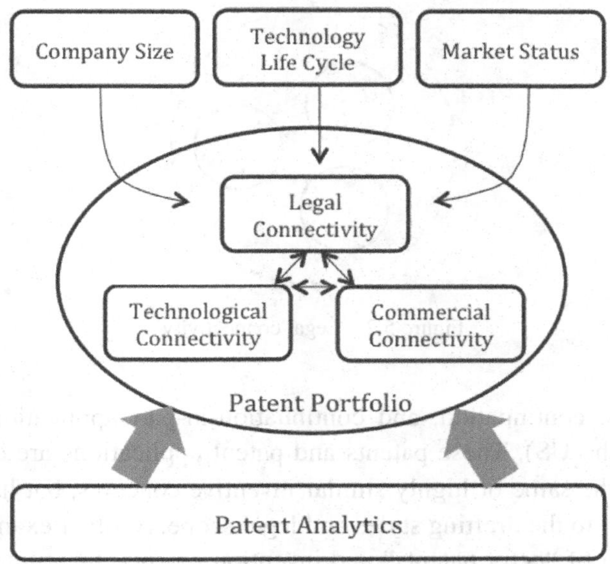

Figure 5.1 Constructing a patent portfolio

token, these three criteria should be the cornerstones for building up a valuable patent portfolio. After fortifying the basic structure of patent portfolios, external factors including technology life cycle, value chain, technology power, and market power need to be considered to provide the context for application. Patent indicators can be used to support the formation of such patent portfolio structures and patent analytics help to put the portfolios in context (Figure 5.1).

5.2.1 The intrinsic structure of patent portfolios

5.2.1.1 *Legal connectivity*

The closest connectivity between patents in a portfolio is legal connectivity. This relationship refers to patents sharing similar if not the same inventive concept. They differ only in the variation of legal characteristics (Figure 5.2). A typical example of a patent portfolio having legal connectivity is one with provisional applications, non-provisional patent

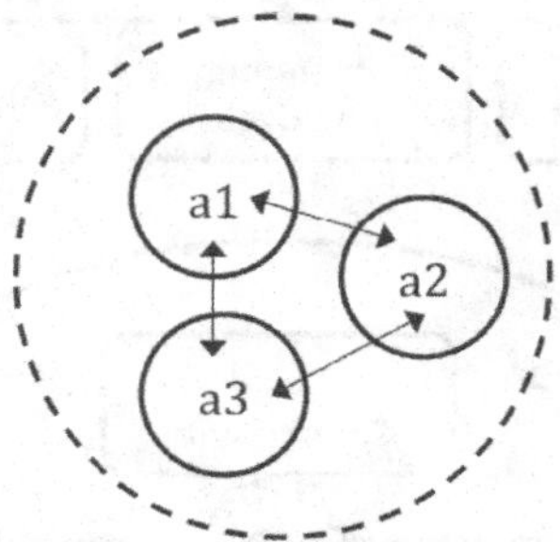

Figure 5.2 Legal connectivity

applications, continuation, and continuation-in-part applications (in the context of the US). These patents and patent applications are essentially describing the same or highly similar inventive concepts, but have minor variations as to the drafting styles and legal scope. Another example is the combination of "petty patents" and invention patents. In countries where petty patents or innovation patents, such as utility models (e.g., China, Japan, Korea, and Taiwan) are available, companies can file both the petty and invention patents pertaining to the same technology simultaneously. Only one can be retained, however, if both are to be granted eventually.

The strength of having legal connectivity within a portfolio is in building up the legal strength of the invention by allowing the patent owner to refine the legal scope over a period of time. This in turn builds up a better association between a product feature and the corresponding patents. Companies often file patents hastily due to pressure to launch their products quickly. The drafting quality of the patents is thus compromised. It is also almost impossible to file a perfect patent encompassing all the foreseeable claims and specifications. Thus, continuation and continuation-in-part applications are good vehicles to address such problems. In addition, the validity of a single patent may also be challenged due to more definite interpretation of law over time. An example would be the interpretation of 35 U.S.C. §112(f). It mentions that,

> *"An element in a claim for a combination may be expressed as a means or step for performing a specified function without the recital of structure,*

material, or acts in support thereof, and such claim shall be construed to cover the corresponding structure, material, or acts described in the specification and equivalents thereof."

This is the law that governs the means-plus-function doctrine. Over time, more cases help to define the requirements of a means-plus-function claim. In the case of software, WMS Gaming, Inc. v. Int'l Game Tech., 184 F.3d 1339 (Fed. Cir. 1999) ruled that the specification must disclose corresponding structure in the form of an algorithm for performing the claimed function. This algorithm may be disclosed in various forms, such as mathematical formulas, flowcharts, prose, or in any other manner that provides sufficient structure. Disclosure of a general purpose computer, however, by itself is not sufficient to satisfy the rule of algorithm. Therefore, software patents that were drafted without clearly stating the algorithm for performing the claimed function may be considered invalid. If there are other patents in the portfolio that may describe the algorithm or if there is a utility patent, the invention can still be protected.

In Williamson v. Citrix Online, LLC, 792 F.3d 1339, 1343 (Fed. Cir. 2015), the *en banc* Federal Circuit overruled the traditionally applied presumption that claim terms that do not include the word "means" are not to be construed as means-plus-function elements. The court determined that the standard going forward should be "whether the words of the claim are understood by persons or ordinary skill in the art to have a sufficiently definite meaning as the name for structure." Under this situation, if there is another patent that can rectify this claim construction problem, the patent right of the patent owner may still be protected over the particular technology.

Besides cementing the legal standing of the patent, a patent portfolio with legal connectivity may also prolong the monopoly period of an invention. This is especially important for pharmaceutical companies. After the patent term which is about 20 years in most countries the drugs may become generic and the price of the drugs may fall drastically–a phenomenon known as "patent cliff." Patents such as continuation-in-part are filed later than the parent patents and thus they have a later expiry date.

5.2.1.2 *Technological connectivity*

The next level of connectivity is technological connectivity. Patents covering different inventive concepts can be grouped together based on their technological characteristics. Patents covering complementary technologies are one such example. They cover various distinctive inventions and yet are all needed to produce the final products. Another example would be between patents that cover a fundamental technology and those that cover its different applications.

In order to illustrate the concept of technological connectivity, we exemplify pictorially using Figure 5.3. A company that wants to produce product P requires some essential technologies, for example, *a, b,* and *c.* Therefore the company needs to build up a patent portfolio with technologies *a, b,* and *c* with complementary relationship among them. This is very often the case for manufacturing hand phones. The telecommunication patents relating to standards, such as the Long Term Evolution technologies or the Wi-Fi technology are very often essential. Technologies like that relating to touch screen and user interface may be nice to include because they improve the functionality and quality of the product but may not be that essential for a hand phone. These are technologies *d* and *e* in Figure 5.3. Thus, if a company builds up a patent portfolio consisting of technologies *a–e,* it is said to have built up a portfolio with technological connectivity.

Building onto this, a smartphone may be further integrated with a music player (R). The combined product is a multi-functional smartphone, S. Therefore, a patent portfolio with technologies *a, b, c, d, e, k, l, m,* and *n* are considered as having technological connectivity as they contribute to producing S.

Besides producing just one core product, a technology may be essential for producing multiple products. This is the case for the Wi-Fi technology. It can be used in smartphones. It can also be used in computers and notebooks. Many tablets also include Wi-Fi functionality. The Wi-Fi technology is represented by *a* in Figure 5.3. It is seen as a core technology that has multiple applications for products P, Q, and O. Products P, Q, and O may be computers, notebooks, and tablets. All the other technologies such as *b, c, f,* and *g* that are needed to make products P, Q, and O can be considered to have indirect technological connectivity since all of them are related to the basic technology *a.*

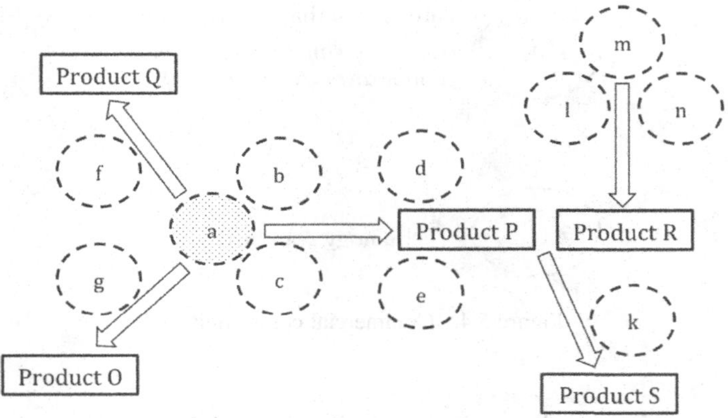

Figure 5.3 Technological connectivity

5.2.1.3 *Commercial connectivity*

In addition to legal and technological connectivities, patents may also have commercial connectivity as well. Commercial connectivity may take many forms (Figure 5.4). A few examples are briefly mentioned below.

One expression of commercial connectivity is through patent pools. In most cases, a patent pool includes patents from various patent owners, who may be upstream or downstream players; collaborators or competitors. Such commercial connectivity accords patents commercial powers. For example, patents from upstream and downstream players could be presented together for patent licensing. This may potentially achieve a better licensing outcome.

Another form of commercial connectivity occurs when a patented technology has been incorporated into a technology standard. This connectivity could improve the patent's enforceability, as it is easier to establish infringement of the standard essential patent.[2] It is also easier to license these patents as players in the industry must adopt such technology.

Despite these advantages, standard essential patents are subject to the fair reasonable and non-discriminatory (FRAND) royalty rate

[2] A product that claims to fulfill a technology standard is deemed to infringe the standard essential patents unless the alleged infringer can prove otherwise (e.g., the SEP is in fact not essential to the standard).

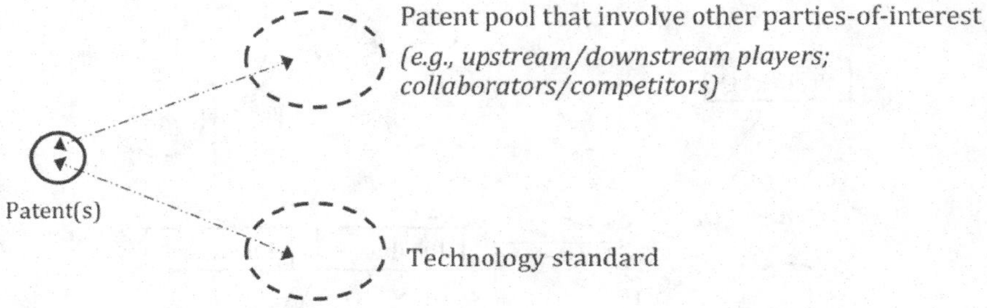

Figure 5.4 Commercial connectivity

requirements. Patents in pooling and alliances might also be subjected to antitrust scrutiny. Licensing contracts found to be in violation of antitrust issues may not be enforceable.

Commercial connectivity is a very diverse and encompassing relationship among patents. It can be realized via many different forms. Patents with commercial connectivity may also show legal and technological connectivity. The structures may be arranged based on the six patenting strategies suggested by Granstrand (1999). In this chapter, we will provide more examples of how patent portfolios can be organized effectively around these three structures.

5.2.2 The extrinsic factors of patent portfolios

The extrinsic factors also shape the patenting strategies. Patenting strategies are the legal arm of technology strategies and they must go hand-in-hand to provide the maximum returns for companies. As such, one of the most important factors to consider is the technology life cycle. Companies need to understand how their core competency fits in the technology life cycle. Next, the market power of the company has to be considered. The market power consists of two parts: the monetary power and the technology power of the company. The monetary power is closely related to the company size, while the technology power depends on whether the company is a first mover or latecomer in the use of the technology. As a whole, deriving patenting strategies is like planning product development projects.

Companies need to balance the budget for building the patent portfolio with the potential returns of monetizing the portfolio.

5.2.2.1 *Technology life cycle*

Technology development follows an evolutionary process. Seldom can technologies, especially radical technologies, burst into existence and be applied immediately and successfully to products. Between the birth of the technology and the final successful implementation lies a long road of improvement and refinement. Similarly, patent portfolios — being the legal counterpart of technologies — will also evolve with technologies. It is not unusual to find patent portfolios in the early stage to focus primarily on the core fundamental technology while being applicable to many different products in the future. The patent portfolios found at this stage are often connected by just legal connectivity. As the technology evolves, new inventions would be more focused on addressing the problems of the "new" technology. More patents on neighboring technologies would be filed. The patent portfolios would evolve with increasing technological connectivity. Eventually when the technology is at the commercial stage, patents would be filed relating to the applications of such technology. As such, commercial connectivity comes into the picture. Thus, we see an evolution in the structure of patent portfolios.

The evolution occurs not only in the structure of patent portfolios along the technology life cycle, but in the patenting strategies as well. In many cases, the evolution in the patenting strategies occurs naturally in companies that have established IP management practices. At an early stage of the technology life cycle, many companies, be they multinational or small and medium, would tend to be on the defensive. At that stage, the technology is uncertain; it may not be easy to patent anything that is far from the core fundamental invention. It is also not easy to pinpoint what the future technology is. Hence, at this stage, it is easier and safer to file patents that describe their invention. As the technology matures a bit more, the technology direction can be more distinctive and discernible and the strategies shift toward proprietary patenting. This means that companies find their core competence and niche to start building up patent portfolios around them. Eventually, when the technology matures, the patenting strategies employed might sometimes be derived from the past patents that have built up over time. Companies that begin development when the technology is at a mature stage may be forced to patent around the core technology. Therefore, we see that patenting strategies change along the technology life cycle. There will be more illustrations in the subsequent sections.

5.2.2.2 *Market power*

5.2.2.2.1 Monetary power

It is important to recognize that patenting strategies depend a lot on the budget that the company has to file and maintain their patent portfolios. Large companies with more cash flow, have more options on strategies for filing patents. The strategies that are usually used by companies with large market power are *blanketing/flooding*, *fencing* and, sometimes a *combination* of strategies. On the other hand, companies with smaller budgets on patents usually use *ad-hoc blocking*, *strategic patenting*, and *surrounding* strategies. In the course of this chapter, we will show how monetary power affects the strategies along the technology life cycle.

5.2.2.2.2 Technology power

Another factor that influences the choice of structure is when companies start to get involved in the technology. Companies that invest early in the research of a technology have the option to get the core patents right from the beginning. For companies that enter late, they only have the choice to either purchase the core patents or they are forced to build up the patent portfolios around the core patents. It is important to understand these external factors that affect patent portfolio formations but intrinsic factors of companies that inevitably shape the patent portfolios.

5.3 Structuring the Framework

The focus of the following sections will be on mapping the six patenting strategies: *ad-hoc blocking and inventing around, blanketing or flooding, strategic patent searching, fencing, surrounding, and combination*, along the technology life cycle of a chosen technology.

In this book, such patenting strategies are manifested using patent classifications. For convenient referencing, we include the following structured hierarchy of the CPC classification scheme here.

- Section (one letter A to H and also Y)
  - Class (two digits)
    - Subclass (one letter)
      - Group (one to three digits)
        - Main group and subgroups (at least two digits)

For example, in the case of H04L 67/00,

- Section **H**
  - Class **04**
    - Subclass **L**
      - Group **67**
        - Main group **00**

Essentially, the choice of *ad-hoc blocking* and *inventing around* strategies are the result of limited resources. This is manifested in companies filing in various neighboring CPC groups but under a major subclass. This is contrasted with *strategic patent searching* strategy where the patent filing is very directed. Even a single patent has a large blocking power for doing business within a specific product area. The company filing in a specific sub-group of a main group manifests such strategy.

In comparison, the *fencing strategy*, which is defined as blocking a certain line of R&D using a series of patents, is manifested by filing a series of patents via the broad range of CPC subgroups to block the line of R&D for the main group. Both the *strategic patent searching* and *fencing* concern the lower hierarchy classifications.

In contrast to *fencing*, *blanketing, and flooding* are strategies that randomly fill the patent landscape in a particular technology, which creates the possibilities of knocking out minor inventions. This is manifested in companies filing in various main groups or subgroups in several key subclasses.

Surrounding strategy relates to a group of patents that may be unimportant individually but may block some commercial implementation of the key patents owned by others. A company filing almost evenly in various subgroups under the same subclass manifests this.

Combination is a careful planning and building up of patent portfolios that can eventually strengthen the overall protection and increase the bargaining power of a company. They are the results of combining any of the above five patenting strategies.

Existing literature on IP strategies almost always focuses on deriving new strategies but neglects the importance of an overview for application of the various strategies under context. It is the objective of this book to address this gap. In this chapter, these six strategies are mapped onto the technology life cycle. The process flow of analyzing the macroscopic environment of technology life cycle and deriving the corresponding strategies is illustrated in Figure 5.5.

5.3.1 Cloud computing history

There are three milestones in cloud computing: "Advanced Research Projects Agency Network" (ARPANET), the launch of Napster and the launch of Amazon Web Services. Cloud computing originated from the idea of an "intergalactic computer network" that was introduced in the sixties by J.C.R. Licklider. He was responsible for enabling the development of ARPANET (Advanced Research Projects Agency Network) in 1969 (Mohamed, 2009). However, some experts attribute the cloud computing concept to the computer scientist John McCarthy. He proposed the idea of computation being delivered as a public utility, similar to the service bureaus that date back to the sixties. The word "cloud computing" was first coined by information system professor Ramnath Chellappa in 1997 (Cantu, 2014).

The next milestone for cloud computing was the launch of Napster from Salesforce.com that delivered enterprise applications through a simple website in 1999. This was then followed by Amazon Web Services, which launched the Amazon Mechanical Turk in 2002. This was a suite of cloud-based services including storage, computation, and even human intelligence (Salesforce.com, 2011). In 2006, Amazon enhanced

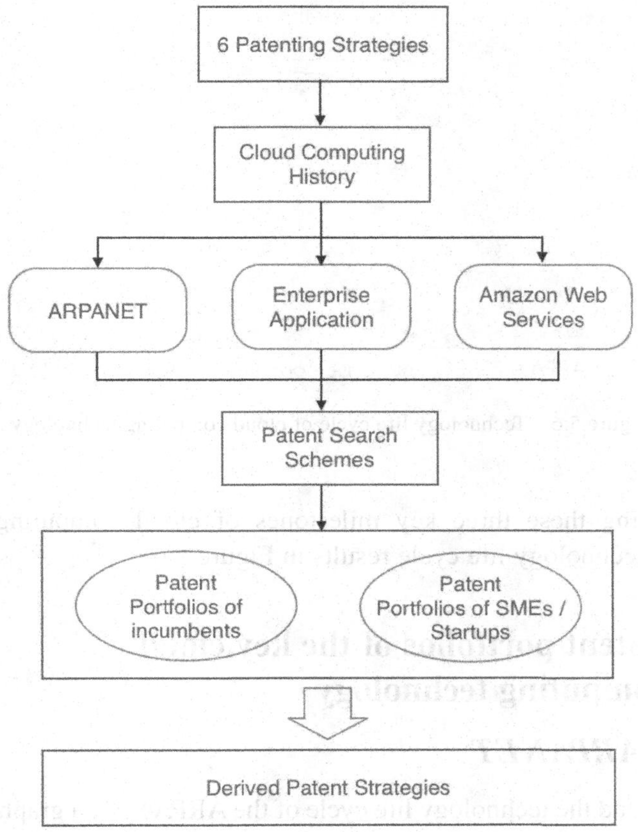

Figure 5.5 Deriving patenting strategies along the technology life cycle

the infrastructure to make cloud computing further accessible by launching its Elastic Compute Cloud (EC2). It is a commercial web service that allows small companies and individuals to run their own computer applications by renting computers to them.

In 2009, Web 2.0 became more popular as Google, Microsoft, and other giants started to offer browser-based enterprise applications through services, such as Google Apps. By this stage, virtualization technology, the development of high-speed bandwidth, and the evolution of universal software interoperability standards had matured enough to make cloud computing accessible to all.

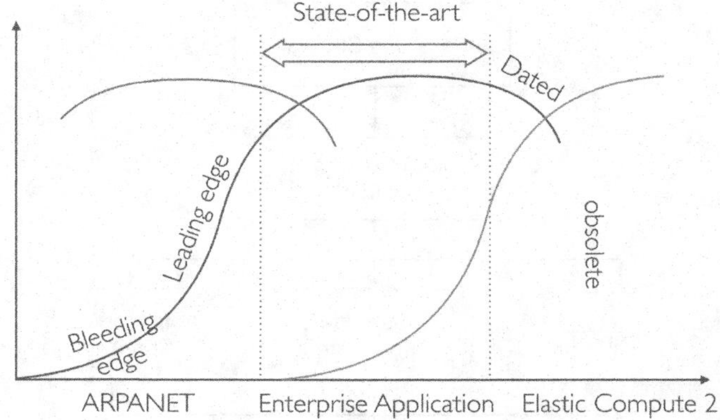

Figure 5.6 Technology life cycle of cloud computing technology

Matching these three key milestones of cloud computing history along the technology life cycle results in Figure 5.6.

5.3.2 Patent portfolios of the key cloud computing technology

5.3.2.1 *ARPANET*

To understand the technology life cycle of the ARPANET, a graph of number of patents against company count was plotted as shown in Figure 5.7. It can be seen that the number of companies researching in ARPANET started to increase dramatically from 1999 to 2006. 2002 was the peak of this development. After 2006, the number of companies researching in this technology declined drastically. The pattern is typical of a technology that has reached its obsolescence. The date referred is the application date.

An early player in this technology was Bell Lab. It filed the majority of the patents in the early 1990s. However, its success was not as strong as the latecomers. Today, Bell Lab is no longer in the value chain of cloud computing. The relative latecomers at that time were Verizon, Hewlett-Packard (HP), and IBM. Most of Bell Lab's and AT&T's ASPANET patents are now under Verizon Patent Licensing Inc. Verizon, HP and IBM

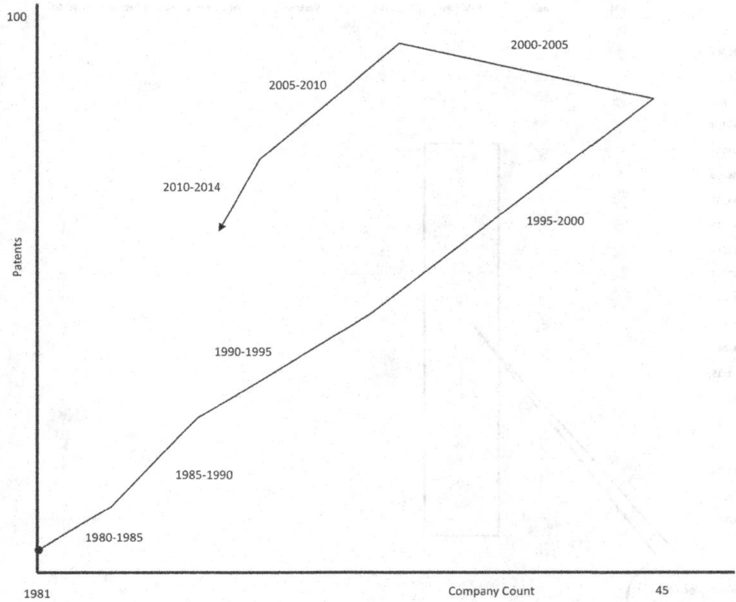

Figure 5.7 Technology evolution of ARPANET

are the incumbents in providing the network facilities for cloud computing today. Palo Alto entered this field after the others. A further check on Palo Alto's patent portfolio revealed its focus on providing enterprise security platforms.

An analysis of this ARPANET patent portfolio in terms of CPC classifications is shown in Figure 5.8. Verizon's patent portfolio includes Bell Lab's patents and depicted as Verizon here. As can be seen in Figure 5.8, Palo Alto's patent portfolio is mainly in CPC areas that are away from Verizon's and AT&T's patent portfolio. For example, Palo Alto's patents are in CPC H04L 45/00 (Routing Or Path Finding Of Packets In Data Switching Networks), H04L 67/32 (for scheduling or organizing the servicing of application requests, for example, requests for application data transmissions involving the analysis and optimization of the required network resources), and H04L 65/10 (Signaling for real time communications). These are the areas of

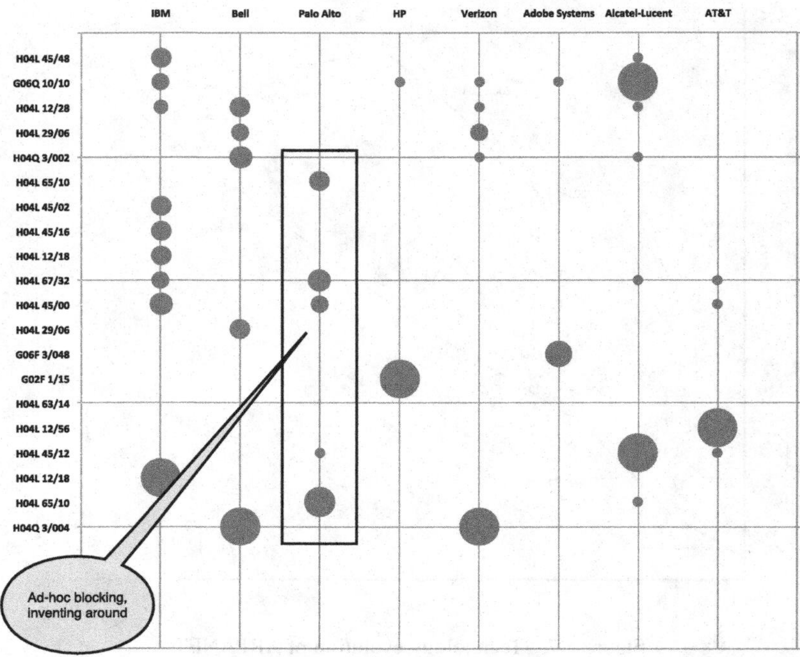

Figure 5.8 Ad-hoc blocking, inventing around Patenting Strategy of Palo Alto compared to Verizon and AT&T

modern cloud computing. On the other hand, Verizon's patent portfolio is in the original ARPANET technology — H04Q 3/04 (Circuit arrangements for receivers of routing digits) and AT&T's in the H04L 12/56 (Packet switching system/Networks). These are the more fundamental infrastructural technology. From the CPC distribution pattern in Figure 5.8, Palo Alto's patent portfolios are not in the same areas as that of Verizon and AT&T as shown in Figures 5.9 and 5.10. Its patenting strategy can be termed as *ad-hoc blocking*, *inventing around* the incumbents' patent portfolios. In addition, Figures 5.11 and 5.12 show that Bell Lab, AT&T, and Verizon together have filed in many groups under the same subclass; whereas Palo Alto has filed only very few subclasses it has filed more patents in a specific subgroup than Bell, AT&T, and Verizon.

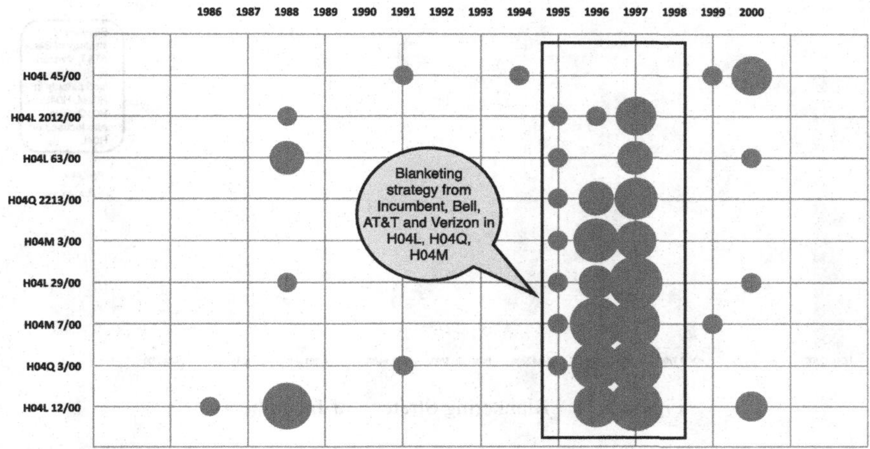

Figure 5.9 Top CPC groups of Bell, AT&T and Verizon by filed year

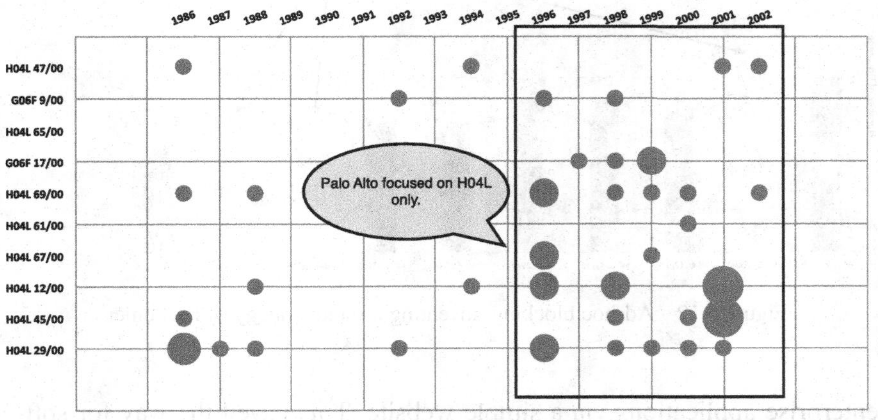

Figure 5.10 Top CPC groups of Palo Alto by filed year

5.3.2.2 *Enterprise applications*

The second milestone in the cloud computing history is the arrival of Salesforce.com in 1999. Salesforce pioneered the idea of delivering

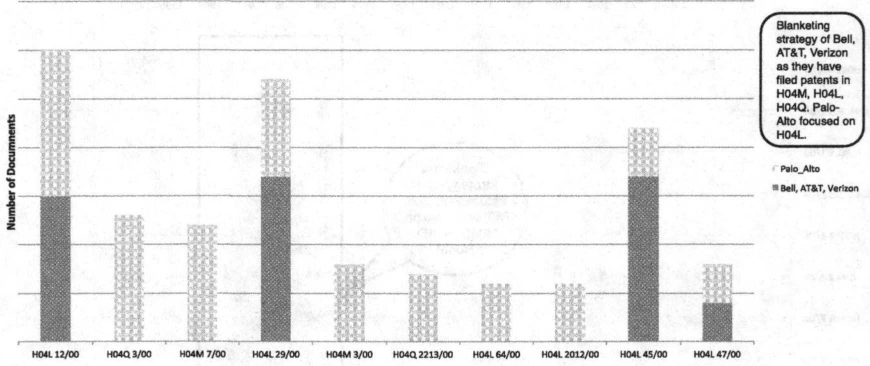

Figure 5.11 Blanketing Strategy of Incumbents

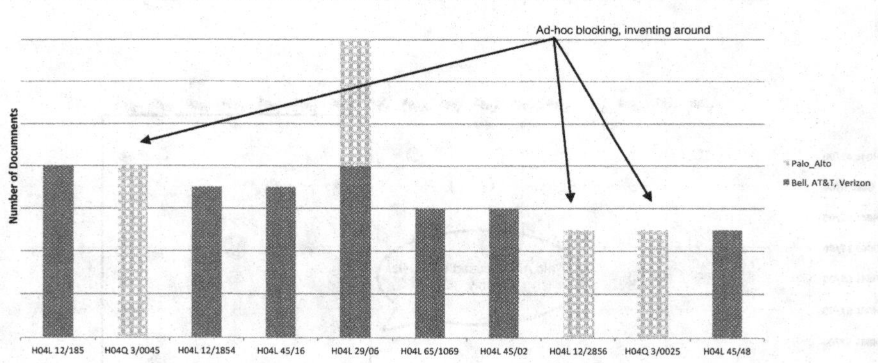

Figure 5.12 Ad-hoc blocking, inventing around strategy of latecomer

enterprise applications via a simple website. This paved the way for software firms to deliver applications over the Internet.

The number of patent count against the number of companies for Enterprise Application Technology is shown in Figure 5.13. The date referred is the application date. In recent years, the number of patents and companies involved in the technology are decreasing. This is typical of a technology that is reaching the state-of-the-art stage.

Salesforce was the company that pioneered this technology. At that time, it was just a start up. Not long after Salesforce's product "Napster"

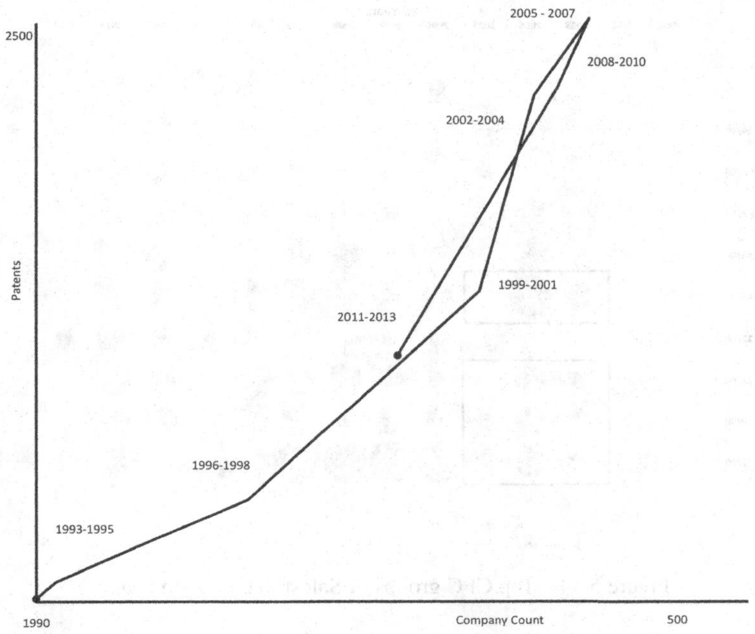

Figure 5.13 Technology life cycle of Enterprise Application related technology

was launched, its competitors launched their own versions. One of Napster's major competitors was Microsoft. Therefore, the patent portfolios of these two companies were compared and analyzed. The top CPC groups for Salesforce over the years are shown in Figure 5.14. The top CPC groups for Microsoft are shown in Figure 5.15. The overlapping areas between the two highlighted rectangles show the CPC groups that the company was focusing on at the time when Salesforce first launched the Napster service. Comparing the two graphs, it can be seen that both Salesforce and Microsoft were filing patents in the same CPC groups. They were mainly related to network communications and network applications.

A comparison at a level down on the CPC codes of Salesforce and Microsoft, however, shows the differing patenting trends of the two companies. They are shown in Figures 5.16 and 5.17. It can be seen from Figure 5.16 that although both Salesforce and Microsoft filed mainly in

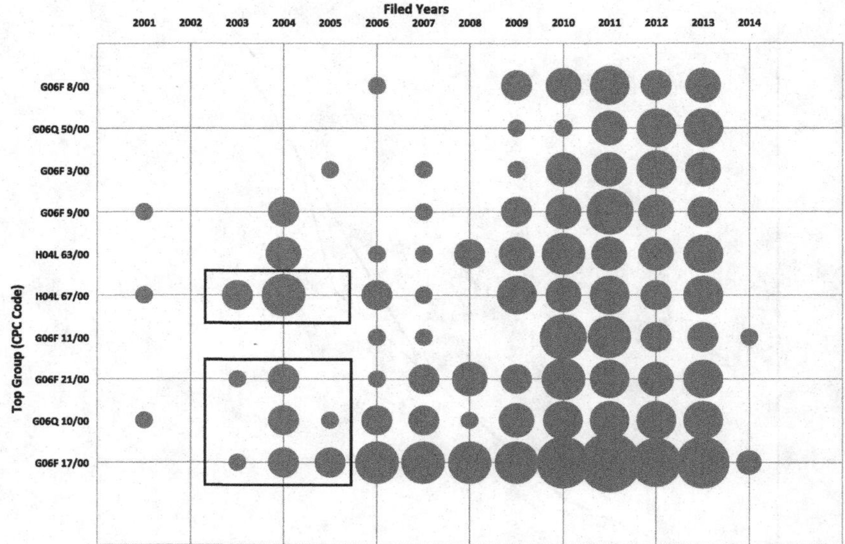

Figure 5.14 Top CPC groups of Salesforce by filed years

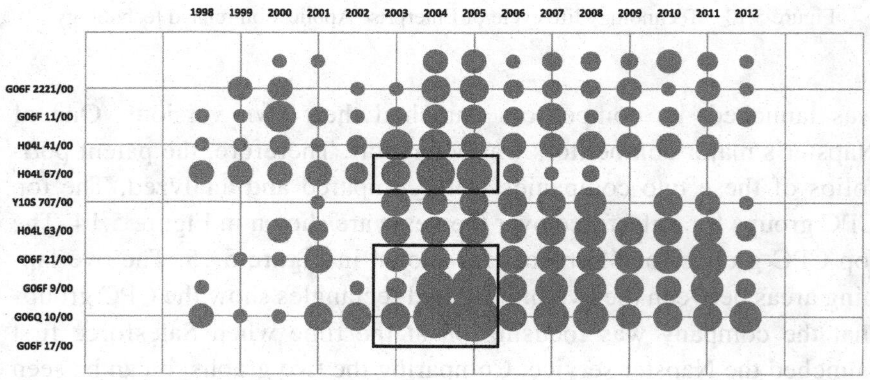

Figure 5.15 Top CPC groups of Microsoft by filed year

CPC H04L 67/00 (networked applications), Salesforce was very focused in filing in H04L 67/02 (web-based technology, e.g., Hyper Text Transfer Protocol [Http]) and H04L 67/306 (user profiles). On the other hand, Microsoft has equal filing over a broad range of CPC codes. Similarly, for

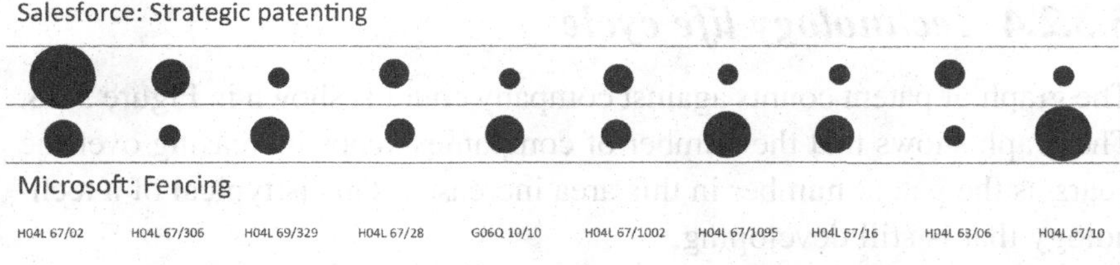

Figure 5.16 Strategic Patenting of Salesforce in CPC H04L 67/00

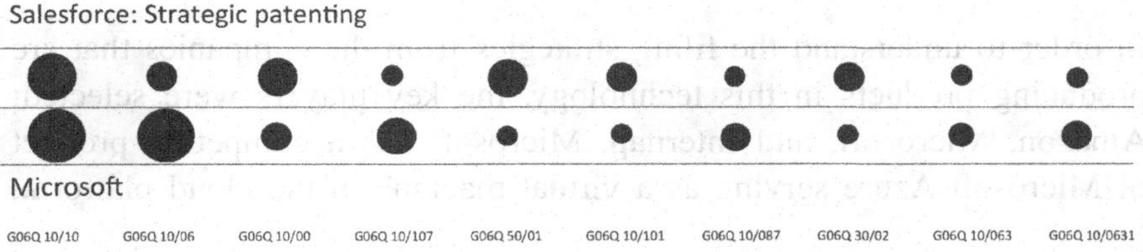

Figure 5.17 Strategic Patenting of Salesforce in CPC G06Q 10/00

the CPC codes G06Q 10/00 (systems or methods specially adapted for administration; management), Salesforce strategically focused on G06F 10/10 (office automation), G06Q 50/01 (social networking), G06Q 10/101 (collaborative creation of products or services), G06Q 30/02 (market research and analysis). Salesforce's portfolios are bigger than Microsoft in these areas. These demonstrated the *strategic patenting* strategies of Salesforce and the *fencing* patenting strategies of Microsoft.

5.3.2.3 *Web services*

The third milestone in cloud computing history is the launch of the Elastic Compute (EC2) by Amazon. This service is the central part of Amazon's Web Services that provide a cloud computing platform. Amazon Web Services (AWS) is a collection of remote computing services (also called web services) that form a cloud computing platform. AWS provides online services for other websites or client-side applications that are not seen directly by end users. These services are functionalities that other developers can use in their applications. EC2 allows customers to rent virtual computers to run their applications.

5.3.2.4 *Technology life cycle*

The graph of patent counts against company count is shown in Figure 5.18. The graph shows that the number of companies keeps increasing over the years as the patent number in this area increases. This is typical of a technology that is still developing.

5.3.2.5 *Current overall patent filing strategies*

In order to understand the filing strategies from the companies that are producing products in this technology, the key players were selected: Amazon, Microsoft, and Internap. Microsoft has a competing product of Microsoft Azure serving as a virtual machine in the cloud platform.

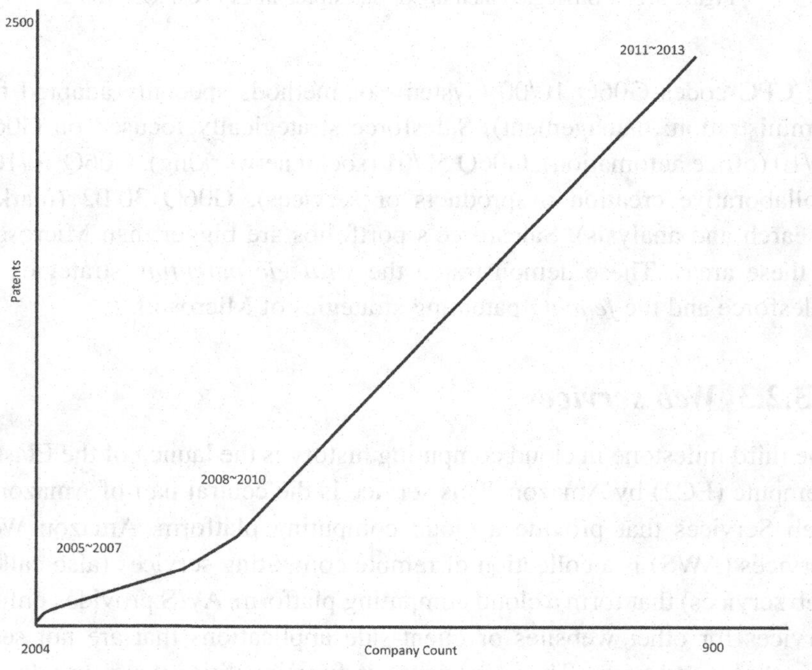

Figure 5.18 Technology life cycle of EC2 related technology

Both Amazon and Microsoft are incumbents. Internap is a latecomer in this area with a smaller patent portfolio.

Figure 5.19 shows the patent portfolios distributions of these three companies. The patent portfolios of Amazon and Microsoft are very diverse. Other than the key sub-group G06F 17/00, which describes the digital computing or data processing method, both Microsoft and Amazon have a diverse filing of other sub CPC classes (G06Q, H04L, Y10S). For Internap, all the subgroups that it has filed are in H04L, which is related to the transmission of digital information. Comparing the pattern of patent portfolios between the incumbents Amazon, Microsoft, and that of Internap, Internap's patenting strategy is surrounding a key classification subclass while that of Amazon and Microsoft are launching a blanket filing across different subclasses. This may be because they have more resources and their businesses are more diverse.

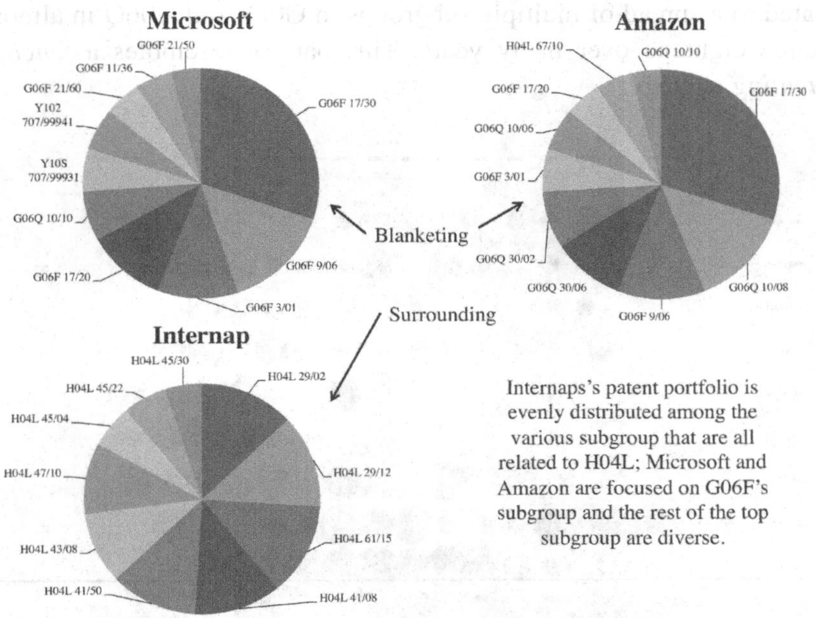

Figure 5.19 Patent portfolio distributions of Amazon, Microsoft and internap

5.3.2.6 *Incumbents' patent filing strategies in virtual computers*

In order to understand the filing strategies of Amazon and Microsoft in the developing technology of their Elastic Cloud 2 and Microsoft Azure, the CPC sub-group G06F 17/00 on digital computing or data processing equipment was investigated. Within this CPC sub-group, the main classification for the virtual machine technology is G06F 17/30, "Information retrieval/database structure." Therefore, the filing pattern of Amazon and Microsoft in G06F 17/30 was plotted as shown in Figures 5.20 and 5.21. Two different patterns can be observed from these two graphs: Amazon does not file patents in all areas, but focuses on specific groups, such as G06F 17/00, G06Q 30/00 and Y10S 707/0, and files patents strategically in these areas. On the other hand, although Microsoft also files patents in the particular areas of G06F 17/00, G06Q 30/00, and Y10S 707/0, Microsoft's patents in G06F 17/30 are also related to a spread of multiple subgroups in G06F and G06Q in almost equal weightage over many years. This pattern resembles a *fencing patenting* strategy.

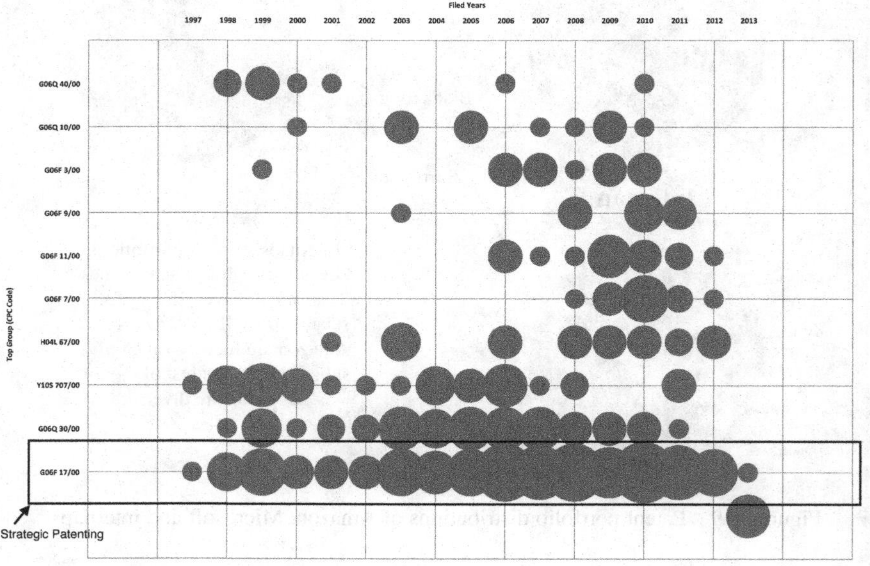

Figure 5.20 Amazon's strategic patenting in G06F 17/00

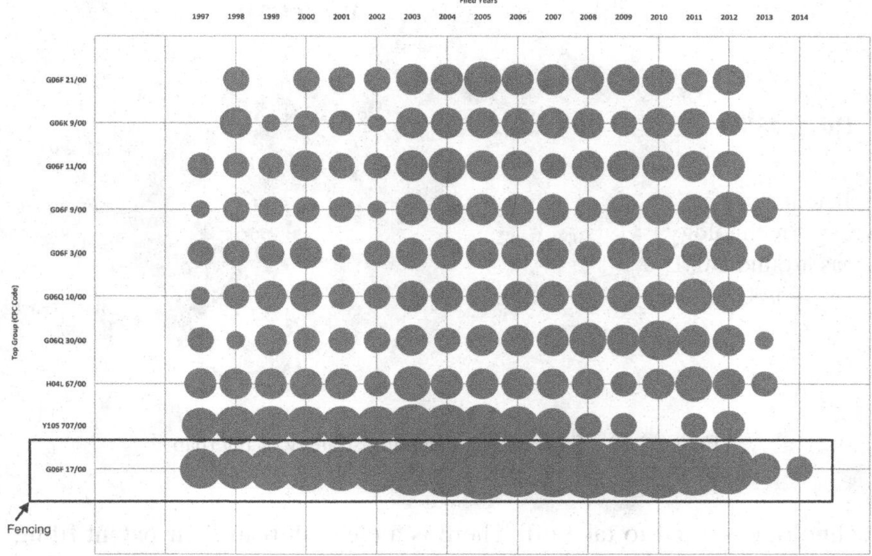

Figure 5.21 Microsoft's fencing patenting strategy in G06F 17/00

5.3.2.7 *Latecomers' patenting filing strategies in virtual computers*

For Internap, most of its patents were filed in the technology classification H04L 45/00. A further analysis of the patents within this group shows that they are distributed over diverse sub classifications related to H04L 45/00 as shown in Figure 5.22. This is typical of a *surrounding patenting* strategy.

5.3.3 Incumbents' patenting strategies over the years

Amazon and Microsoft also demonstrated their evolving patenting strategies over the years. Both companies filed patents in the data processing, database, and file management areas in the 90s and early 2000s. However, their filing directions started to change to network applications as the development of the third milestone in cloud computing–virtual computing

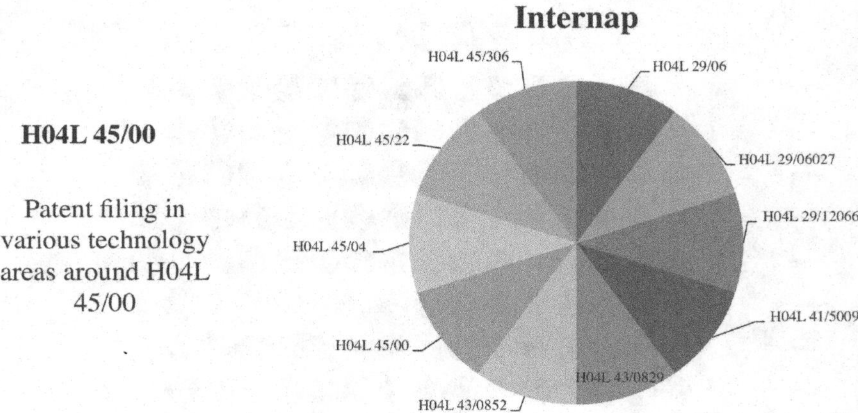

Figure 5.22 Surrounding patenting strategy of Internap

technology, started to take off. There is a clear shift in their patent filing focus from infrastructure, which is an upstream technology, to system integration, which is a downstream technology. For Amazon, one of its core businesses is in E Commerce and it has been filing patents in this area throughout these years. These changes are shown in Figure 5.23.

5.3.4 Technology latecomers' patent filing strategies over the years

In contrast to the *strategic and fencing patenting* strategies of Amazon and Microsoft, Internap's patenting strategy over the years is markedly different. Internap focuses on developing the core technologies in network specific arrangement in H04L 67/00 and G06F 17/00 since the early 2000s. In recent years, it has started to file patents in surrounding technologies such as interface arrangements for transferring data, systems for specific business sectors and network security in G06F 8/00, G06Q 50/00, and G06F 3/00, respectively. In addition, it has also become active in interface technologies, such as arrangement for program control in G06F 9/00. The filing trend of Internap is shown in Figure 5.24.

Based on the analysis of the patent filing strategy of Internap, the following *surrounding* trend can be observed in Figure 5.25.

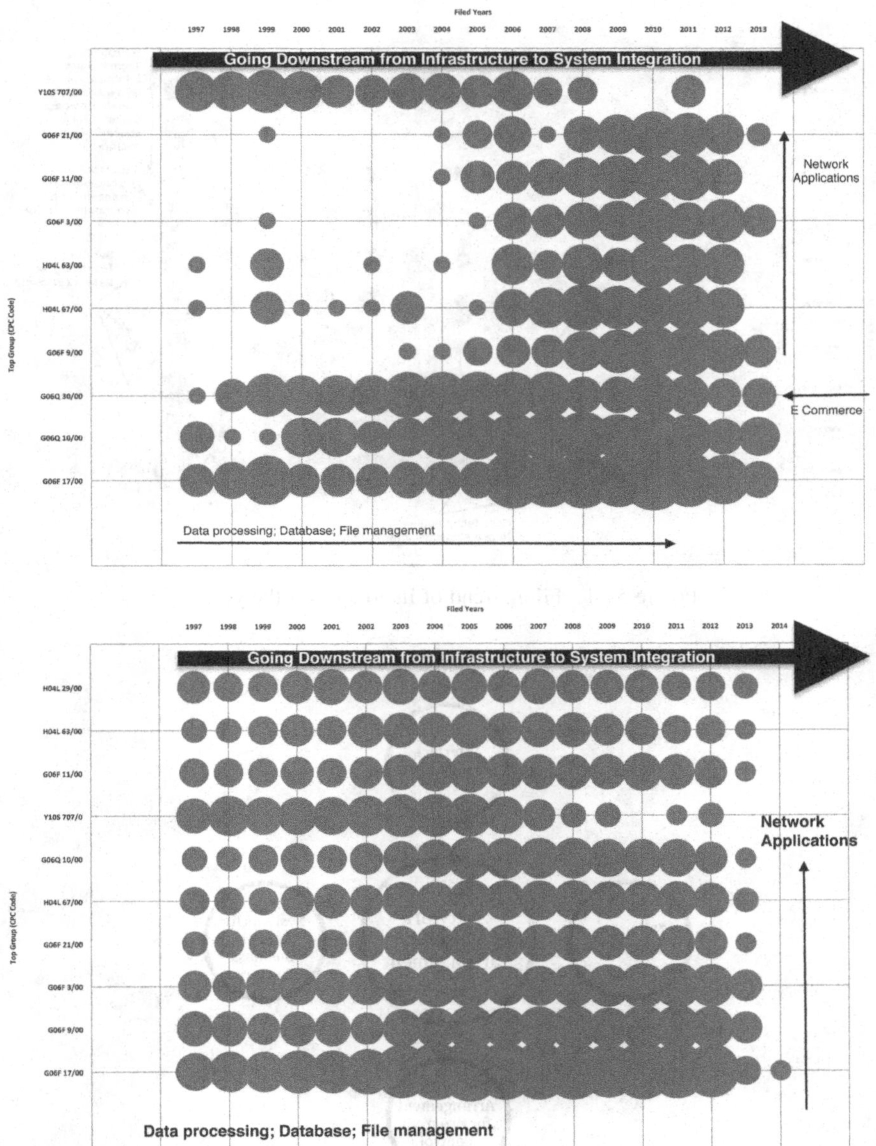

Figure 5.23 Shifting filing focus for Amazon and Microsoft over the years

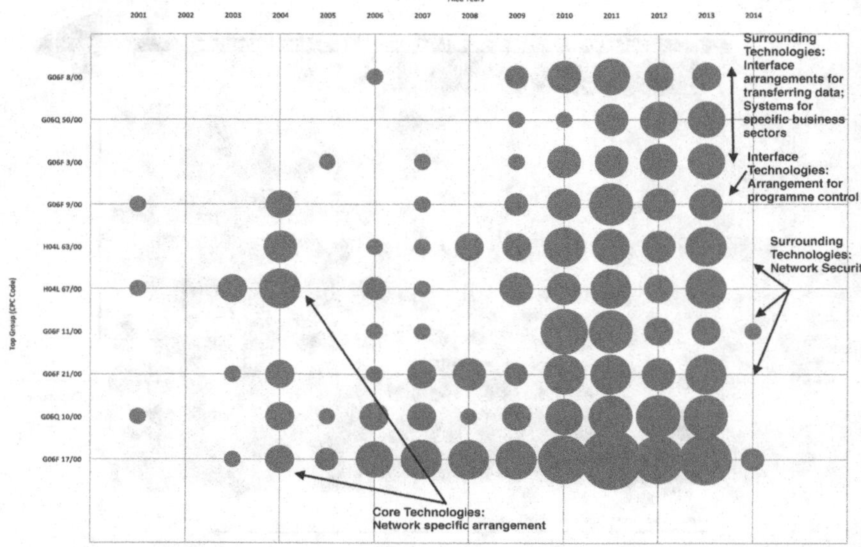

Figure 5.24 Filing trend of Internap over the years

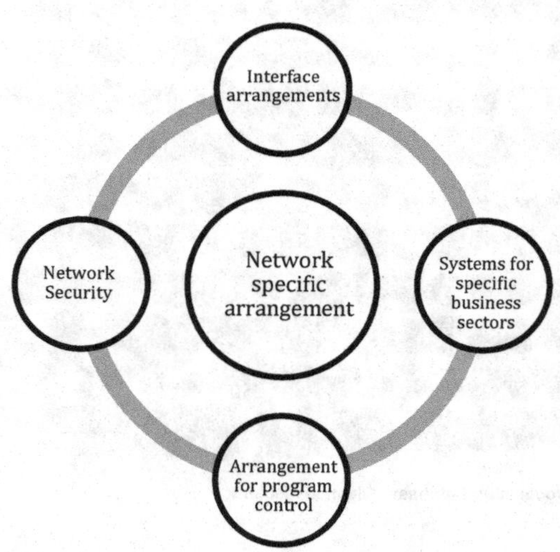

Figure 5.25 Surrounding patent filing strategies of Internap

5.4 Making use of the Frameworks

The above analysis on the various patenting strategies of incumbents and latecomers has provided a framework for companies to consider when developing their own patent filing strategies. Table 5.1 summarizes the patenting strategies of the incumbents and relative latecomers along the technology life cycle.

These strategies can be broadly categorized into defensive, proprietary, and leveraging strategies. At the emerging stage of the technology life cycle, the strategies used are usually defensive in nature because they are not yet ready to be commercialized extensively and there are still a lot of uncertainties. Incumbents with more resources will usually diversify their research to increase the probability of one of their technologies finding success. Therefore, they adopt *blanketing and flooding* strategies. Latecomers, that do not have resources to build up a forest of patents, face higher risks to identify an area that has the highest potential of success and adopt *surrounding* strategies to either block or go around the key areas occupied by the incumbents.

At the development stage, companies start to identify the direction to focus on and more strategic planning takes place. This is the stage when companies use proprietary patenting strategies. This means that the company has a better idea of the filing direction that it wants to pursue.

Table 5.1 Patenting strategies of incumbents and latecomers along the technology life cycle.

Technology life cycle	Examples	Strategies	Incumbents	Latecomers
Initial	ARPANET	Defensive	Blanketing or flooding	ad-hoc blocking & inventing around
Developing	Enterprise Applications	Proprietary	Fencing	Strategic patenting
Mature	EC2	Leveraging	Combination	Surrounding

So while incumbents would still use their resources to file many patents in many areas, they will be focused on certain groups of CPC and build their fences in these key groups. And, once latecomers have a clearer idea of the role they can play in this upcoming technology, they can file specifically in those areas, which is the *strategic patent* strategy. The patent portfolios of both incumbents and latecomers, are shaped into the company's identity.

By the time the technology matures, companies would have already built up a substantial amount of research results and patents. At this stage, companies have more bullets to leverage on the values of these accumulated assets. Therefore, *leveraging* patenting strategies will result. Incumbents, that have already built up a large patent portfolio over the years tend to make use of their patent portfolios in multiple combinations. Their patenting patterns are more diverse and complicated. In contrast, smaller players, maintained focused patenting strategies all along the technology life cycle, have been very focused. Now at this mature stage of technology life cycle, they can skew and organize their patent portfolios to the support of the key technology areas occupied by the incumbents and provide added value to them. These broad patenting strategies need to be deployed in line with the company's business strategies and core competencies.

5.5 Benefits of the Framework

This framework helps companies understand the external environment, in which their R&D operates and better positions companies to manage risks. The external environment overview helps companies derive macroscopic strategies that serve as the foundation for other microscopic strategies.

5.5.1 Competitive relationships between incumbents and latecomers

Considering the technology life cycle, and their position in it, helps companies derive strategies that can better leverage on collaboration opportunities with other players. Latecomers can understand the key technology areas and the patent portfolios of the incumbents through analyzing the technology life cycle. With that information, they can strategically direct their patent filing resources to providing a complementary addition to the whole patent landscape.

This is an opportunistic approach. Latecomers now have other options to monetize the IP, besides product commercialization. Nevertheless, in the context of product development, the usual role of latecomers and the smaller companies is to build up the "infrastructure" to commercialize the final products. If one looks at product development as a full process, different companies, big and small, come together to co-develop the product, not necessarily with regards to the same technology. The common goal is the product. The latecomers and smaller companies get the rewards through monetization of the IP, either by licensing, transaction, and — sometimes by less desirable means — through litigation. In any case, it opens up another means to retrieve monetary rewards.

The development of ASPANET and enterprise web applications, were milestones that enabled more players to enter the industry and help push the cloud computing industry to the next level of development. In the cloud computing industry, an upstream player can reach end consumers by providing storage to customers. It can also develop products that help other companies address various needs in the market.

Each milestone is like the main branch of a tree from which smaller branches spout out. There is not much of an early mover advantage in the cloud computing industry. Instead, every milestone creates an opportunity to expand the current addressable market and open new market in other segment of the value chain. Among the incumbents, there may be competition. But among the incumbents and latecomers are not necessarily in competition. They are in fact co-operating with each other to gain a larger individual market size.

5.5.2 Open innovation

With a means to profit from the IP, more structured open innovation involving smaller companies can take place. This, in turn, encourages entrepreneurship. Eventually, any participant who wants to contribute to the product development can find a way to recoup the resources spent. It may be true that the patents may not attract venture capital funding (Hoenig & Henkel, 2014; Mann & Sager, 2007). However, patents provide a way for the company to sell off assets in the future. It also offers options for new business ventures or, at least, to reduce losses. This was the case when the multinational telecommunications and data networking equipment manufacturer Nortel went bankrupt but still managed to sell its patent portfolio in a USD 4.5 billion deal to a consortium made up of Apple, Microsoft, Blackberry, Ericsson, and Sony.[3]

Besides being acquired as a developed patent portfolio, latecomers and can play a part in co-development of improved technology. Very often, latecomers and have very little power to negotiate a licensing deal. Therefore, the stick approach of licensing through initiating litigation is not very effective for them. Very often, the licensing deals from latecomers would involve technology transfer agreements. There will be a period for such technology transfers to be completed. In the process, some new ideas may arise to solve new problems that appear in the implementation process. In this case, the latecomer can co-develop with the incumbent. Ultimately, whether the newly generated IP belongs to the incumbent or the latecomer, depends on the licensing contract governing improved technology. Still, in this way, co-development between incumbents and latecomer is possible. Open innovation can also occur in the context of new technology that is not already in the patent domain.

5.6 Concluding Diagram

In this chapter, the incumbents and the latecomers different patenting strategies to survive and prosper in the evolution of the technology. Bigger companies, such as Amazon and Microsoft, have the resources to apply for many patents to flood the patent landscape so as to build up their patent portfolios. Smaller companies, such as Salesforce and Internap, diversify their patent portfolios strategically to stay in the value network. They use the *surrounding patenting* strategy to build fences around their core technologies. This helps them survive the waves of competition evolving the industry.

---

[3] http://www.wsj.com/articles/SB10001424052702303812104576440161959082234 (Last accessed 21st November 2016).

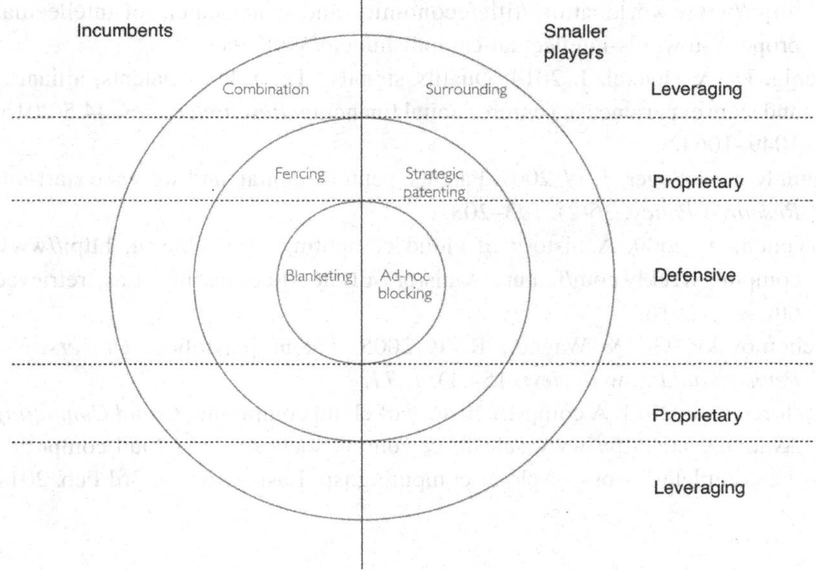

Figure 5.26 Derived patenting strategies along the technology life cycle

Through the history of cloud computing technology, incumbents and SMEs can exist in harmony because the value network allows the upstream players to reach the consumer directly. Incumbents have the option to co-operate with latecomers to extend the value chain and increase the value network. Prompt responses and corresponding strategies from both incumbents and SMEs are possible only because they can understand the evolution of the technology. The framework for positioning the company in the technology life cycle is provided in Figure 5.26.

Bibliography

Cantu, A. 2014. *The history and future of cloud computing*. Elgar Pub., Cheltenham, UK: Northampton, MA, USA. Available at: http://www.worldcat.org/title/economics-and-management-of-intellectual-property-towards-intellectual-capitalism/oclc/39981948

Granstrand, O. 1999. *The economics and management of intellectual property*. E. Elgar Pub., Cheltenham, UK: Northampton, MA, USA. Available at:

http://www.worldcat.org/title/economics-and-management-of-intellectual-property-towards-intellectual-capitalism/oclc/39981948

Hoenig, D., & Henkel, J. 2014. Quality signals? The role of patents, alliances, and team experience in venture capital financing. *Research Policy*, 44.5(2015), 1049–1064.

Mann, R. J., & Sager, T. W. 2007. Patents, venture capital, and software start-ups. *Research Policy*, 36(2), 193–208.

Mohamed, A. 2009. A history of cloud computing. Available at: http://www.computerweekly.com/feature/A-history-of-cloud-computing. Last retrieved: 6th Sept. 2016.

Parchomovsky, G., & Wagner, R. P. 2005. Patent portfolios. *University of Pennsylvania Law Review*, 154(1), 1–77.

Salesforce.com. 2011. A complete history of cloud computing, *Cloud Computing*. Available at: http://www.salesforce.com/uk/socialsuccess/cloud-computing/the-complete-history-of-cloud-computing.jsp. Last retrieved: 3rd Feb. 2014.

Chapter 6
R&D Strategies

6.1 R&D Strategies for Bridging the R&D and Product Markets

This chapter crystallizes the results of scouting information from the patent landscape, academic journals trends and marketing intelligence to derive R&D strategies. Most companies have R&D plans or technology road maps. However, the gap between these plans and the consumer desired products is still considerable. We propose that a good grasp of systematic, purposeful patent analysis is the key to bridging the R&D and Product markets. This chapter focuses on crossing the chasms between the R&D, Patent, and Product markets. We place special attention on R&D strategies that lead to research being applied successfully to the products. The resulting R&D strategies are usually directly applicable to incremental innovation. However, if multiple patent portfolios are analyzed and correlated, R&D strategies for radical innovation may also be derived. Radical innovations usually result from new discoveries in science. The route to eventually applying such new inventions to products may be unclear. Therefore, it warrants more sophisticated analysis for deriving R&D strategies for radical innovations. With the end products in mind, the derived R&D strategies for radical innovation may lead to higher chances for the technologies to be applied to the Product market in a shorter time. Therefore, it is important to understand the market to derive relevant R&D strategies that bridge the R&D and Product markets.

6.1.1 The role of patent analytics

Current methods of developing technology road maps usually do consider the demands in the Product market. However, the chasm between the R&D market and Product market still exits. This is because these methods usually leave out the Patent market. Deriving R&D strategies without considering the Patent market may potentially result in with products encountering patent thickets or patent landmines controlled by competitors. This increases the risk of patent disputes. In addition, leaving out the Patent market runs the risk of patent information being left out. This may lead to reinventing the wheel. It also risks a research direction that is technically infeasible. Thus, information from the Patent market is necessary to optimize R&D strategies.

In essence, the Patent market is a necessary stepping platform to solving the chasm between the R&D and Product markets. Although a result of organizational restructuring, the Patent market is the platform that connects the R&D and Product markets. With the rise of the Patent market, more intelligence can be deduced from the embedded information in the aggregated patent database. This is because an awareness of the importance of patents is higher among companies. Many companies, including start-ups, are diligently filing patents as a means to protect their inventions. This provides a valuable resource for deriving R&D strategies. In order to bridge the R&D and Product markets, analysis from both the R&D and Product perspectives is required. From the R&D perspective, for every invention included in the patent document, there is an associated technology with a function to solve a technological problem. This technology and *function* pair forms another dyad. If these two dyads are paired together, we will be able to link the product feature with the associated technology.

6.2 R&D Strategies and Patenting Strategies

R&D strategies and patenting strategies go hand in hand. Sometimes patenting strategies will affect R&D strategies. At other times, it is the other way round. As R&D results are often protected by patents, R&D

strategies can influence the patenting strategies by pinpointing the specific technology field to file. On the other hand, by considering patenting strategies, a company might have to do more research in a particular direction if patent acquisition is not a viable option. In addition, since patent information is the key to bridging R&D and Product markets, R&D, and patenting strategies are partly derived from a shared database.

R&D strategies for every company are unique. Depending on the size, the industrial value chain and the technology life cycle of the technology, the strategies will be different. Patenting strategies are the same. However, as these influencing factors for R&D strategies are well known, this book will not discuss them. However, as these factors are less discussed for patenting strategies, this chapter will now turn to them.

6.3 Patent Micro-Reading

Deriving R&D strategies relies heavily on the intelligence gathered from patent data and non-patent literature. To derive R&D strategies that are useful to the companies in particular, it is important to maintain the balance between the macroscopic and microscopic views. The patent analytic scheme discussed in chapter 3 provides a macroscopic overview from the technology life cycle and value chain. It is the first step towards scouting a comprehensive patent portfolio for analysis. Such view is useful for governments to chart out national R&D directions. It guides proposals for corresponding policies to build up the industries. At an industrial level, the macroscopic view helps to foster more collaboration among companies. Research institutes and corporations with large R&D centers benefit from this macroscopic analysis to identify the new direction of R&D. However, further processing to obtain a comparatively microscopic view is needed if the analysis is to serve companies. A microscopic view calls for detailed understanding of smaller but key patent portfolios. Usually, the patents selected for such microscopic views would be the company's own patents and those from its competitors. The technical field for analysis will also be contextual and carefully chosen to serve a specific purpose.

Further processing can be based on patent maps. Chapter 3 has introduced the various types of patent maps and the general applications. This chapter focuses specifically on using the matrix patent map to derive specific R&D strategies. In order to derive a meaningful matrix patent map, patent micro-reading is required. It allows the company to systematically analyze the chosen patent portfolio. Patent micro-reading is useful to analyze a company's own patents too. Most of the time, the person drafting the patents will not be the one who does patent analysis for deriving R&D and patenting strategies. Therefore it is important to have an effective way to understand the company's patent portfolio. Even if the patent personnel who derive the R&D strategies follow the patent filing of the company closely or draft most of the company's patents, especially in start-ups, a systematic way to understand the patents, statistically is still needed. The concept of micro-reading is the same as drafting. Every patent is related to a technical field. Within the technical field, the patent seeks to solve a problem through a technical means to achieve the intended result. This is illustrated in Figure 6.1. By analyzing patents in this manner, the patent analyst will be able to understand the use and the value of the company's patents. Patent micro-reading of the company's patent portfolio also helps to identify areas of technology for further micro-reading analysis. The objective of the matrix patent map is to analyze a highly selective patent portfolio. However, such analysis requires each patent to be analyzed and categorized. The cost is high. Therefore it is important to include only the relevant patents for analysis. Understanding the purpose of analysis and identifying the corresponding patents are the two fundamental steps for deriving meaningful R&D strategies.

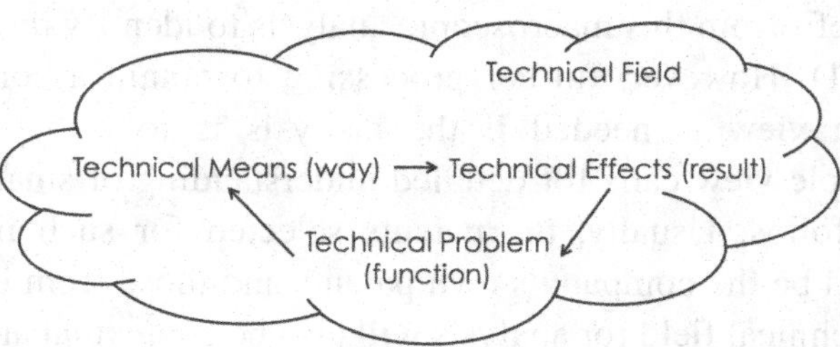

Figure 6.1 Extracting key information in micro-reading

6.4 Quantified Qualitative Analysis

Current research on patent analysis focuses on quantitative methods to obtain an overview of the trends. Quantitative methods may suit a macroscopic analysis. However, it may not be able to address the needs of companies. Qualitative methods, such as patent micro-reading may be a better approach to address the needs of companies. But qualitative analysis is time-consuming and micro-reading patients without understanding them statistically will not provide the trends needed to derive R&D strategies. Therefore, an efficient and comprehensive methodology for patent analysis combines both the qualitative and quantitative information of the patent documents. Using the qualitative information identified for each patent document, patent networking matrix maps can be generated to serve as technology road maps as shown in Figure 6.2. With such patent networking maps, patent portfolios can be analyzed more effectively.

6.5 A Scheme for Deriving R&D Strategies

Through patent micro-reading, a coding method has been developed to analyze the full patent documents of the selected set of patents. This

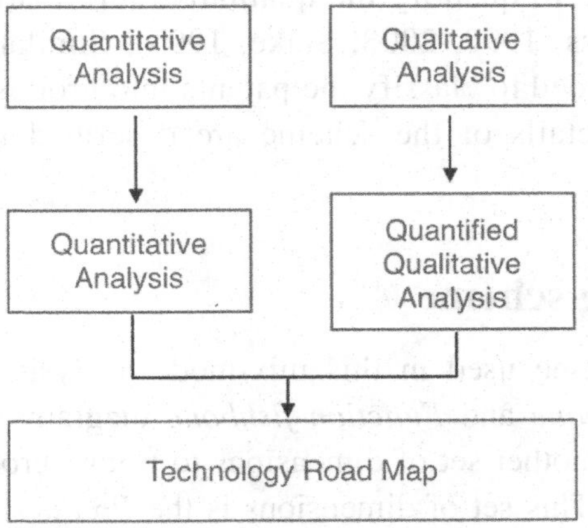

Figure 6.2 Quantitative and refined qualitative analysis for technology road map

coding gives an overview of the contents of the patents. The codes are further analyzed and categorized into clusters of main *technology*, *function*, *product features* and *uses*. From the patent coding analysis, a patent portfolio landscape map can be generated. This map can double up as the technology road map for R&D planning in formulating R&D strategies, such as identifying the relevant patents for licensing, increasing the awareness of patent thickets, and potential infringement areas. Existing patent landscape maps provided by commercial patent analysis software uses quantitative method of visualizing the patent portfolio and lose important information relating to the purpose of the invention, which is important for R&D planning. Experts can extract the information from patents using qualitative analysis. However, this method is usually time-consuming and very costly. Therefore, our method aims to extract the technology and function information inherent in the patent documents in a systematic and efficient manner to relate technology to products in the market.

To obtain qualitative information from the patent portfolio, this method uses the mixed mode qualitative and quantitative analysis employed in social science research to analyze the patent portfolio. In this case, the analysis of patent documents is likened to analyzing interview transcripts. Researchers can obtain insightful themes from the interviews. To obtain statistical information, the interview transcripts are coded to quantify the qualitative information (Berg, 2004; Corbin & Strauss, 1990, 2008; Stake, 1995). Similarly, patent documents will be coded to classify the patents into groups for quantitative analysis. The details of the scheme are described in the following sub-sections.

6.5.1 Coding scheme

The coding scheme used in this mix-mode analysis is based on the *Technology fishbone* and *Function fishbone* diagrams. In addition, we propose to add another set of dimensions to bridge product information and technology. This set of dimensions is the *Product Feature fishbone* and *Use fishbone*. These two classifications are better descriptions for products. The *Technology fishbone* and *Function fishbone* are descriptions that are closely related to technology. By introducing this new set of dimensions to codify a patent document, the link between technology and product can be established.

Therefore, the four major codes used are:

1. *Technology*
2. *Function*
3. *Product Feature*
4. *Use*

In each of these dimensions, the fishbone diagrams were generated in order to subdivide the dimensions into finer classes. Instead of predefining each subdivision at the beginning of the analysis, a progressive way of building up the fishbone diagrams is suggested here. A commercial mixed mode analysis software "Dedoose[1]" was used in this book to demonstrate the coding to be done. There are other available software, such as "MAXQDA[2]" and "QDA Miner[3]" that can provide a platform for multiple coders to code documents. These software tools allow codes to be generated and modified while reading the documents.

6.5.2 Coding the patent documents

For every patent document, there are four codes, one from each of the dimensions of *technology*, *function*, *product feature*, and *use*. The patent portfolio was arranged in groups based on their IPCs. Two or more coders who are familiar with patent management and the technology should be engaged to read through the patents. Every coder may be assigned a portion of the portfolio for analysis and coders should cross-check each other's work to ensure correct codes are used.

---

[1] http://app.dedoose.com

[2] http://www.maxqda.com

[3] http://provalisresearch.com/products/qualitative-data-analysis-software/

6.5.3 Mixed mode analysis

After the patent portfolio has been codified, the codes are then analyzed statistically to give an overview of the patent portfolio. The analysis can be divided into company level and technology level. As the strength and novelty of this analysis scheme is in deriving the R&D direction through the interconnections between the matrices or network of patents, only the technology level analysis is discussed here. Company level analysis using the same method can be useful for companies to understand their standing compared to competitors.

After coding, the relationship between the patents and the corresponding codes are analyzed using existing matrix tools to generate a tool for technology road-mapping and patent strategies formulation. The matrices illustrate the relationships between the classifications: *Technology/Function* Matrix, *Function/Uses* Matrix, and *Uses/Product Features* Matrix. The process flow of this analysis scheme is shown in Figure 6.3.

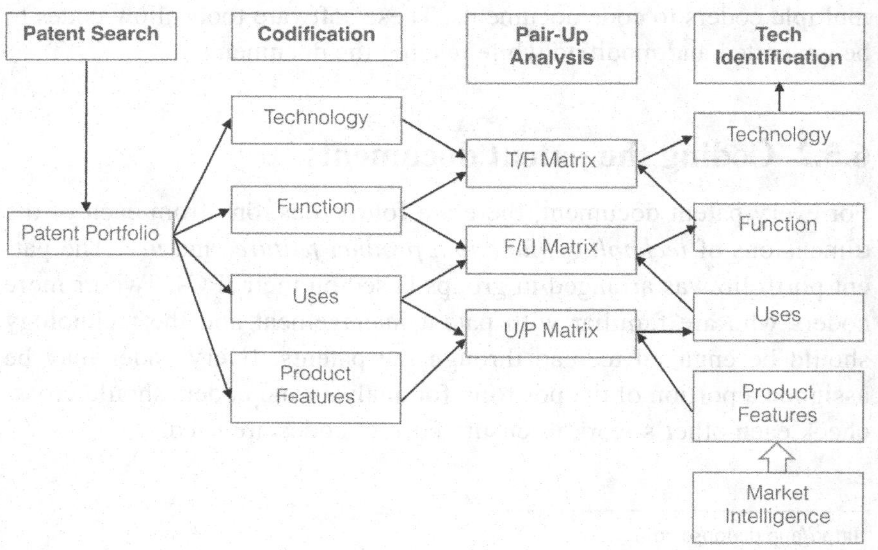

Figure 6.3 Process flow of the patent classification module

6.6 Implementation of Scheme using Touch Screen

6.6.1 Patent search dataset

In order to illustrate how the proposed scheme can be used for deriving R&D strategies, we analyzed US granted utility patents related to touch screen technology from January 1st, 2007 to December 31st, 2012. Analyzed patents were limited to these 5 years of granted patents because the technology only took off with Apple's first iPhone in 2007. Other companies also started to intensify their research in this area at around the same time. For companies to have proper intellectual property protection of their products, they would have had to file filed patents before 2007.

Keywords that describe both the touch screen and the components in touch screen systems were used to search for the set of patents to be analyzed. Although there are criticisms of the reliance on keywords as the searching criteria (David Hunt, 2007), it is adequate for this case because the aim of analyzing this set of patents is to find out the distribution of the technology focus and to zoom in on areas of interest to conduct further analysis for patenting strategies. As the purpose of the patent search in this analysis is a background understanding of the general landscape of the technology, the keyword search is sufficient. The total number of patents searched is 1160. After some screening, 818 patents were found to be relevant.

6.6.2 Codification

After codifying the 818 patents, the codes were further clustered to reduce the complexity. The major clusters are shown in Table 6.1. For each cluster, there are subclasses to further define the patent documents. They are shown in Appendix A–D.

It can be seen from this table that the majority of the technology of these patents is related to detection technique and software methods. The most desirable functions of these technologies are improving the

Table 6.1 Coding schemes clusters and the corresponding number of codes

Technology		Function		Product feature		Use	
Assembly	66	Operational enhancement	162	Accepting touch	222	Operation	28
Electrical circuits	116	Quality enhancement	175	Text	80	Display	113
Mechanical parts	71	User experience enhancement	193	Security	25	Control	37
Detection technique	237	Improve physical features of device	98	Image	25	Detection	35
Display technique	66	Operational functions	51	Navigation	12	Touch	125
Computation	76	Additional functions	64	Selection	64	Measurement	27
Methods	186	Cost	75	Management	48	Editing	12
				Display	110	User experience	90
				Automotive	11	Touch screen assembly	161
				Soft functional features	7	Input	115
				Detection	19	Capture image	5
				Physical function features	144	Management	15
				Components	39	Security	15
				Music	5	Entertainment	29
				User experience features	2	Other uses	11
				Non-textual inputs	5		
	818		818		818		818

user experience and, in particular, the operational enhancement of touch screens.

The *Product Feature* and *Use* dimensions, are related to accepting some forms of touch and some physical function features, such as 2D and 3D interface or connections to a second device. A majority of the patents are used for display, touch screen assembly, and, as inputs.

6.6.3 Pair-up analysis

Based on the coding exercise above, the *Technology\Function* Matrix, *Function\Uses* Matrix, and *Uses\Product Feature* Matrix were tabulated as below in Figure 6.4. The matrices below show the first level classification. The *Technology\Function* Matrix has the x-axis representing the various *Technologies* and the y-axis representing the *Functions*.

The *Function\Uses* Matrix is represented in Figure 6.5. The *x*-axis represents the *Functions* and the *y*-axis represents the *Uses*. The *Uses*

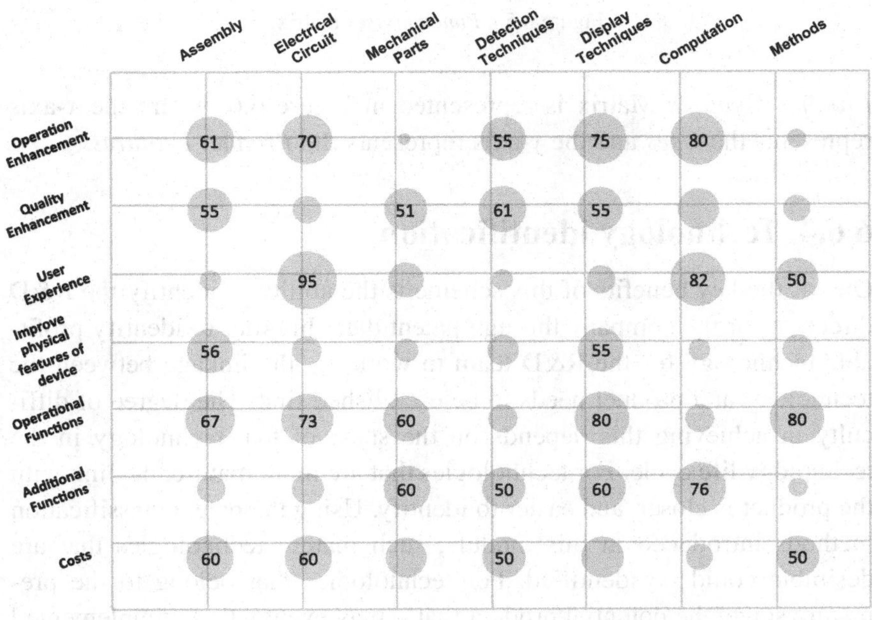

Figure 6.4 Technology\function matrix

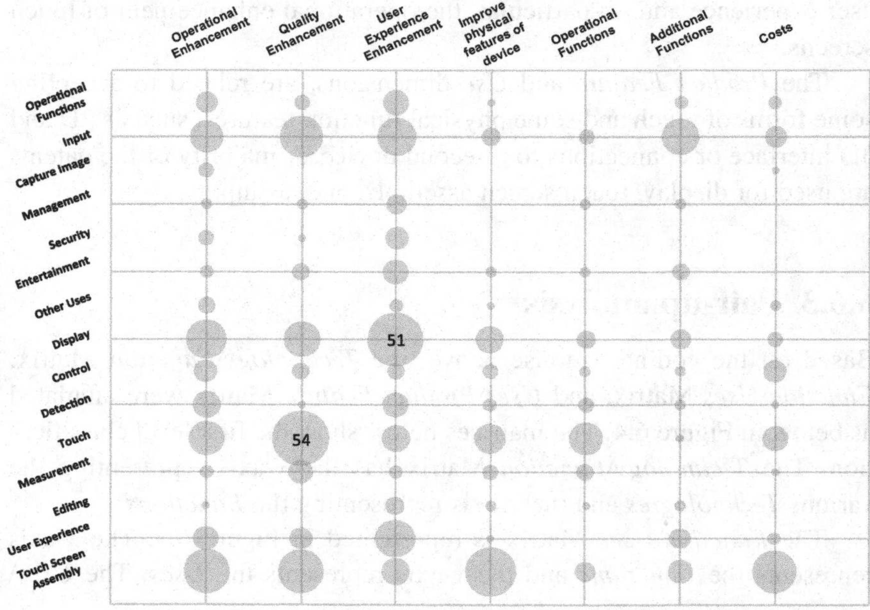

Figure 6.5 *Function\uses* matrix

Product Features Matrix is represented in Figure 6.6, where the *x*-axis represents the *Uses* and the *y*-axis represents the *Product Features*.

6.6.4 Technology identification

One of the key benefits of this scheme is the ability to identify the R&D direction for the company through patent data. In order to identify profitable technology for the R&D team to work on, the linkage between the technology and product needs to be established first. The degree of difficulty in achieving this depends on the stage of that technology in the technology life cycle. For technologies that are more mature, the link with the product is closer, and easier to identify. Using the patent classification methods introduced in this module, such mature technologies that are desirable could be identified. For technologies that belong to the premature stage, the potential product that it may eventually be implemented

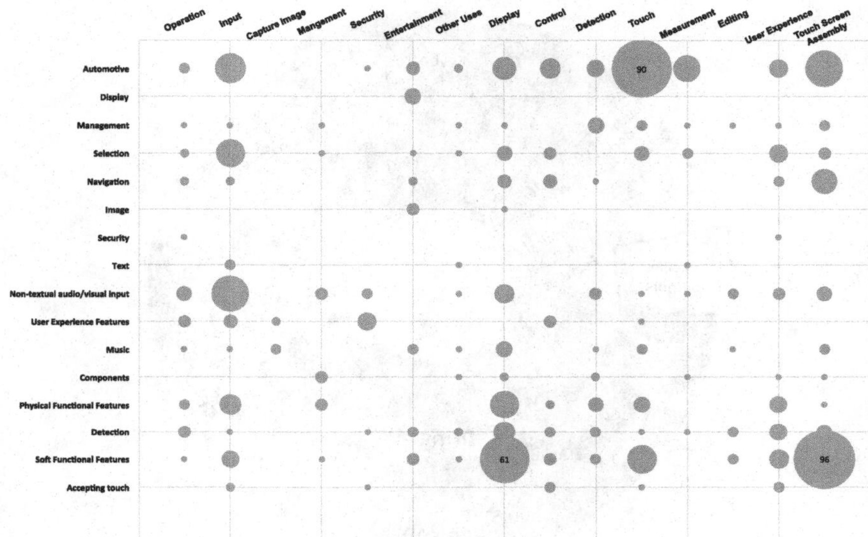

Figure 6.6 Uses\product features matrix

in may not be clear and so the patent drafter would not have put this into the patent document. Nevertheless, it is still possible to check out the application areas in the patent documents.

This tool is to be combined with market information, such as the hot product features that customers are looking for in purchasing. The process flow is illustrated in the following steps:

6.6.4.1 *Getting information from market news*

The desirable product feature can be found through some Internet posts or industry guru analysis. In this example, the *product feature* chosen is "tactile outputs" as shown in Figure 6.7. This chart shows the various types of *product features* coded for the patent documents. The size of the pie is proportional to the number of documents coded under the code. The inner circle is the first level classification and the outer circle is the second level classifications.

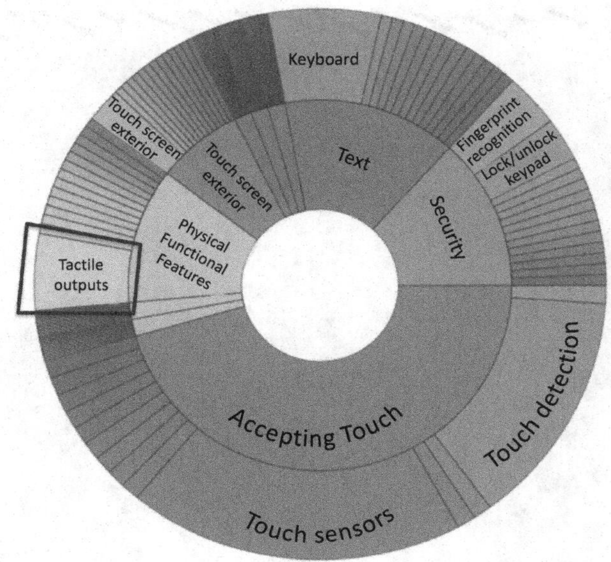

Figure 6.7 Identified desirable *product features* from market information

6.6.4.2 *From product features to "uses"*

The identified *product feature* from market information is then linked to the *Uses* through the *Uses\Product* Features matrix. The most *Uses* specified in this matrix in relation to tactile outputs are then identified. This is shown in Figure 6.8. Most of the *Uses* are for "providing touch input."

6.6.4.3 *From "uses" to "functions"*

From the previous step, it is identified that providing touch input was the key *Uses* for the *product feature* of "tactile outputs." Referencing the *Function\Uses* matrix would lead to the *Functions* that such uses are mostly meant for. This is shown in Figures 6.9 and 6.10. The most *Functions* identified are being accurate and providing haptic feedback.

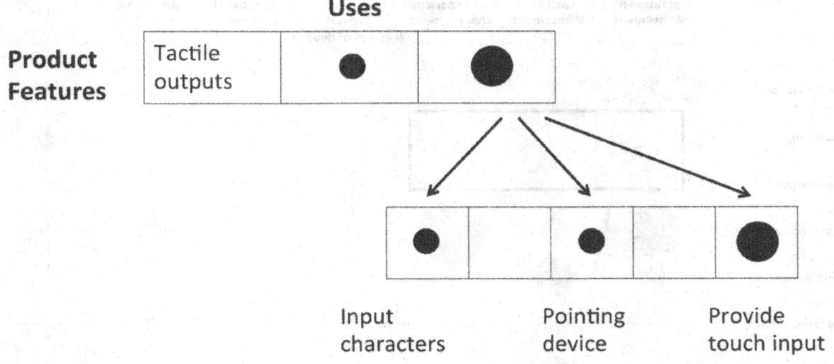

Figure 6.8 Identifying the most "Uses" from the desirable product features

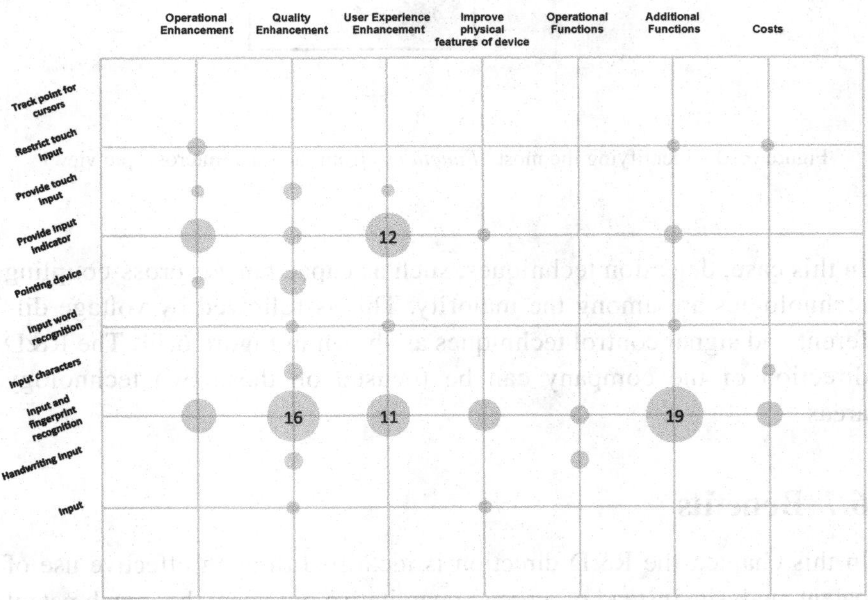

Figure 6.9 Identifying the most "*Functions*" from the *uses* (macroscopic view)

6.6.4.4 *From "Functions" to "Technology"*

From the *Technology\Functions Function* matrix, the desirable technologies that correspond to the identified *functions* can be determined.

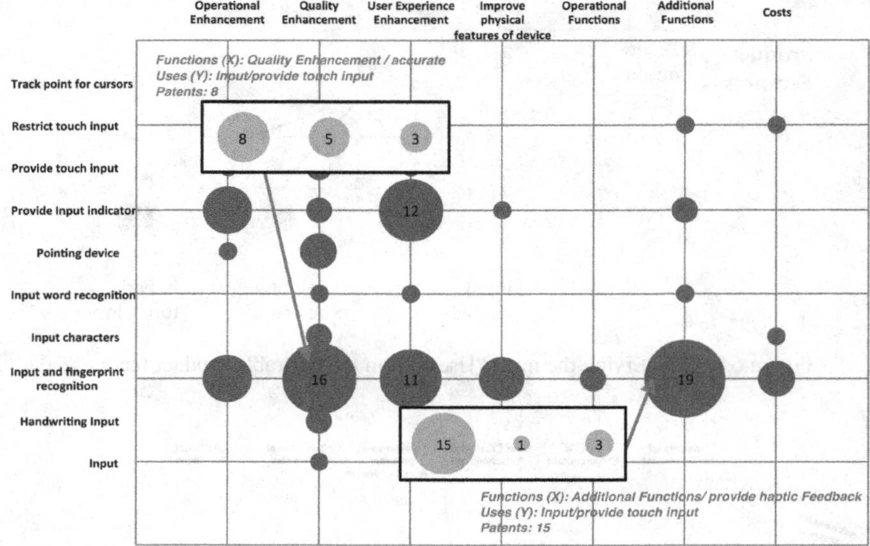

Figure 6.10 Identifying the most "*Functions*" from the *uses* (microscopic view)

In this case, detection techniques, such as capacitances, cross-coupling technologies are among the majority. This is followed by voltage different and signal control techniques as shown in Figure 6.11. The R&D direction of the company can be focused on these two technology areas.

6.7 Benefits

In this chapter, the R&D direction is identified through effective use of patent analysis. Instead of a broad quantitative overview that much patent analytic software provides, this method provides an efficient way of coding the patents and linking the codes through matrices to draw up the link between products and technologies. This method can also identify potential licensees for the company's patents.

This method focuses on combining the qualitative and quantitative information that patent portfolios can reveal. In this digital age of

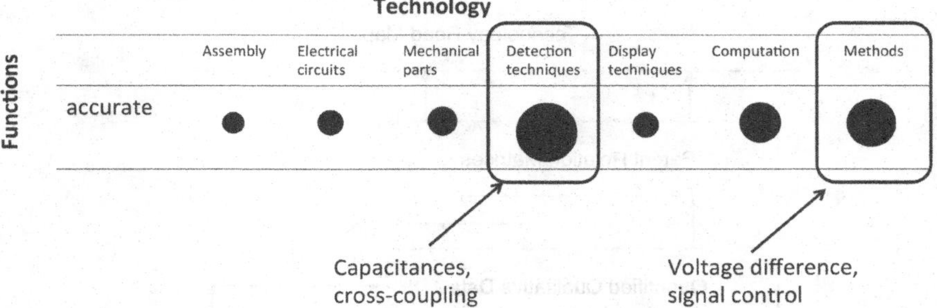

Figure 6.11 Identifying the most commonly used "*Technology*" from "*Functions*"

data explosions, efficient ways are needed to analyze this information. Using the mixed-mode methods, this module presented a methodology to develop technology roadmaps for R&D managers to understand the technology trend. This methodology can be extended to include non-patent literature and citations of the selected patents in the future.

The previous chapter draws additional information from journal data. This chapter draws market information and integrates that with the patent information. Many companies that do their own patent analysis would classify their patents according to their internal classification codes. If the above matrices are taken into account in analyzing the company's patent portfolio, resources can be managed more efficiently.

6.8 Conclusion

An efficient and effective patent analysis is crucial to making sense out of the large quantity of patent documents. Existing patent analysis tools make use of the quantitative information of patent documents, such as the assignees, the patent filing date, the number of citations or international classifications, and are just able to provide the landscape of the technology. The insights are usually drawn among the patent data. In this chapter, external information is drawn to link the important quantified qualitative

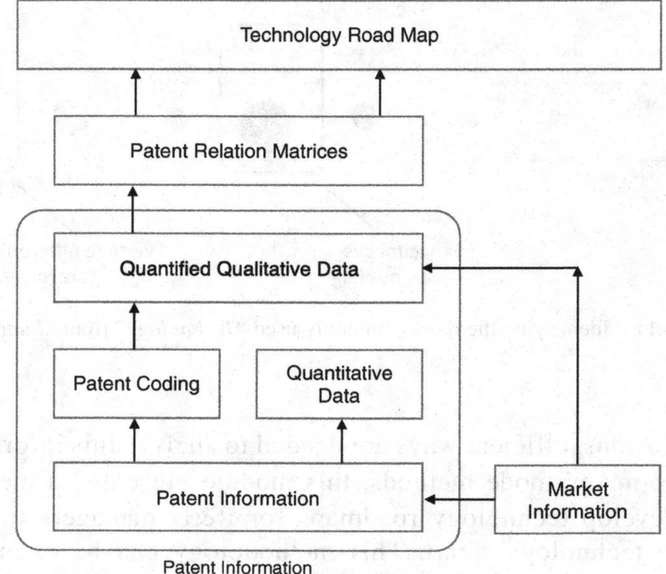

Figure 6.12 Drawing technology road map from patent classifications

information with the quantitative information. This is summarized in Figure 6.12.

1.1. Appendix A Technology sub-classifications

Technology

1. Assembly
   - transparent panel
   - TFT substrate
   - adhesive part
   - adjustable housing
   - adjusting dimensions of frames
   - bezel frame
   - black bordering
   - case and touch screen coplanar
   - extension
   - fastener supports
   - flexible sensor substrate
   - glass substrate
   - high index layer
   - injection molding
   - ink trail
   - insulation substrate
   - ion-dielectric
   - light altering material
   - liquid crystal layer
   - molded body
   - monolithic substrate
   - nanoparticles
   - optical film
   - optically transparent base and shield film
   - piezoelectric substrate
   - plastic film
   - recess frame
   - rendering vertex
   - rotating assembly
   - seal

2. Electrical circuits
   angular pattern of resistive material
   anntenna array
   bi-dimensional input pattern
   bonding flex circuits
   boundary line
   bridge crossing two electrodes
   clock circuit
   clustering sensor pads
   combination of touch cells
   compensating force sensor for baseline error
   conductive belt
   control lines
   coupling of electrode
   cross-over sensing patterns
   dummy sensig series
   electro-optic medium
   encrypting circuit
   gate lines
   graphic controller
   graphic signals
   groove
   haptic driver
   haptic region
   haptic simulator
   hollow-out patterns
   image pickup elements
   interconnection of networks
   light pulse emitting units
   patterned surface
   pixel structure
   polarizer
   resistive chain
   shield electrode
   spacer dots
   transparent carbon nanotube (CNT) electrode

transparent conductor layer
triangular shape electrodes

3. Mechanical parts
   actuator
   actuator to deflect the housing
   antenna probe
   concave and convex portions
   curved material
   deforemable member
   directional optical microprisms
   flexible material
   locking plate
   memory alloy wires
   modular unit connector
   optical fibers
   organic LED
   photoconductor
   press-fit pins
   shock-absorbing cushion
   tethering cord
   touch sensitive fabric
   touch sensor protrusion
   touch switch
   vibration-damping element
   wiring harness

4. Detection technique
   Surface Acoustic Wave
   analyse facial features
   atmospheric pressure detection
   biometric sensors
   capacitive sensor
   closed loop sensing
   conductive cap
   conductive coupling
   conductive doped silicon

cross-coupling capacitances
detect eyeglasses
detect pressure using load detection unit
detect tap gesture
detecting edge of object
driving sensor
fingerpint sensing
fingerprint recognition sensor
gavity sensor
gesture processing
infrared light
intensity-sensitive touch-sensing
light detector
motion and voice detection
multiple contact point discrimination
mutual capacitances
non-linear edge sensing
optical flow
position movement
pressure sensing
radio frequency
rotating tension
sense direction of dragging signal
sense object proximity
sensing electric characteristic of fluid
shockwave detector
simultaneous touch sensing
speech recognition
temperature sensing
text-to-speed technology
touch force
vibration sensors

5. Display technique
   2D screen translation heuristic
   3D trajectory

VoIP
based on orientation of device
detecting humidity
display animation of LED
display files with shared attributes
image sensor
more than one display
partition display
projective mapping
sequential image display process
slidable screen
stackup display pixels
wireless transmission

6. Computation
DAC
calculate a running average
calculate rotating direction
calibration and validation of pixel coordinates
capacitance-to-digital converter
coding
correction coefficients
delay time-difference
delta sigma modulation
determine low noise simulation frequencies
determine operating frequency
determine reflective index
difference in voltage potential
eccentricity threshold
estimate velocity
fingerprint parameters
frustrated total internal reflection
generate pixel coordinates
identify touched sensors using frequencies and phase
measure luminance
measure relative amount of contact

offsets
parameter setting
pixel processing
precharge voltage
process object information
retention period
sampling
set increase or decrease from reference value
weighing factor

7. Methods
   LED selector
   SOP workspace
   annotation
   biometric templates
   changing display attributes
   character set
   circular volume image
   color filtering
   consonant letter
   content magnifier
   continuous lamina of light
   demarcating shooting areas
   determine matched zoom mode
   displaying phone numbers on latitude and longitude location on map
   enlarge characters
   expand localized area
   frequency of use
   function setting
   identify active area
   image and sound
   image manipulation
   indicator to selected key
   interface application control
   irradiates light towards translucent panel

keysets
memory storing chord data files
memory storing graphical information
non-letter character keys
optical response to light
pass code
plurality of sensing zones
progress bar
scrollable character wheel
scrollable list
selection technique
software
stroke
substrate-retaining mechanism
suggested replacement
switching input mode
using control signal
using web service environment
viewing angle control
virtual key buttons

1.2. Appendix B Functions sub-classifications

Functions

1. Operational Enhancement
   - allow Shift key function
   - automatic
   - confirm finished action
   - continuous key operation
   - continuous operation
   - detachable
   - easy installation
   - efficient text entering
   - fast sensing cycle
   - high operational security
   - improve analog frontend
   - improve functionality of touch based device
   - improve input with visual observation
   - improve reflectance difference between sensing patterns
   - increase detection cycle
   - increase light transmissibility
   - increase text entry speed
   - indicate operation status
   - indicators
   - maximize detection time between adj sensor signals
   - measurable by small microcontroller
   - minimize electronic processing
   - more explicit indication of key functions
   - multiple tasks may be performed
   - no need general purpose computer for touch screen
   - no outside sensor
   - operate during malfunction
   - organized
   - oversee operation
   - prevent leakage of fingerprint marks
   - provide control while in locked mode

reduce calculation burden
reduce idle waiting time
reduce interfacial reflections of visible light
solve mismatch between coordinate of touch pad and display
stable measurement

2. Quality Enhancement
account for nonlinear characteristics
accurate
avoid inadvertent user input
discard unrelated touch
improve calibration
improve coupling stability
improve display quality
improve fingerprint resolution
improve pen-based input
improve sensitivity
increase durability
increase reliability of sense signal
less interference
linear calibration
protect flat screens against vibrations
reduce input errors
reduce noise
satisfactory resolution
secure safety in driving
versatile

3. User Experience Enhancement
better user interface for touch screen
customized
easy edit macro
easy option change after installation
easy to operate
easy to select menu option
effective use of complicated functions

enlarge text-based items
help visually impaired
interactive
intuitive
non-linear edge User Interface
open up internet to non-textual universe
personalize user interface
proactive
work for gloved fingers and stylus
zoom function

4. Improve physical features of device
   accommodate very narrow border region
   flexible
   improve space flexibility
   improve touch screen assembly
   increase transparency
   less cameras
   overcome slippery surface
   prevent damage to products
   prevent foreign materials
   reduce circuit complexity
   reduce device height
   reduce device size
   reduce thickness
   reduce visibility of conductive elements
   reduce weight
   reduce worn-out
   resistant to damage by delamination
   resistant to scratching
   save display space

5. Operational Functions
   detect contact object even with insufficient conductivity
   detect object in z direction
   detect object position
   determine image of touch

determine distance between user and touch screen
determine edge coordinates
determine position of touch by multiple users
displaying keys
dynamic detection of transients and repeating inputs
high precision identification of point of contact
integrate touch panel with system
integrated system
manipulation without identifying physical object
measure relative position between objects
movement in angle around an axis perpendicular to screen
prevent rotation of tablet
provide both visible and mechanical output
real-time
remote inputs from users
remote simulation
resolve locations of simultaneous touch
simultaneous set on/off state
track movement

6. Additional functions
   3D image support
   ability to detect EM stylus
   adapt keys to the language
   adjust analog clock
   capable of playing different games
   compatible with common portable devices
   doubled up as household network
   ergonometric
   facilitate Hindi characters input
   find users with common interest
   for both dynamic and static game
   freedom to choose orientation
   gives variety
   input emoticons
   input various character sets

maintain flight crew awareness of actions taken
provide haptic feedback
provide immediate information on incident
suitable for vehicles
toggle volume feature
user unaware of image acquisition
viewable even with polarized sunglasses

7. Cost
   cost effective
   energy conservation
   low cost force sense feedback function
   reduce power

1.3. Appendix C Uses sub-classifications

Uses

1. Operation
   - activate operation
   - activate screen
   - adjust image on screen
   - avionic operation
2. Display
   - browsing collection of digital images
   - display content of page
   - display executable functions
   - display hyperlink
   - display image
   - display list
   - display medical record
   - display text entry interface
   - flat panel monitor
   - for emissive display
   - information presentation
   - liquid crystal display
   - rescaling display
   - video display
   - virtual browsing
3. Control
   - control access
   - control power supply
   - control space conditioning equipment
   - controller circuit
4. Detection
   - detect acceleration
   - detect operation of passenger
   - detect/emit light
   - determine angular position

determine gesture
determine material of object
determine position of object on screen
determine two or more simultaneous touches
dimension detection

5. Touch
   localize touch events
   touch contact
   touch location
   touch shape
   touch zones

6. Measurement
   calculate traveling route
   calibration
   measure capacitance
   measure pulse rate
   sensing noise
   set sensitivity
   simulating touch
   test connections
   touch sensitivity measurement

7. Editing
   capture image
   download data
   edit documents
   extract metadata from image
   files management
   handling multiple text fields
   macro editing
   manipulate graphical objects

8. User Experience
   generate GUI
   haptic system

provide visual feedback
reconfigurating GUI
user interface
user terminal

9. Touch screen assembly
   RFID circuitry
   additional keyboard
   anti highlight
   backlighting
   bi-directional communication
   conductive materials
   connect two sections of frames
   connecting two conductive layers
   forming electrodes
   forming laminate
   interferometric modulator
   keyboard overlay
   light modulator
   locate frame center
   manufacture substrate of touch screen
   manufacture touch screen assembly
   optical waveguide
   programming touch screen
   protective enclosure
   removable keyboard
   sealing system
   storing stylus
   support
   thin films
   touch sensor switch

10. Input
    handwriting input
    input and fingerprint recognition
    input characters

input word recognition
pointing device
provide input indicator
provide touch input
restrict touch inputs
track point for cursors

11. Capture image
    fingerprint scanner
    signature capture
    taking photos

12. Management
    allocate keys on keyboard
    inspection
    menu for creative works
    monitor other users' location
    navigation through a plurality of features
    provide list

13. Security
    encryption
    password registering
    protection from access-sensing region
    security system
    touch-based authentication

14. Entertainment
    create web-clip widget
    gaming
    gaming machine
    music composition
    produce chord sounds
    synthetic guitar

15. Other Uses
    audio presentation from text
    making calls

modify surgical procedure
originate emergency call
robot
secure point-of-sale (POS)
targeted search
traffic jam guide

1.4. Appendix D Product Features sub-classifications

Product Features

1. Accepting touch
    - Sensing
        - force sensors
        - inductive sensing
        - light diffusing and sensing
        - light sensing
        - near-proximity sensing
        - produce toggle signal
        - resistive sensing circuits
        - touch sensors
        - variable capacitance sensors
    - fingernail touch
    - movement input
    - multi-input manner
    - multi-touch
    - slide detection
    - speed touching
    - tactile input
    - touch detection
    - touch instruments
        - glove
        - stylus
    - users' touch

2. Text
    - data collection
    - data entry
    - handwriting recognition
    - keyboard
    - language mode switching
    - secure data entry
    - stowable
    - text editing

text messaging
text read out
text selection
translucent on-screen keyboard
voice messaging
word recommendations

3. Security
   biometric authentication
   finger print recognition
   lock/unlock keypad
   password protection

4. Image
   camera to sense touch
   image capture
   image dialing
   photo editing
   picture-in-picture display control
   shutter
   video game

5. Navigation
   GPS
   navigation system

6. Selection
   insertion marker
   navigational object
   option selection
   scroll bar
   virtual wheel

7. Management
   Applications
     map application
     multiple applications

Control
control consoles
control panel
remote control
volume control
artificial intelligence
automation system
conference call
input during calls
manage emergency using wireless communications
manage missed calls
multimedia handling
present instructions
tags
time setting
viewing process

8. Display
LCD
antiglare
change display mode
change orientation of UI
cleaning
control timing of information display
digital photographic display
display virtual objects
  virtual LED
  virtual graffiti
electric dartboard
financial information
flexible display panel
grouped display information
multiple windows
organic light emitting diode (OLED) display
raise portions of display
refractive index

rewritable
touch screen display
touch screen protector
waterproof

9. Automotive
armored vehicles
control element for vehicles
control of vehicle sub-system
lock/unlock door
seat

10. Soft Functional features
lottery
phonebook
playing cards
wager

11. Detection
detect and track multiple objects
detect defects
detect motion of cellular
determine orientation of finger
drop target gestures
object position detection
object recognition

12. Physical functional features
2D and 3D interface
Calibration
browsing web
connection to second device
counterbalance armature
flashlight switch
payment transactions
social networking
spectrum analysis of noise

tactile outputs
transmittance uniformity

13. Components
    Indium Tin Oxide (ITO)
    MEMS
    PCB
    PCB bridge connectors
    accelerometer
    elevators
    folding computer
    mechanical buttons
    on/off button
    power switch
    thermostats
    touch screen exterior
    transceivers used to support wireless communications in unlicensed spectra
    wireless devices

14. Music
    Arpeggiator
    electronic music instruments

15. User experience features
    children-friendly
    interfacing with customers at store

16. Non-textual audio/visual input

Chapter 7

Licensing, Litigation and Alliance Strategies

7.1 The Roles, Interactions and Effects of the Licensing, Litigation and Alliance Strategies

Licensing, litigation, and alliance strategies are the components of the patent portfolio planning. They are strategies by which the company can operationalize the revenue generation mechanisms of patents. Most legal instruments and business models are variations that fall under these three broad umbrellas. Although the three strategies may sound different and distinct, particularly licensing and litigation strategies — one being cooperative while the other competitive — they are in fact interconnected. All three mechanisms are meant to bridge the Patent and Product markets. Their common goal is to extract the most value out of patents. Each one of these strategies carries distinguishing features that allow them to best applied to various circumstances.

7.1.1 Licensing

Licensing is a cooperative patent monetization strategy because it sets out to reach agreement between two or more parties (see Figure 7.1). The formalities of licensing strategies are realized through contracts, which stipulate the existence of offers, acceptance, considerations, contractual

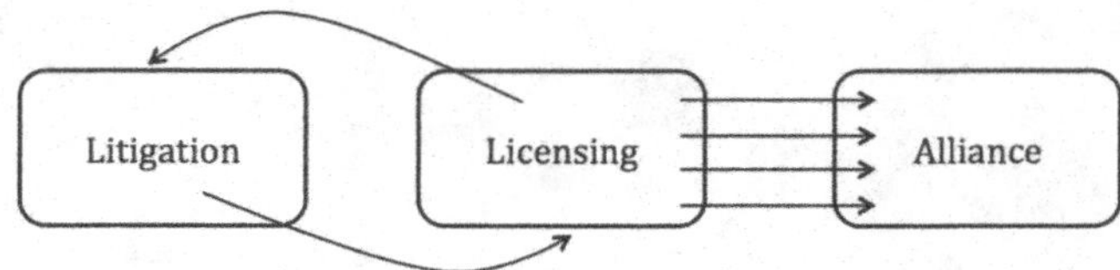

Figure 7.1 The three main categories of patent monetization strategies and their relationship

intention, and forms. For licensing strategies, the licensors offer their work on the technology and seek to gain monetary rewards. On the other hand, licensees accept the offer by providing considerations, usually in terms of monetary values. In return, licensees benefit from the use of the technology. Therefore, licensing is an effective mode to commercialize patents because both parties potentially meant to gain in the contracts.

In addition to the win-win nature of licensing strategies, it also offers the tool for business model innovation through the flexibility in drafting licensing terms. There are five rights conferred by a grant of patent. In principle, these five rights can be offered together or selectively to form exclusive or non-exclusive licenses. The licensing terms can be drafted to catch potential contributory infringement or to give more control to licensors by taking care of the allocation of rights such as who can make and use the patented technologies for the licensee. From the Product market perspective, licensing strategies can be sought when companies want to acquire technologies instead of developing them from scratch. Licensing thus, brings advantages to Product markets. From the licensors' point of view, licensing will help to create market power because successful licensing out the technology signifies acceptance of the merits of the technology. Therefore, licensing is the preferred mode to commercialize patents and it is the desired and ultimate outcome of Patent Portfolio Management.

7.1.2 Litigation

Litigation, on the other hand, is competitive and cacophonous. The immediate and prima facie intention of litigation is to seek redress from potential infringers. In effect, litigation is a legal tool to enforce the rights conferred, be it the five rights of patents or those that have been conferred through licensing contracts. In the past, it was the latter that constituted the bulk of the IP cases. Increasing litigation cases on infringement of patents have overshadowed the IP litigation landscape. Traditional patent litigation cases intend to exclude competitors from using the same technologies in order to create market advantage. A typical case is the smartphone war with Apple suing Samsung for the use of "slide-to-unlock" patents and the rounded corner design patents of the smartphones. Apple wanted to have market advantage of these distinguishing technologies. *It was a "world war" between the two giants, with patent lawsuits in Germany, Australia and the U.S.A. Apple had an initial success. But patents related to the slide-to-unlock feature were eventually found invalid in Germany and Australia.*[1] *In the United States, Apple was awarded USD 129 millions damages and the verdict has been upheld by the Court of Appeal for the Federal Circuit.*[2] *At the time of this book, there is still a pending case for the design patents in the Supreme Court. It is estimated that Apple and Samsung paid their lawyers more than USD 400 millions*[3] *even at the district court level. With the case going to the Supreme Court, they would probably spend more than a billion dollars in this fight.*[4]

Recently, however, litigation has increasingly been used as an initial step to get attention from third parties. Despite the advantages of licensing, most companies will not easily accept or be outright to look for licenses. Some stimulation is necessary. Litigation can be such stimulation. The ultimate aim of the litigation is to get the other party to agree to license the technologies. Around 65–68% of patent litigation cases are settled at the district court level, even more settled on the appeal level.[5] This phenomenon has now come to be known as "litigation for licensing."

---

[1] http://www.redmondpie.com/this-infographic-explains-the-patent-war-between-apple-and-samsung/

[2] https://9to5mac.com/2016/10/07/samsung-apple-120-million-court-slide-to-unlock-patent/

[3] http://www.bloomberg.com/news/articles/2012-03-29/apples-war-on-android

[4] http://www.beemonpatents.com/2016/04/what-everyone-should-know-about-apple-slide-to-unlock-patent-vs-samsung/ (Last accessed 21st November 2016)

[5] Megan M. La Belle, Against Settlement of (Some) Patent Cases, 67 VAND. L. REV. 375 (2014).

This is often the case when the technologies have already been adopted by the other party and they would not respond to demands for signing licensing contracts. Litigation, thus, forces the other party to respond and provides the motivation and urgency for both parties to come together for negotiation because of the high litigation costs. The longer the parties are antagonistic, the higher the litigation costs. Such expenses only benefits the lawyers. Therefore, there is incentive to settle the case as early as possible. The ultimate aim is to reach a settlement between the parties. Usually this means concluding licensing contracts for the continued use of the patented technology.

In effect, both licensing and litigation encourage collaboration among players in the value chain for increasing profits and market influence by exerting ownership of implemented technologies. Licensing and litigation also function hand-in-hand to exclude competitors and to extend influence along the value chain. Depending on the market power of the companies, a certain degree of influence along the value chain can be realized through licensing terms. However, such licensing clauses need to be drafted with great care to avoid potential antitrust violations.

7.1.3 Alliance

An alliance is licensing with a strategic purpose. It usually involves more than two parties. The results of such multi-party alliance can be far reaching compared to a two-party patent licensing. Alliance is not only an aggregate of licensing power through a single contract, which alleviates the transactional costs of licensing. Alliance also provides a solution to the deficiencies of the patent system and simple licensing. The patent system has been conceived to encourage innovation by disclosing the enablement of technologies in exchange for the monopoly of rights. However, there are limitations to such a monopoly. These limitations are necessary because patent law provides the patent owners much stronger remedies than contract law. For example, there is injunctive relief for patent owners whereas the remedy for a breach of contract is monetary. Even for monetary remedy, patent owners are allowed up to treble the damage amount in the event of willful infringement. Patent law is also binding on everyone regardless of whether they have contractual relationships with the patent owners. Therefore, it is only natural that there are limitations in place. For example, the patent term is limited, usually to 20 years in most countries. Patent rights are also jurisdictional which makes the decision to file patents in different jurisdictions a major headache for most companies, especially for start-ups who work on shoestring budgets. There are also limits to the scope of protection. The technology is confined to the descriptions in the patent documents. More precisely, the conferred rights are limited by the approved claims of the granted patents. Words, however, may not be sufficient to encompass every technical aspect. Thus, the document may not fully capture the essence of the technology. The patented technologies are often at the mercy of the drafters who give meaning to patented technologies. The drafter, however, may not understand the technology completely because they are not the inventors. This is the chasm that has been described in earlier chapters. In summary, the patent system has put in place restrictions to the monopoly conferred. In addition, with the increase in filing and continual exponential growth of patent grants, problems arise with patent thickets, royalties stacking, and patent hold ups if parties refuse to pay the royalties. These highly controversial outcomes of the patent system may be resolved by alliance.

Licensing has limitations too. Licensing contracts cannot be drafted to allow licensors to extend the power of the patents without limits. The law of contracts shapes how licensing contracts should be interpreted. There are two main types of licenses: implied or expressed. Sometimes the language used and the conduct by the licensors may result in an implied license, which can be used as a complete defense to the charge of patent infringement. There is also exhaustion of patent rights that is incurred by expressed license or in patent sale through implied license. All these legal concepts keep licensing in control.

Just as the objective of licensing and litigation is to secure common goals and interests in the use of technologies, so it goes with alliance. It is not uncommon to find many companies coming together to form an alliance, especially when the technology is commonly used and broadly applied across the platform for multiple categories of products. Through patent alliance, the transaction costs for reaching licenses can be reduced. It saves parties the money, time, and effort to negotiate multiple contracts from various parties. Licensing confers great power because it not only helps companies gain monetary values through collecting royalties, it also helps to extend market power. However, there are legal mechanisms in place to prevent it from manifesting its full potential. Alliance solves some of these issues.

7.2 Functions and Use of Licensing Strategies

In this book, we advocate licensing as the core strategy for patent monetization and licensing contracts as the tools to realize the various licensing strategies. Therefore, one needs to appreciate and master the art of drafting licensing contracts to maximize profits. In the following sections, we provide some fundamental concepts of licensing contracts and extend it to more complicated licensing models. A discussion on licensing contracts will not be complete without understanding the limitations such as the exhaustion of patent rights and ways to avoid these constraints. The application of licensing strategies will be exemplified using a case study on the Light Emitting Diodes (LEDs).

7.2.1 Reasons for implementing licensing strategies

Licensing strategies can be considered as a business model for business units with patents as the commodities. Its monetary licensing terms may range from lump sum payments to running royalties. It may also take the form of an exchange of rights between IP owners as in the case of cross licenses. While there may not be monetary gain in such arrangements, however, the parties can gain in cost savings.[6]

Licensing is a good vehicle for recouping R&D investments, especially when it is not advisable to produce products directly by the company. Very often, this is the case when the core competence of the company is in design. Successful examples of such companies are Qualcomm and ARM, who do not manufacture their designs; neither do they sub-contract to third parties for manufacturing. Their products are their design architecture and they license the technology out. With the increasing segmentation

---

[6]Alexander I. Poltorak and Paul J. Lerner: Essentials of Licensing Intellectual Property.

of the modern economy, many companies only focus on their core competence of design and do not want to venture into manufacturing. Thus, licensing is a good business model for instant commercialization of technology to recoup early financial rewards. Licensing strategies may also be welcomed by companies who do not want to risk going into certain geographical locations. By licensing the technology out, it will help the company strengthen their market position and increase the awareness of the technology globally without taking on too much risks. Allowing more players to use the technology would also help to proliferate the use and adoption of the technology, which is needed especially when the technology is applied industrially and at an early stage of development. If required, this may eventually lead to the incorporation of the technology into an industry standard. Licensing of technology at its early stage would also help to reduce the concerns of potential antitrust laws.

However, there are also disadvantages to licensing, such as losing partial control of the technology and lowering the level of involvement for the inventors. This may prevent the inventors from further developing the technology at the implementation stage. On the other hand, since the licensees have since been implementing the technology, it may not be surprising that they will eventually come up with more customized versions of the technology that are eventually implemented into products. Sometimes, this may even lead to licensees coming up with design-around alternatives to avoid using the patents by the licensors. In addition, licensing usually will generate less financial returns compared to product-based commercialization. Therefore, when deciding whether to use licensing as the vehicle of commercialization, the careful evaluation of the companies' goals and strategies is essential.

7.2.2 Key issues in licensing negotiation

When considering licensing as the mode for monetization, several determining factors have to be evaluated. Internally, companies need to identify the subject matter to be licensed. They may be patents, copyrights, or even trademarks. In this book, we focus on patent portfolio deployment.

Therefore, we are concerned with patents being the subject matter for licensing (see Figure 7.2). For most product-producing companies, the patent portfolios for licensing are usually found among non-core patents of the companies. Sometimes, companies involved in consumer products, such as personal care and cleaning agents may choose to license out even their core patents. However, they only do so after an interval. For example, P&G typically licenses out its best selling technology three years after the launch of a product or five years after a patent was issued on that technology. This is because competitors would copy the technology if it is popular.[7] It is faster and cheaper for them to license than to research on the same technology. On the other hand, P&G would have taken the early-mover advantage. Licensing helps to monetize their patents to lower the maintenance burden of patents.

Besides patents themselves, the know-how may also be part of the assets to be licensed. The definition of know-how needs to be carefully drafted to avoid ambiguity. Besides defining the assets, the price at which the assets are to be licensed needs to be stated too. In connection with the

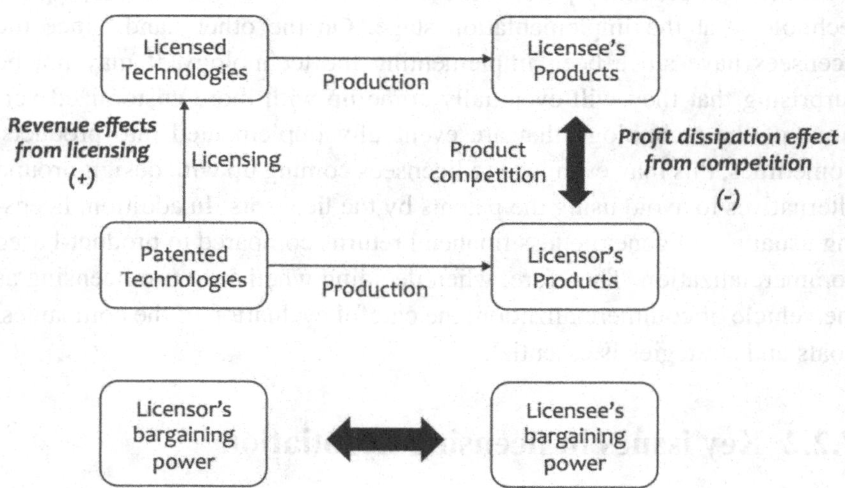

Figure 7.2 Understanding the advantages and disadvantages of licensing

[7] Bruce Berman, "From Assets to Profits. Competing for IP Vale & Return".

price are the payment schedule and the royalty audits details. Companies need to select the potential licensees carefully. Not only should the consideration be about the specific licensee, it should also include the position along the value chain in order to understand the macroscopic effects of one having the license. For example, should licenses be granted to manufacturers along the value chain? Or should they be granted to smaller competitors in countries where the licensors have no, or only small, operations? Or should licenses be granted to all parties in the ecosystem to produce the products, such as in the case of standard essential patents (SEPs)?

On top of these internal factors that companies need to contemplate before launching the licensing program, it is also vital to understand the licensing terms that can be and should be negotiated with the potential licensees. For example, the licensors should try to analyze the purpose of licensing from the licensees' perspective. Some licensees use the licensed technology to do further research. Some use it directly for manufacturing. Some licensees need the licenses for distribution. Determining this would help one to focus on the key terms for negotiation (see Figure 7.3). The duration of the licensing contract is another important factor to be negotiated. Usually it will just be a few years and the amount of royalties to be received for each year may vary. It is also common to receive an initial upfront payment for the first year and royalties for subsequent years, usually

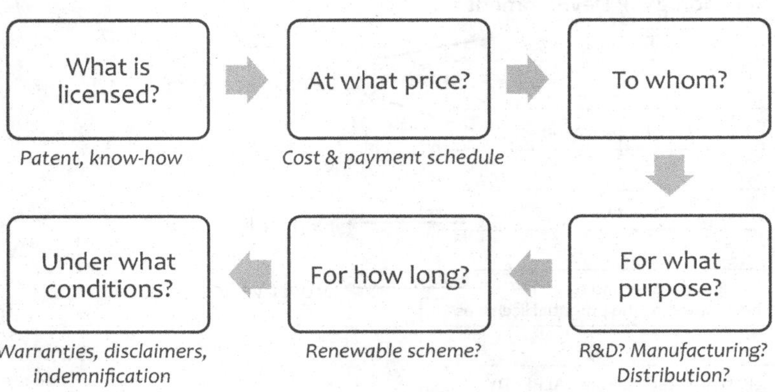

Figure 7.3 Understanding key issues in licensing negotiation

with diminishing rates. Other terms to be negotiated are the warranties, disclaimers and if necessary, whether there will be indemnification against future infringement lawsuits from third parties for the licensees.

7.2.3 Progressive nature of patent licenses

At different stages of technology development and IP development, there will be different objectives and concerns for the licensing contracts (see Figure 7.4). At the R&D and patent application stage, the license to be negotiated is an *ex ante* (before the event) license. This is the stage when the success of the technology is unknown and there are higher risks involved for the potential licensees. Licensees at this stage needs a lot more persuasion because the technology has not yet been adopted. However, licensees do enjoy first mover advantage if licenses are taken up at this stage. If the licensor is a start-up and urgently needs extra funding for the next stage of development, the potential licensees may take up some shares or they may be able to take up licenses at a lower rate compared to the stage when the technology has been adopted. There are even non-practicing entities who are willing to fund the IP development stage in return for a share of the ownership of IP or having favorable rights to sub-license to others.

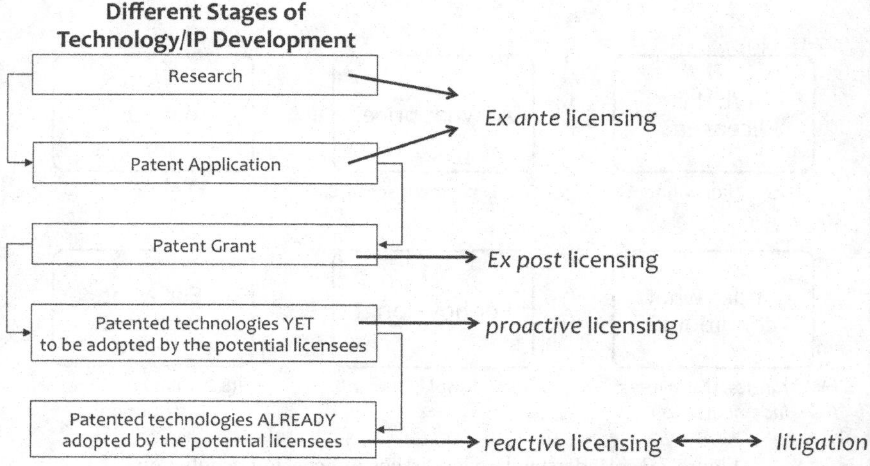

Figure 7.4 Progressive nature of technology licensing

When the patent is granted, it would be *ex post* (after the event) licensing as compared to *ex ante*. However, there are still differences to the licensing negotiations depending on whether the technology has been adopted. If the technology has yet to be adopted by potential licensees, the licensor needs to be proactive in pursuing licensing agreements with the potential licensees. On the other hand, if the technology has been adopted, such as P&G's case or in the event of SEPs, the type of licenses would be reactive. Licensees would be more willing to look for the licensors for licenses. In the event when licensees are unwilling to do so, litigation may be the only recourse. This is a natural progression for "litigation for licensing" that was mentioned in the earlier part of the chapter.

7.2.4 Basic principles of licensing contracts

The intention of signing licenses is primarily to avoid arguments in a business relationship by writing down the parties' expectations in advance.[8] Licensing contracts can therefore be seen as tools to manage risks in business operations. Contracts are promises that are legally enforceable. The basic elements of contracts include offer and acceptance, competent parties, considerations, and legal purposes. An offer arises when one party proposes a bargain (the offer) and the other party agrees to the (the acceptance). However, the agreement cannot be indefinitely drafted. The agreement itself must contain all the necessary terms and any unnecessary terms will be supplied by the court. The existence of the licensing agreement is evaluated by an objective test in which a reasonable person would have concluded an agreement reached from the acts of the two parties.

Another requirement of lawful licensing contract is that the parties must be competent and proper. The competent parties are those of undiminished mental capacity. Most people are considered competent to contract, but there are exceptions such as those who are mentally infirm or intoxicated. Minors may enter into contracts, but these contracts may be voided (or terminated). Only upon reaching majority (usually age 18 or 21 depending on the countries), may the minor ratify or reject the contract.

---

[8] David W. Tollen: The Tech Contracts Handbook — Software Licenses and Technology Services Agreements for Lawyers and Business people.

If ratified, the contract would then have the same status as that originally entered into by competent parties. The parties must also be proper parties. This means that the ownership of the patent properties should have written representation. If the patents have been previously licensed on an exclusive basis, the patent owners will not have the right to license the patents to another third party again. For licensees, if it is written in the license agreements that they are allowed to sublicense the patents to others, then these licensees are proper parties too. In the event that the licenses are to be acted upon by organizations, the parties representing the parties must have representative capacities and there must be proper execution. The names of the organizations and the titles of the representatives must be clearly stated in the licensing contracts.

Furthermore, like any contract, there must be consideration. "Consideration" is the price each party agrees to carry out his or her part of the contract. The licensor allows the licensee to utilize some rights under certain intellectual property. In return, the licensee promises to pay royalty or cross license some rights to the licensor. The exchange does not have to be of equivalent value, but lack of this consideration will cause the contract to be regarded as a gift and therefore unenforceable.

In addition, a contract must have a legal purpose. It must not be for the performance of an activity prohibited by law; otherwise, enforcing the contract would be contrary to public policy. In the case of intellectual property, the license must not be in violation of antitrust law and franchising laws, for example.

Even if the contract fulfills all these basic elements, it may not be enforceable if it does not follow the doctrine of unconscionability. This means that if the provisions in the contract are so unfairly drafted that they go against the conscience of the court, the court may refuse to enforce the contract or the particular unconscionable provision. The court may also limit the application of any unconscionable provision. Another level of unconscionability requirement to be satisfied is substantive unconscionability, meaning the provision cannot be truly unfair or one-sided. Examples of substantive unconscionability may appear unreasonably large amount of monetary remedies, and having liquidated damages. Besides the terms of the contract, the procedure in which the contract is entered into must satisfy the procedural unconscionability. The contract will not be enforceable if one party is induced to enter into a contract without having an alternative such as the case when the parties are of vastly different economic powers (contracts of adhesion).

The above introduction on the principles of licensing contracts is brief but it serves to give start-ups and small and medium enterprises (SMEs) who may not have in-house legal counsel to have some understanding of contract law, which helps to execute licensing strategies. If the reader would like further information on this area, books specifically on the law of contract or in particular, licensing contract should be consulted.

7.2.5 Basic structures of licensing contracts

The basic principles of licensing contracts can be reflected in the following general structure for licensing contracts:

1. Introduction — The Preamble
2. Definitions
3. Grant of Rights
4. Royalties
5. Representations and Warranties
6. Term and Termination
7. Assignment and Transfer
8. Miscellaneous Terms
9. Signature

In this section, we will have an overview of these elements. Each of these elements is a term to be discussed and determined by both licensing parties. They would also provide rooms for negotiation in the licensing contract.

7.2.5.1 *Introduction — The preamble*

Licensing contracts always start with the identification of the contracting parties. If the contracting parties are corporations, identify the states and countries in which they are organized and their principal places of business. This can form the basis for claims to legal jurisdiction over the organization. In the introduction, it is also important to include the "whereas" clauses. These are facts leading to the formation of the contract and provide the intentions of the parties for concluding the licensing contract. The descriptions in this part also supply any omitted contract terms, which will be considered when questions of unconscionability are raised in disputes.

7.2.5.2 *Definitions*

The next important part of the contract is the definitions. Parties should define the terms to their own benefits. If the terms are not defined properly, potential legal disputes will arise. The definitions can be expressed inclusively, with the defined terms clearly stated. They can also be expressed exclusively, describing what is not included. In either case, the definitions can be in an open or closed format. An open format will allow for the inclusion of further unstated items or terms to be interpreted while a closed format is limited to the stated definitions in the contract.

7.2.5.3 *Grant*

The grant section specifies the rights, in terms of scope and nature that the licensor bestows on the licensee for the permission of use by identifying the licensed rights or properties, the limits on the extent or the manner of their use, the geographical and temporal bounds of the license. Besides the basic rights to be granted, it also specifies the ability or inability of the licensor to grant further licenses. This determines whether the licensing contract is an exclusive or non-exclusive contract. For a non-exclusive contract, the licensor remains free to use the licensed right and grant additional licenses to others. For exclusive licenses, the licensor cannot grant further licenses of the same rights; neither can the licensor use the rights. However, if the license is a sole license, the licensor can utilize the rights even though he cannot grant further rights to third parties.

In addition, the grant section also specifies the assignability nature of the license. In an assignable license, the licensee may transfer or assign licenses to third parties. If the license is a paid-up license, which means that the royalties are paid in a lump sum at the stipulated date of the license, the license should be non-assignable. For licenses with running royalties, they may be assignable. However, it can be uneconomical for the licensor to administer or unduly burdensome on the licensee. Therefore, assignable licenses are best to be avoided. In cases when the licensee really needs to assign the right of the license such as in a merger and acquisition case, the licensor should consider limiting the use of the patents by any assignee to the level of use of the assignor immediately preceding the assignment.

For running royalty licenses, it is generally not a problem to assign such licenses except for running the risks of future assignees to the licensing contract being dishonest, unreliable, or financially unsound. Therefore, it is best to draft the assignment term such as "subject to the approval of the licensor, which shall not be unreasonably withheld." For bankruptcy cases, it is common to follow that a license will automatically be terminated if the licensee becomes illiquid or otherwise exhibits conditions suggesting that bankruptcy is inevitable.

7.2.5.4 *Royalties*

The section on royalties stipulates the amount to be paid for by the licensees. Various schemes are commonly used depending on negotiation. Royalty may be quantity-based, revenue-based, or profit-based. It may also be a flat fee/lump sum payment or a combination of running royalty and lump sum payment (two-part tariff regime). Usually licensors would request for an upfront payment either to secure funding for further research or to minimize risks in subsequent payment schedules by a stepwise payment scheme. Royalties may also be paid in equity. On the provision of royalty collection, it is important to specify the audit methods to assess this, such as allowing the licensor to access the licensee's financial records through an external auditor. There should also be provisions for penalties for late royalty payments.

7.2.5.5 *Representations and warranties*

Representations are statements on the current state of affairs that are relied upon as the basis for the agreement between the parties. If they were untrue, it would constitute misrepresentation, which is the basis for termination.

Warranties are promises that the agreed statements are true and will remain so. If they are broken, the licensee is entitled to damages. Oral statements of promises, however, are excluded, following the parole evidence rule in contract law.

7.2.5.6 *Term and termination*

The term of the license is the duration, which may be for a fixed period with or without extensions or renewals. It may also be triggered by the occurrence of some future events such as when the research has reached another stage, especially in the case of pharmaceutical patent licenses.

Termination clauses allow for the disposal of inventories or work in progress. They can be executed upon fulfillment of existing contracts and warranty obligations. In the termination clauses, it can stipulate the licensees to return all the confidential documents and pay up all the accrued royalties.

7.2.5.7 *Miscellaneous terms*

Many other terms can be put in place in licensing contracts. For example, the most favored nations clauses can be added to ensure that the licensee can enjoy at least the same favorable treatment as those previously or thereafter granted to any other licensee. The more favorable term can be required to be made retroactive. Care has to be taken in negotiating these terms as they may seriously limit the licensor's flexibility in negotiating with potential licensees in the future.

It is also common to specify the choice of jurisdiction governing the contract, such as "the contract is to be construed, interpreted, governed in accordance with the laws" of a state or nation. The mode of settling disputes of the licensing contract in the future should also be included, such as the arbitration and mediation clauses. There should also be a non-waiver clause to ensure that a party's failure to enforce its contractual rights, intentionally or unintentionally, does not result in a waiver of those rights or remedies for their breach. The non-waiver clause provides that the licensor does not waive its rights to insist upon strict compliance with terms of the contract in the future even if it has deviated from the enforcement of those terms in the past.

7.3 Limitations of Licensing

7.3.1 Express and implied license

Licenses can also be expressed or implied. Express licenses arise whenever the negotiated and consented language and conduct of the two parties are being reduced into writing on papers to be signed. Implied licenses result from the behavior of patent holders regarding the licensing of the patents. However, these have not been reduced to writing. There are four doctrines of implied license: acquiescence, conduct, equitable estoppel, and legal estoppel.

Acquiescence and conduct are the more abstract theories. They may be inferred by the language and behavior of the licensor. Legal estoppel is invoked when the patent owner derogates from the licensing, assignment agreements, or any arrangements with considerations. In determining the existence of legal estoppel, a court considers the scope of the rights granted and whether the licensor's actions impact those rights. If the remedies sought by the licensor impact what is granted under the license, an implied license would be granted based on legal estoppel.

The principle of legal estoppel has been illustrated in *TransCore, LP v. Electronic Transaction Consultants Corp., No. 08-1430 (Fed. Cir. Apr. 8, 2009)*. In 2000, TransCore sued one of its competitors, Mark IV Industries ("Mark IV"), for infringement of three of its patents, including '924 patent. The parties entered into a settlement agreement ("the TransCore-Mark IV agreement"). In the agreement, TransCore "covenants not to bring any demand, claim, lawsuit, or action against Mark IV for future infringement" of certain patents, specifically on ten patents, including the three asserted patents. The agreement, however, excludes other patents issued on the effective date of the TransCore-Mark IV agreement or those to be issued in the future. The '924 patent falls under the category of patents issued in the future. The Federal Circuit considered whether TransCore's rights to the later-issued '924 patent, were exhausted by Mark IV's authorized sales under an implied license to practice the '924 patent by virtue of legal estoppel. The Court concluded that, the '946 patent was broader than, and necessary to practice at least one of the patents included in the TransCore-Mark IV agreement, therefore, TransCore was legally estopped from asserting the '946 patent against Mark IV. The same principle was articulated by the court in *AMP Inc. v. United States*, 389 F.2d 448 (Ct. Cl. 1968), and *Wang Laboratories, Inc. v. Mitsubishi Electronics America, Inc.*, 103 F.3d 1571 (Fed. Cir. 1997).

The doctrine of equitable estoppel is explained in Integrated Global Concepts, Inc. v. J2 Global, Inc., No. C-12-03434-RMW (N.D. Cal. June 28, 2013). The court explained that:

> *"An implied license by equitable estoppel requires that: "(1) the patentee, through statements or conduct, gave an affirmative grant of consent or permission to make, use, or sell to the alleged infringer; (2) the alleged infringer relied on that statement or conduct; and (3) the alleged infringer would, therefore, be materially prejudiced if the patentee is allowed to proceed with its claim." Winbond Electronics Corp. v. Int'l Trade Comm'n, 262 F.3d 1363, 1374 opinion corrected, 275 F.3d 1344 (Fed. Cir. 2001)."*

Therefore, equitable estoppel is determined by the misleading conduct of the patent holder, such as suggesting that he will not advocate or enforce such patent rights. It is necessary to analyze the "entire course of conduct" between the patent holder and the other parties in order to determine the application of the doctrine.

7.3.1.1 *Implied license as a defense*

Implied licenses constitute a complete defense to a charge of patent infringement. This principle is illustrated in *Anton/Bauer, Inc. v. PAG,*

Ltd., No. 02-1487 (Fed. Cir. May 21, 2003). Anton/Bauer owns US Patent No. 4,810,204 ("the '204 patent"). It is directed to a battery-pack connection that allows replacement of a battery pack to be quick and efficient. Every claim of the '204 patent is concerned with a combination of a female plate and a male plate and requires a "releasable locking means." Anton/Bauer allowed Camcorder manufacturers to sell the female plate to consumers with no attached conditions and at the same time, Anton/Bauer also manufactured and sold battery packs. The court ruled that Anton/Bauer had granted an implied license to its customers to use '204 patent's combination. Therefore, defendant, PAG, Ltd. ("PAG") who sold the accused battery packs that could be used in combination with Anton/Bauer's female plates, did not commit direct, induced, or indirect infringement against Anton/Bauer. The conditions for using implied license as a defense for infringement is that the patent holder must sell the components separately and unconditionally. In addition, the only function of the components is to exemplify the claims in the patent.

Implied licensing also arises due to sublicenses. In *Jacobs v. Nintendo of America, Inc., No. 03- 1297 (Fed. Cir. May 28, 2004)*, the federal circuit illustrated this principle. Jacobs owns US Patent No. 5,059,958 ("the '958 patent"), which concerns a tilt-sensitive joystick for a video-game controller. In July 2001, Jacobs settled a case against Analog and agreed to grant a license of the '985 patent to Analog. After this settlement, Jacobs sued Nintendo for infringement of the '958 patent. As Analog's customer, Nintendo moved for a summary judgment of non-infringement based on Jacob's '958 patent license with Analog. The district court ruled that the settlement agreement between Jacobs and Analog in fact granted Analog's customers implied sublicenses. On appeal, the Federal Circuit agreed with the district court's decision and stated that it is the basic contract principle that a party may not assign a right, receive consideration for it, and then take steps that would render the right commercially worthless. It was known to Jacobs that Analog was not in the business of making game controls, so there was no reason to believe that Analog would have bargained for a right that would not protect its customers.

From the illustrations of these two cases on implied licenses, it is clear that licensors need to pay special attention to their licensing contracts. Therefore, in the next part of this chapter, we will focus on the special issues in licenses, especially the exhaustion of patent rights, because the use of patent licensing to manage the power of patent holders is a main focus of this book. It is important for the patent holders to understand what the law conscripts on the patent owners to prevent them from overexerting their patent rights.

7.3.2 Exhaustion of patent rights

The patent exhaustion doctrine is an exhaustion of rights that limits the extent to which patent holders can control an individual article of a patented product after an authorized sale.

> ".. In the essential nature of things, when the patentee, or the person having his rights, sells a machine or instrument whose sole value is in its use, he receives the consideration for its use and he parts with the right to restrict that use. The article, in the language of the court, passes without the limit of monopoly." *(Adams v. Burke, 84 US 453, 456 (1873)).*

Patent exhaustion is also known as the first sale doctrine because the first unrestricted sale of a patented item exhausts the patent holder's control over that particular item. In other words, "the initial authorized sale of a patented item terminates all patent rights to that item" as articulated in *Quanta Computer, Inc. v. LG Electronics, Inc., 553 US 617 (2008).*

An exhaustion of patent rights can be incurred by licensing (express license) or patented product sale (implied license), which embeds with implied license of product patent in the use, sale, offer for sale, and possibly import (international exhaustion). Other circumstances when there is an exhaustion of patent rights are exclusive licenses. In such cases, patent exhaustion is asserted as an affirmative defense to charges of patent infringement, though it is less commonly asserted affirmatively in a declaratory judgment action.

It can also be a defense to indirect infringement of partial elements of a claim. In the case of *Anton/Bauer, Inc. v. PAG, Ltd., No. 02-1487 (Fed. Cir. May 21, 2003)* that we have discussed earlier, the Federal Circuit concluded that sales by Anton/Bauer of the unpatented female plate have extinguished Anton/Bauer's right to control the future use of the plate because it can only be used in the patented combination and the combination is inevitably completed by the purchaser, which is PAG in this case.

7.3.2.1 *Process patents and patent exhaustion*

The case of *United States v. Univis Lens Co., 316 US 241 (1942)* may illustrate the application of the doctrine of patent exhaustion to process patents. Univis manufactured lens blanks and sold them to licensees. The licenses required the licensees to sell the lenses at fixed prices controlled by Univis. The court concluded that the only use of the blanks would be to manufacture the licensed lens and the only objective of the sale of the lens blanks was to enable the manufacture of the patented lenses. Sale of lens blanks by the patentee in itself is a complete transfer of ownership of the blanks, and a license to practice the final stage of the patent procedure was also completed with consideration by the licensee paying the purchase price. In this case, the sale of the blanks exhausted the patents. Therefore, "the patentee may not thereafter, by virtue of his patent, control the use or disposition of the article," such as by fixing the price of the article to be sold subsequently. In this case, the court ruled that exhaustion of patent rights does extend to process patents that cover unfinished products.

7.3.2.2 *Method patents and patent exhaustion*

The doctrine of patent exhaustion extends to method patents as illustrated in the decision in *Quanta Computer, Inc. v. LG Electronics, Inc., 553 US 617*. In this case, LG Electronics ("LG") owned patents describing techniques for efficient communication between computer components. It then licensed them to Intel Corporation to use in the manufacture and resale of microprocessors. However, the license prohibited third parties from combining LG's patents with non-licensed items. Quanta purchased microchips from Intel under a license restricting them from breaching the Intel/LG agreement. Quanta then combined the microchips with other parts in order to produce computers. LG sued Quanta, alleging Quanta's conduct infringed their patents and breached the terms of the licensing agreement. The Supreme Court of United States concluded that LG's license did not restrict Intel's right to sell their microprocessors, but instead "broadly permit[ted] Intel to 'make, use, [or] sell' products free of LG's patent claims." Applying Univis' case on exhaustion of method patents, the Court reasoned that chipsets and microprocessors have substantially embodied LG's patents. Thus, it is conclusive that Intel's products "had no reasonable non-infringing use and included all the inventive aspects of the patented methods." As such, since Intel was authorized to sell to any party, "the doctrine of patent exhaustion prevents LG from asserting its patent rights with respect to the patents substantially embodied by those products."

This judgment extended the doctrine of patent exhaustion to method patents. However, the Court did not actually rule on the contractual issues in LG and Intel's licensing agreement. In fact, the Court explicitly raised the possibility that Quanta might have been susceptible to liabilities based on contract law had this argument been advanced. This remark leaves open the possibility that parties might be able to recover damages under contract even when patent exhaustion does not allow them to do so.

In the case of LG, the licensing agreement required Intel to give notice to its customers, including Quanta, that LG had not licensed those customers to practice its patents. But LG did *not* mention that it licensed Intel to make, use, and sell microprocessor products ONLY in the field of microprocessor products combined with other LG-licensed products. Without an explicit field-of-use limitation on Intel's manufacturing, using, and selling rights, LG failed to go straight to the point to expressly deny Intel any license to make microprocessor products that would be combined with other products. Should there have been such clauses in the licensing agreement, LG could have invoked to sue under breach of contract. Therefore, even though Quanta's case has confirmed the doctrine of patent exhaustion for method patents, there are ways to cope with the limitations using carefully drafted contracts.

7.3.2.3 *Coping with decision in Quanta*

As mentioned, LG could have sought damages through contract law. In the licensing agreement, LG may require manufacturers to structure sales contracts to grant the patentee the right to sue purchasers as third party beneficiaries. For example, semiconductor design houses, who only license their designs to be manufactured by chip manufacturers and handset makers, may devise the licensing scheme such that it licenses both chip manufacturer and handset makers for its entire portfolio. Chip makers are forbidden from selling to unlicensed handset makers, and handset makers are forbidden from purchasing chips from unlicensed chipmakers.

Alternatively, a design house may choose not to license the entire patent portfolio. Instead, they may divide the portfolio into separate smaller portfolios and license them according to the role they play in the value chain. In reality, such licensing strategies may be difficult to implement. If the patents are interconnected, the potential licensees may require them to be licensed as a portfolio anyway. Licensees may also have implied licenses of patents not in the licensing agreement but as interlocked with the licensed patents. This requires the licensors to build up a patent portfolio that covers various stages in the production of the product and have a good understanding of the limitations and rules of contract law. Thus, it is important to have the concept of patent portfolio development and deployment in mind in order to tackle the limitations posted by licensing patents.

7.3.2.4 *Conditional licensing and patent exhaustion*

Conditional licenses may not lead to patent exhaustion, whereas unconditional licenses usually lead to patent exhaustion. The Supreme Court allowed for the possibility of an authorized, but conditional sale (*Keeler v. Standard Folding Bed Co., 157 US 659, 1895*). However, such conditions are to be enforceable under contract law, not patent law. Thus, as illustrated in the Quanta case, patentee could only enforce licensing contracts or sales conditions against original and subsequent purchasers who had been informed of the conditions or who agreed to the conditions. Operationally, it may make it difficult for the patent owner to enforce these conditions against all downstream purchasers in the value chain.

7.3.2.5 *Exclusive licensing and patent exhaustion*

Exclusive licenses grant some of the proprietary rights of a patent to the licensee. In so doing, the patentee has exploited the patent right given by statue so that he cannot prohibit subsequent activities of exploitation anymore. A non-exclusive license is, however, in effect a "bare" license. In determining whether a non-exclusive license is subject to patent exhaustion, the court checks whether an authorized sale has occurred. A purchaser who acquires a patented article through an authorized sale enjoys the patent rights with no additional costs. For non-exclusive license, the court will focus on whether the sale of the patented article is within the scope of the license, and therefore authorized. If the sale is authorized, the doctrine applies, and the patent rights are exhausted in the licensed product. Otherwise, the doctrine does not apply, and the patent rights are not exhausted. This principle can be illustrated by the two US Supreme Court cases.

In Adams v. Burke, the licensee was authorized to make, use, and sell patented coffin lids within a designated geographical area of the United States. An undertaker purchased the lids from the licensee within the designated area as stipulated by the licensing contract and used them outside the designated area. The patentee objected to the use, because the undertaker was competing with the patentee in an area originally thought to be reserved for the patentee. The Supreme Court decided that since the value of the patented article was in its use, the patentee should have received full consideration from the sale of the lids regardless of where they were used. Since the licensee's sale of the lids to the undertaker was authorized, the sale has therefore exhausted the patent rights in those lids. The patentee, thus, could not enforce the patent against the undertaker even though the lids purchased from the licensee were used outside the authorized area.

In General Talking Pictures v. Western Electric, the licensee was authorized to make and sell patented amplifiers within a designated and for private use market in the United States. The licensee sold the amplifiers to a customer, even after knowing that the customer planned to use the amplifiers for commercial use in the motion picture industry. The patentee had licensed the same patent in the commercial market to different licensees, who wanted to preserve the patent's value in the commercial market. The Court found that movie theaters did not belong to the private use market. The licensee, thus, violated the terms of his license and the sale was therefore unauthorized. As a result, the patent rights of the patentee in the amplifier were not exhausted. The patent could be asserted against the sale of that amplifier in the commercial market.

7.3.2.6 *Covenant-not-to-sue and patent exhaustion*

Unconditional convenient-not-to-sue invokes patent exhaustion as mentioned by the Federal Court of US *in TransCore, LP v. Electronic Transaction Consultants Corp., No. 2008-1430 (Fed. Cir. Apr. 8, 2009)*. According to the court, this is equivalent to a non-exclusive patent license and thus implicates patent exhaustion. In this case, the Federal Court of US followed Quanta's footstep that "an unconditional covenant-not-to-sue" does authorize sales "by the covenantee for purposes of patent exhaustion." The court concluded that a covenant-not-to-sue "for future infringement," without further restriction, "thus authorizes all acts that would otherwise be infringements: making, using, offering for sale, selling, or importing." The court pointed out that TransCore could have limited this authorization (e.g., to just "making" or "using") but did not do so. Therefore, it is unclear whether a conditional covenant-not-to-sue will invoke the doctrine of patent exhaustion.

7.4 Licensing Disputes and Litigation

The focus of this book is patent portfolio deployment to extract its maximum value. Such an attempt to extend power is not without risks as it seems to go against competition law, especially antitrust law. The law will not permit the misuse of patent rights if it is against the protection of the public. The special note on patent exhaustion discussed in the earlier section is just the tip of an iceberg for more complicated issues in licensing. In this section, we will look at issues that arise when licensing is applied on a bigger scale involving more players, market power, and the extension of patent rights.

Antitrust issues may appear to restrict the expansion of the power of patent rights. However, both laws aim at "promoting innovation and enhancing consumer welfare."[9] They are not in conflict, but the licensors should fully understand the implications of some actions to prevent possible violation of antitrust law.

7.4.1 The governing law and doctrine

The antitrust law in the United States has three main elements:

1. Prohibit agreements or practices that restrict free trading and competition between business entities. This includes, in particular, the repression of cartels.
2. Ban abusive behavior by a firm dominating a market, or anti-competitive practices that tend to lead to such a dominant position. Practices controlled in this way may include predatory pricing, tying, price gouging, refusal to deal, and many others.
3. Supervise the mergers and acquisitions of large corporations, including some joint ventures. Transactions that are considered to threaten the competitive process can be prohibited altogether, or approved subject to "remedies" such as an obligation to divest part of the merged business or to offer licenses or access to facilities to enable other businesses to continue competing.

The enforcing agencies for antitrust laws are the US Department of Justice (DOJ) and the Federal Trade Commission (FTC). DOJ and FTC generally work together while FTC has extra jurisdiction over unfair competition in interstate commerce.

7.4.1.1 *Sherman Act*

Sections 1 and 2 of the Sherman Act are the most relevant provisions related to intellectual properties. Section 1 of the Sherman Act prohibits

[9] "1995 Antitrust Guidelines for the Licensing of Intellectual Property", U.S. Department of Justice and the Federal Trade Commission.

agreements between two or more unrelated entities that unreasonably restraining trade. Section 2 of the Act prohibits the willful acquisition or maintenance of a monopoly as distinguished from growth or development "as a consequence of superior product, business acumen, or historical accident" (United States v Grinnell Corp., 384 US 563, 570–71 (1966).

7.4.1.2 *Clayton Act*

The Clayton Act aims to strengthen the antitrust laws by conferring enforcement power against transactions that are likely to affect competition even before they actually happen. Sections 3 and 7 are more relevant to intellectual property. Section 3 deals with "tie-out" issues, meaning the seller conditions the sale or lease of a product by making an agreement with the buyer to not to use or deal with competitive products. The burden of proof for liability is lower for the Clayton Act but it introduces the concept of "relevant market" which must be proved.

Section 7 is generally applied to mergers and acquisitions between companies. Exclusive license is the acquisition of assets that are considered by Section 7 of the Clayton Act. Thus, any exclusive license has to be submitted to the FTC and DOJ for approval.

7.4.1.3 *The FTC Act*

Finally, Section 5(a)(1) of the Federal Trade Commission Act grants FTC the power to enforce anti-competition matters. FTC has the power to investigate and prosecute "unfair methods of competition in commerce, and unfair or deceptive acts or practices in commerce." (U.S.C. §45(a)(1) (2000)).

7.4.2 Evaluation rule

The conduct that may lead to antitrust issues is evaluated by the per se rule or the "rule of reason."

7.4.2.1 *Per se rule*

Per se rule is generally applied to price-fixing and market division among competitors, which are practices that impose unreasonable restraints on competition. It generally applies when intellectual property is licensed as a pretext for a market allocation scheme or when an intellectual property holder ties the sale of one product to the sale of a product protected by an intellectual property right.

7.4.2.2 *"Rule of reason"*

The rule of reason is the most common rule to evaluate antitrust conduct. It evolved from the Supreme Court judgment in *Standard Oil Co. of New Jersey v. United States (US 1 (1911))*. The Court held that only contracts that "unreasonably" restrained trade were violations of the Sherman Act. Under this rule, a relevant market is defined and the pro-competitive benefits of the alleged conduct are weighed against the anti-competitive harm. If, on balance, the conduct is pro-competitive, the conduct is lawful; otherwise, the agreement unreasonably restricts competition. The "rule of reason" in effect requires facts and expert opinions on the relevant market as evidence.

7.4.2.3 *The relevant market*

The relevant market consists of a relevant product and a relevant geographic area. The intellectual property owner's market share is then determined by the relevant market and assessed on whether it possesses monopoly or market power. If the relevant market share exceeds 50%, the patent owner might be considered to possess market power. The key to determining the relevant market is whether the product in question has substitutes that customers could economically switch to. If yes, these substitutes should be included in the relevant market assessment.

In the 1994 IP Guidelines, markets can also be characterized as "technology" or "innovation markets." A technology market is a market that consists of "the intellectual property that is licensed ... and its close substitutes." An innovation market is a market that "consists of the research and development directed to particular new or improved goods or processes, and the close substitutes for that research and development."

Market definition is a threshold issue that must be addressed before further inquiry in any antitrust cases. (In re Schering-Plough Corp., No. 9297 (FTC 27 June 2002). In technology and innovation markets, the IP Guidelines state that if there are "four other independently controlled entities that possess comparable capabilities and incentives to undertake research and development," then it is unlikely that there could be an adverse effect on competition (IP Guidelines §§ 3.2.3, 4.30. If, on the other hand, an intellectual property holder possesses monopoly or market power in a relevant antitrust market, then further analysis is required to determine whether its conduct violates the antitrust laws.

7.4.3 Application of US antitrust laws to intellectual property rights

7.4.3.1 *Exclusive licensing*

As mentioned earlier, exclusive licenses are subject to the scrutiny of Section 7 of the Clayton Act. Exclusive licenses can be found to be per se violations of the antitrust law if the licensing is merely a sham or pretext for horizontal price fixing or market allocation. For vertical exclusive licenses, which are between entities at different levels of the market, most of the time they are considered lawful under the US antitrust laws. Vertical exclusive licenses that contain non-price restrictions are analyzed under the rule of reason. If the vertical license attempts to set minimum price levels at which the licensee may sell products, the license will attract antitrust scrutiny. However, the exclusive licenses in different fields may not be an issue of antitrust violation. Only when there is evidence that the patent owner deliberately extend its patent rights beyond what is conferred by the patent right will there be an antitrust violation issue.

7.4.3.2 *Refusal to license*

The patent owner, in general, has the right to refuse granting license to any party unless it is a concerted effort to refuse to grant a license to a particular party, similar to a group boycott, then it would be a per se antitrust violation case.

In Image Technical Services Inc v Eastman Kodak Co, 125 F.3d 1195 (9th Cir. 1997), the Ninth Circuit Court of Appeals held that the following elements must be shown to establish a monopoly:

1. possession of monopoly power in one market;
2. refusal to license technology to competitors in a second related market, and
3. specific intent.

However, the Federal Circuit Court of Appeals rejected this assessment in In re Independent Service Organizations Antitrust Litigation, 203 F.3d 1322 (Fed. Cir. 2000). The Federal Circuit took a simpler approach and stated that the exercise of patent rights in most cases will not bring up antitrust issues for refusals to license, unless the refusal to license is part of an unlawful tying scheme as discussed below, the patent is obtained by fraud, or the enforcement litigation is a sham.

7.4.3.3 *Tying*

Tying is closely related to the extension of patent power as it is about leveraging. It is tying the sale of one product on the condition that the buyer will buy another product from the seller. Tying may be analyzed under the per se rule or the "rule of reason."

A per se tying usually involves the patent owner coercing the licensee to license a tied product or patent. Usually the triggering factor for antitrust violations would be the market power of the patent owner in the principle licensing technology. A "rule of reason" tying requires an actual anti-competitive effect as a result of the tying arrangement without valid business justification. The court is careful not to stifle innovation by applying per se rule to a tying agreement. For example, in United States v Microsoft Corp., 253 F.3d 34 (DC Cir. 2001), the DC Circuit held that

Microsoft's bundling of a browser with the operating system did not warrant per se rule treatment despite its market share.

7.4.3.4 *Patent pooling and cross licensing*

Patent pooling is a type of cross licensing that involves two or more patent owners collectively licensing a set of patents. Most of the patent-pooling arrangements are pro-competitive because they can integrate complementary technologies, reduce transaction costs, avoid, or settle costly licensing litigation, and clear blocking patents. There are, however, situations when the pooling arrangements reduce or restrict competition. For example, if the cross-licensing arrangement is such that it requires the participants' approval for licensing to potential licensees outside the pool, then it may attract antitrust concerns. Alternatively, if the patent pool forces a grant back license for current or future technology without any consideration, innovation may be discouraged and it may attract antitrust concerns too.

Antitrust assessments for patents is generally analyzed under the rule of reason unless it is a sham or price-fixing case. Therefore, the market for the pooled patents must be assessed to determine if the pool creates market power. In order to minimize this power, the patent should only include patents that are necessary for producing the relevant product. In addition, it is also necessary to analyze the relationship between the pooled patents. There are two types of relationships between patents: substitutive and complementary. Substitute patents cover alternative technologies and are non-blocking. They are potentially competing with each other. Complementary patents are patents that must be used together to produce a specific output of the technology and are not substitutes for each other. They are patents that are required to produce the desired output. Two mutually blocking patents are complementary from a legal point of view. Substitute patents compete with each other, thus, they should not be bundled in a pool from a competition point of view. Complementary patents do not have this concern.

7.4.3.5 *Exclusive dealing*

Exclusive dealing refers to the case when a licensor prevents the licensee from selling, licensing, distributing, or using competing technologies or products, which incorporate competing technologies. Most exclusive dealing arrangements are vertical in nature. Thus, they are assessed under the rule of reason, meaning, the market share of the licensor must be assessed. In addition, the degree of disclosure to suppliers of competing goods or technologies, the duration of such exclusive dealing, the possibility that competing technology can enter into the market and the purpose behind the restraint must also be evaluated to determine if there is a case of antitrust.

7.4.3.6 *Standard setting*

Standardization and patent pools are interconnected because many standards are based on complementary technology developed by different firms. A technical standard is an officially established norm or requirement about a technical system that establishes uniform engineering or technical criteria, methods, process and practices. Standards can be important for the wide adoption of new technologies in the marketplace. However, they will create a barrier to entry to the respective market as switching from one standard to another is often not possible or only with substantial efforts. Therefore, this may raise antitrust concerns.

Standard setting is considered pro-competitive because it promotes market efficiencies by ensuring compatibility of products, thus, making it easier to gain market acceptance. Standard setting, however, can raise antitrust concerns if members of the standard setting body use the process to exclude competitors or when a member of the standard setting body manipulates the standard setting process to monopolize the respective market. This latter scenario is demonstrated in In re Rambus Inc, No. 9302 (FTC 18 June 2002).

The FTC brought a case against Rambus, alleging that it failed to make required disclosures to the Joint Electron Device Engineering Council (JEDEC), a standard setting organization that develops standards for computer memory. Rambus was accused of reducing competition by failing to disclose its intellectual property as required when the standard was formed. Rambus later sought to enforce its intellectual property rights in relation to this standard. The Federal Circuit analyzed the language of the JEDEC membership rules and found that there was no "duty" to disclose Rambus's patent applications because applications could not read on the standard and the duty to disclose before the standard was presented to JEDEC members for adoption. As a result of this decision, there is a heavy responsibility for the standard setting organization to "define clearly what, when, how, and to whom the members must disclose [to] provide a firm basis for the disclosure duty necessary for a fraud verdict." Id. at 1002. FTC later reviewed the case and found that Rambus distorted a critical standard-setting process through deceptive conduct and engaged in an anticompetitive "hold up" of the computer memory industry. Rambus was barred from making misrepresentations or omissions to standard-setting organizations and was required to license its SDRAM and DDR SDRAM technology. Limits were set to the royalty rates Rambus can collect under the licensing agreements.

Anyone who wishes to practice the standard must obtain rights under such patents, or else antitrust issues may arise. Standard setting organizations, thus, stipulated that owners of the patents related to the standards must license these patents on fair, reasonable, and non-discriminatory (FRAND) terms. However, which actually constitute FRAND terms? In the case, *Microsoft Corp. v. Motorola Inc.*, No. 2:10-cv-01823-JLR *(W.D. Wash. Apr. 25, 2013)*, which is about the H.264 video coding standard and 802.11 Wi-Fi Standard, Motorola in 2010 offered to license Microsoft its patents essential to the implementation of these standards. A disagreement arose over the royalty calculation that Motorola proposed. Under the rules of the related standard setting organizations, royalties for patents covering H.264 and 802.11 must comply with RAND requirements. Microsoft alleged that Motorola's initial "reasonable" demand royalty would have resulted in royalty payment in excess of $4 billion per year. Microsoft sued Motorola for breach of contract. In 2012 October, Judge Robart ruled that the applicable RAND royalty rate must be determined before a finding can be made regarding Motorola's alleged breach of contract. Thus, the court developed a legal framework for assessing the value of SEPs where a RAND commitment exists. The framework will be discussed in the next chapter when we touch on valuation.

7.4.4 Patent misuse

Patent misuse is an affirmative defense developed through case laws for use in patent litigation. It is used when a defendant has been accused of have infringed a patent. It has also been used to mitigate damages following a finding of infringement. It is also used to provide remedies for patent abuse when there is a violation of antitrust laws and/or improper expansion of the scope or term of the patent, yet the case does not amount to antitrust case. It deals with issues of fair trade in cases of compulsory licensing, parallel import, and price differentiation. There is, however, guidance on the use of the misuse doctrine. In 1988, U.S. the Congress amended the patent laws and added subparagraphs (4) and (5) to 35 U.S.C. §271 (d) of the Patent Laws:

No patent owner otherwise entitled to relief for infringement or contributory infringement of a patent shall be denied relief or deemed guilty of misuse or illegal extension of the patent right by reason of his having done one or more of the following:

(4) refused to license or use any rights to the patent; or

(5) conditioned the license of any rights to the patent or the sale of the patented product on the acquisition of a license to rights in another patent or purchase of a separate product, unless, in view of the circumstances, the patent owner has market power in the relevant market for the patent or patented product on which the license or sale is conditioned.

Market power is defined by the power to charge more than marginal cost (competitive price). For example, the licensor deliberately raises the price by reducing the market wide output, perhaps by reducing its own output, while rivals are unable to make compensating increases in output. Market power is defined by the relevant product or geographic market, and market share. The following factors are used to estimate market power: ease and rate of substitutes, rate of response from other incumbent/current firms, ease, and rate of buyers' control on purchases and entry barriers of new firms.

7.4.4.1 *Tying*

There are various types of patent misuse. One common type is tying. As mentioned earlier, tying is conditional licensing, usually with the purchase or license of a second item. According to 35 U.S.C. §271 (d) (5) of the Patent Law, the existence of market power in the market of the second item in the conditioned license must be determined. Once this is affirmed, the court would consider the three-step analysis of patent misuse as laid out in the Federal Circuit Case *Senza-Gel Corp. v Seiffhart (803 F.2d 661, 231 USPQ 363 (Fed. Cir. 1986).* Step 1 is to consider whether the tying item and the tied items are actually the same item. Step 2 determines whether the tied item is a staple. Step 3 determines whether the tying actually occurred. If these three criteria are not satisfied, there may not be a patent misuse case.

Similarly, tying-out is also a patent misuse and is subject to scrutiny under 35 U.S.C. §271 (d) (5) of the Patent Law. An example of a tie-out arrangement is the licensee conditioning the licensing of patents such that the licensee is not allowed to purchase, use, or sell other products not within the licensed patent scope. Not all non-competition provisions are, however, considered as patent misuse, especially if the provision is not onerous in view of the benefits that the licensee will receive and that the provision only has an effect on the licensee but not the entire market *(County Materials Corp. v. Allan Block Co., 502 F.3d 730 (7th Cir. 2007)).*

7.4.4.2 *Multi-patent licensing*

We emphasize in this book that it is important to consider patents as a portfolio. Similarly, we also recommend patent portfolio licensing. This, however, may amount to patent misuse if the licensor requires the licensee to license the whole portfolio while the licensee is willing to license only some patents but not the entire portfolio. The assessment for patent misuse in this case again requires proof of actual market power and anti-competitive result. An exception would be when the multi-patent licensing involves patents that are essentially covering the same product. Nevertheless, it is also possible for licensors to bundle a portfolio of patents for licensing that are not necessarily interlocking patents reading on one single product. In this case, the licensor may make the licensing fees for each patent known explicitly and the licensee has the option to select which patents to license.

7.4.4.3 *Other types of patent misuse conduct*

There are many other types of patent misuse conduct. The following is a non-exhaustive list. Some of these have been discussed in the antitrust section. They raise patent misuse concerns again because patent misuse can provide remedies in the event that the case falls short of the standards required in antitrust cases.

- Extension beyond Patent Terms (hybrid with know-how)
- Grant back Clauses (improvement may incur blocking)
- Field-of-use Restrictions (avoid free-rider)
- Horizontal Arrangements (pooling with blocking patents, SSO)
- Price Discrimination
- Other Conduct (extends the patent beyond its lawful scope)
  — Double dipping (collects royalties more than once for the same products and patents at two different stages of production: violates exhaustion doctrine)

In summary, antitrust law and patent law are not contradictory. In constructing patent licenses, one should be careful not to invoke antitrust and patent misuse issues. For easy reference, it may be useful to reiterate some of the points mentioned in this section by the nine "NO–NO" in patent licensing. Some of these may no longer be truly a "no–no" ("per se illegal") as the legal regime changes, but they are still relevant in most circumstances and provide a good summary.

The nine "No–No"[10]

1. Royalties not reasonably related to sales of the patented products;
2. Restraints on licensees' commerce outside the scope of the patent (tie-outs);
3. Requiring the licensee to purchase unpatented materials from the licensor (tie-ins);
4. Mandatory package licensing;

---

[10] Bruce Wilson in "Patent and Know-How License Arrangements: Field of Use, Territorial, Price and Quantity Restrictions," a speech delivered on November 6 1970 in Boston.

5. Requiring the licensee to assign to the patentee patents that may be issued to the licensee after the licensing arrangement is executed (exclusive grant backs):
6. Licensee veto power over grants of further licenses;
7. Restraints on sales of unpatented products made with a patented process;
8. Post-sale restraints on resale; and
9. Setting minimum prices on resale of the patent products.

7.5 Patent Alliance

7.5.1 What is a patent alliance?

A patent alliance can be realized through patent pools. According to WIPO's definition, patent pools are "defined as an agreement between two or more patent owners to license one or more of their patents to one another or to third parties."[11] In patent pools, the patent rights are aggregated among multiple patent owners. Usually, members and non-members can take licenses, but with differing fees. Part of the licensing fees collected will be distributed back to the patent owners based on the share of patents that they have contributed.

Patent pools can be categorized into three main types depending on its administration (see Figures 7.5–7.7). The first category is joint licensing patent pools where multiple patent owners in a technology area pool their related patents together to be available for members who join the alliance. There is usually a representative licensor having more patents in that technology field and this licensor would take the lead to gather all related patents to be available for all who are willing to participate in the alliance. For example, Philips, who pioneered DVD technology and has a significant number of patents in the area, would manage such a pool.

The second type is realized through the presence of licensing administrators to minimize administrative fees. The difference between this type of patent pool and the previous is that there can be an independent administrator or multiple patent owners each contributing

[11] Patent Pools And Antitrust — A Comparative Analysis, WIPO, March 2014.

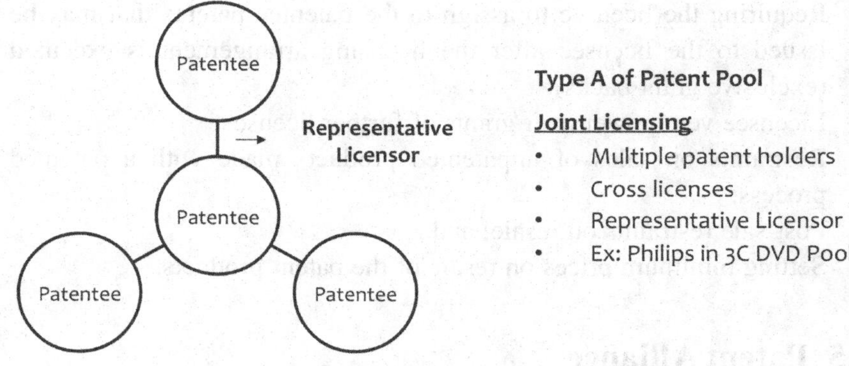

Figure 7.5 Type A patent pool

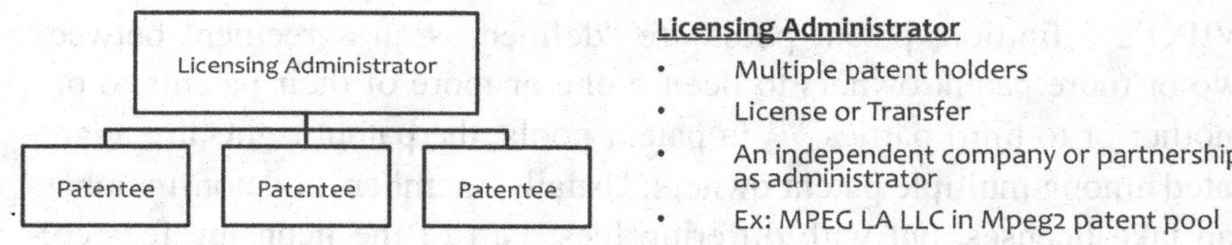

Figure 7.6 Type B patent pool

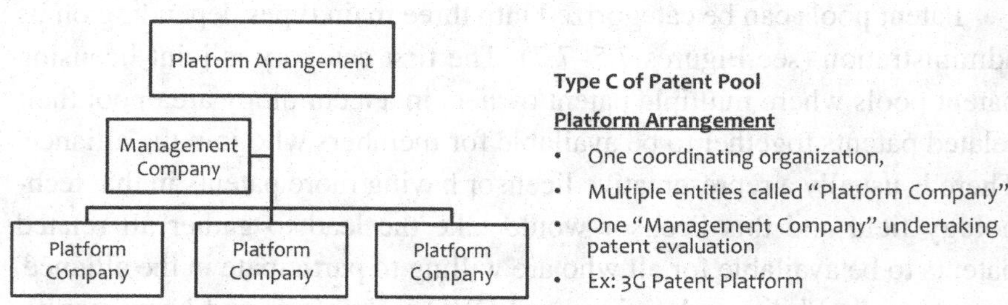

Figure 7.7 Type C patent pool

to the administration. There is no dominant company in charge of the administrator. Such configuration of patent pool usually arises for the case of stand-setting technology.

The third type of patent pool involves more extended collaboration and pooling of patents. It is called platform arrangement. There can be multiple patent pools inside this arrangement and each patent pool consists of different patent owners. A management company would be responsible for the coordination and evaluation or determination of the patents in each platform company. Traditional examples of such patent pools can be found in telecommunication standards like the 3G patent platform. There is a recent trend of new companies setting up management companies, such as, RPX Corp., Allied Security Trusts (AST), and Open Innovation Network.

7.5.2 Evolution of the patent alliance

The patent alliance originated from North America as early as the 1910s. At that time, alliances were formed primarily among the North American companies. However, it did not take long before alliances were formed among North American and European companies as well. In the 1940s, European companies also started forming alliances among themselves. In recent years, alliances have become truly international, involving North American, European, and Asian companies pooling their patents together. This is in response to the needs of a globalized economy.[12] In addition to the trends by countries, there is also a distinguishing trend by industry. In the early 19th century, alliances were formed among diverse industries. Recently, most alliances are in the information and communications (ICT) industry.

In general, the evolution of the patent alliance can be divided into three distinguishing phases, each meant to solve slightly different problems in patent licensing (see Figure 7.8). In the early stage, alliances were formed primarily to build up monopolies and cartels for price controlling. As such, many antitrust complaints arose for these early alliances. Nevertheless, these conflicts provided opportunities to legislation.

7.5.2.1 *Early stage*

The early pools, like those in the early 1900s, were formed primarily to address the problems of a patent thicket. Although there have been many

[12] World Intellectual Property Report 2011, The Changing Face of Innovation, Chapter 3: Balancing Collaboration and Competition, 121, available at www.wipo.int/econ_stat/en/economics/wipr/.

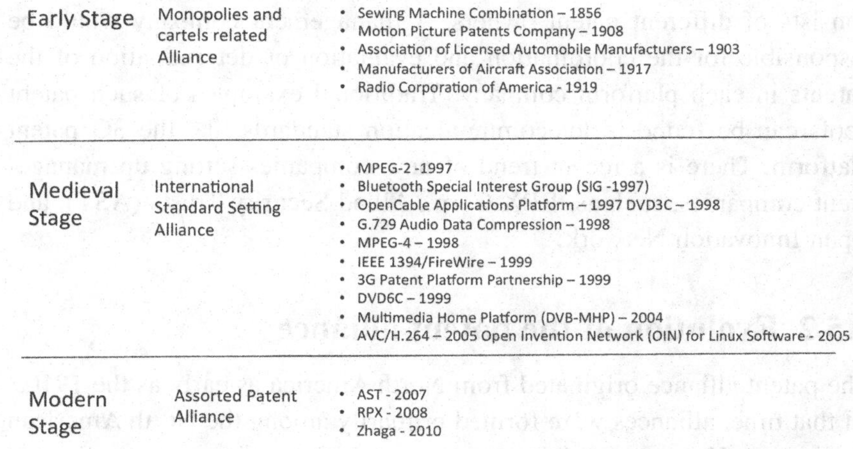

Early Stage
Monopolies and cartels related Alliance
Sewing Machine Combination – 1856
Motion Picture Patents Company – 1908
Association of Licensed Automobile Manufacturers – 1903
Manufacturers of Aircraft Association – 1917
Radio Corporation of America - 1919
Medieval Stage
International Standard Setting Alliance
MPEG-2 -1997
Bluetooth Special Interest Group (SIG -1997)
OpenCable Applications Platform – 1997 DVD3C – 1998
G.729 Audio Data Compression – 1998
MPEG-4 – 1998
IEEE 1394/FireWire – 1999
3G Patent Platform Partnership – 1999
DVD6C – 1999
Multimedia Home Platform (DVB-MHP) – 2004
AVC/H.264 – 2005 Open Invention Network (OIN) for Linux Software - 2005
Modern Stage
Assorted Patent Alliance
AST - 2007
RPX - 2008
Zhaga - 2010

Figure 7.8 Evolution of patent alliance

complaints about patent thickets with the increase media focus on the patent troll business patent thickets are actually not a new problem. In the past, markets were usually not as fragmented and patents were aggregated in the hands of a few patent owners. Yet, the number of patents on a technology can be sufficiently large to threaten the operations of other owners. Therefore, these patent owners formed alliances to share their patents with members. The provisions in the alliance usually allow companies in the alliance to control pricing and lodge patent claims against non-members. The early stage patent alliance was usually realized using the Type A patent pool format, controlled by the patent owner with the largest patent portfolio on that technology. Sometimes, a trust would also be formed to manage licensing activities, which corresponds to the Type B patent pool.

7.5.2.2 *Transitional stage*

Towards the late 1990s, the early patent alliances that focused on having monopoly power and cartels disappeared because a more sophisticated antitrust law and other competition law curtailed them. Patent alliance strategies, however, did not disappear but evolved to cater to the needs of the changing technological environment. During the transitional stage, digital technologies flourished and there was a need for a common platform to ensure interoperability. Therefore, this period is dominated by international standard setting alliances to ensure devices can be used across platforms. Members of the alliance have the license to use the patents from other patent owners in the alliance. They usually also stipulate that members do not sue each other on technology described in that alliance. Such arrangement allows a "one-stop-service" for companies who want to practice the technology, and the technology is available for license under FRAND terms. It reduces transaction costs and is desirable to promote technology development. The managing organization is usually an expert in licensing and negotiation. A large network of contacts is needed to ensure the success of such an alliance. The transitional stage started the adoption of the Type C patent pool, requiring a special management organization to coordinate all the licensing activities. It is important to note that not all technology standards have patent alliances. Many of the telecommunication patents are in the hands of individual patent owners and very often, companies do not even know that they have infringed such SEPs.

7.5.2.3 *Modern stage*

The newer "business model" of patent alliances takes the form of patent aggregators who aggregate patents with higher chance to be litigated and offer licenses to members. In return, members have to pay an annual fee. The two most well-known alliances in this modern stage are AST and RPX Corporation. AST's business model is to "catch, license and release" within a few years. This means AST will not hold the patents for long in order to recoup the initial overlay for purchasing the patents by selling patents to secondary market. AST only purchases patents that its members contribute funds to and licenses to them at more favorable rates. Members who have not contributed to the purchase of that particular portfolio, still take licenses but at a higher rate. AST has a flat rate for membership. The operation of AST belongs to the Type C patent pool with AST being the managing company.

RPX, on the other hand, buys and holds patents. RPX also purchases patents that are highly likely to be the targets of patent trolls. Its business model is to build up an IP library to which all members get an equal term license that eventually becomes a perpetual license after rolling out for two years. All patents acquired by RPX can be licensed by its members with no customized package. However, the annual membership fees vary between companies depending on their size. RPX also operates under the Type C patent pool arrangement with it being both the platform company and managing company. It is important to note that the business models of these companies evolve very fast with changes in the business environment.

7.5.3 LED licensing strategies and alliance

The final section of this chapter provides examples of licensing strategies in the LED industry. The LED industry is an industry that has evolved gradually over the past 30 years. Many companies with various sectors of focus take part in a new industry by developing the upstream technology. Usually these developments were the results of the work of many universities and big corporations. Examples of key incumbents in the LED industry are Nichia, Philips, and Osram. Many of these players are in the upstream. When the industry is in its infancy, the revenue also mainly resided in the upstream market. However, as the upstream technology becomes more mature, the revenue begins to shift downstream.

7.5.3.1 *LED value chain*

The LED value chain and the components that made up each segment along the value chain are shown in Figure 7.9. Profits mean everything. Berman (2008) noted that in order to derive IP strategies for the company, identifying the profit pools (Gilbert, 1998) along the value chain is one of the first steps toward deriving successful strategies. At the moment, the profits in the LED industry are in the upstream. However, as predicted by some of industry reports (McKinsey & Company, 2012; Yole Development, 2012), profits in the upstream will decrease and in the downstream will increase (Figure 7.10).

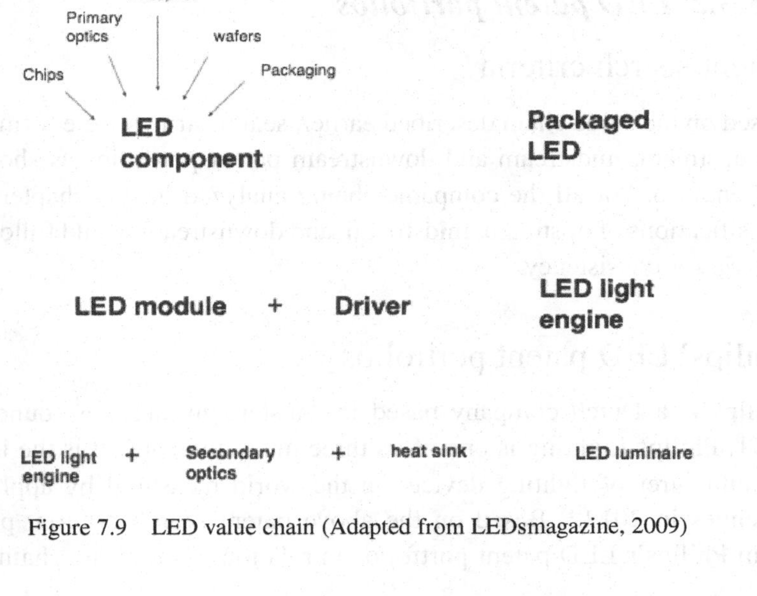

Figure 7.9 LED value chain (Adapted from LEDsmagazine, 2009)

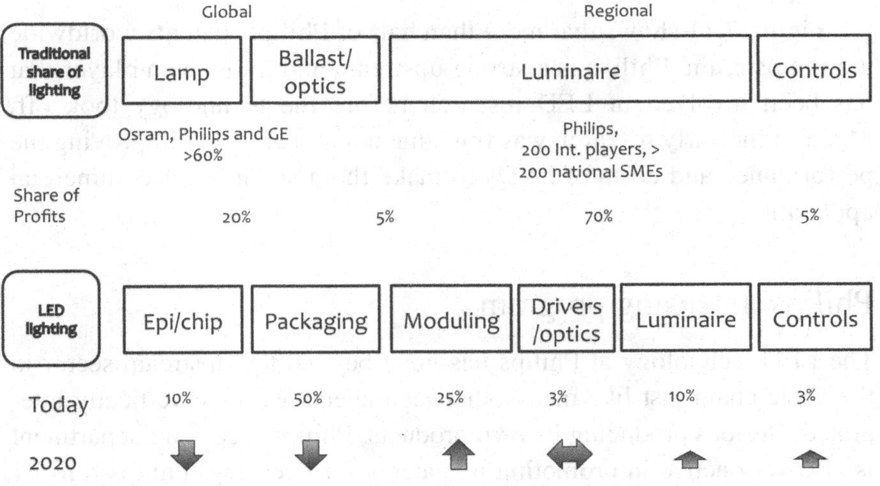

Figure 7.10 Changes in the LED value chain (Adapted from LEDsmagazine, 2009)

In the following sections, we will take a look at the major players of LED and try to derive their licensing strategies and alliances that have thus formed to address the issue of profits shifting from upstream to downstream.

7.5.3.2 *LED patent portfolios*

Patent search criteria

Based on the value chain described earlier, search strings were formed for the upstream, midstream and downstream patent portfolios as shown in Appendix 6. For all the companies being analyzed in this chapter, their classifications of upstream, midstream, and downstream would follow this criteria for consistency.

Philips' LED patent portfolios

Philips is a Dutch company based in Amsterdam and was founded in 1891. Philips Lighting is one of its three main divisions. It is the largest manufacturer of lighting devices in the world measured by applicable revenues in 2012.[13] Based on the above patent search criteria, patents from Philips's LED patent portfolios in relation to the value chain were analyzed.

Figure 7.11 shows that more than half of Philips' patents worldwide are in upstream. Philips is a strong upstream and midstream player that has been involved in LED research before the technology took off. Much of the early research was fundamental and aimed at improving the performance and costs of LEDs to make them suitable for commercial application.

Philips' licensing program

The LED technology at Philips has gone beyond the upstream sector in the value chain just like many other incumbents who are vertically integrated. Besides producing its own products, Philips' licensing department is also very active in promoting its patents for licensing. Philips runs 61 licensing programs as of October 9, 2014. Its LED-licensing program offers over 200 patents for licensing. Although the program is called the

[13] "Lighting maker Philips warns fourth quarter earnings hurt by weakness in European market". The Washington Post. 10 January 2012. Retrieved 13 January 2012.

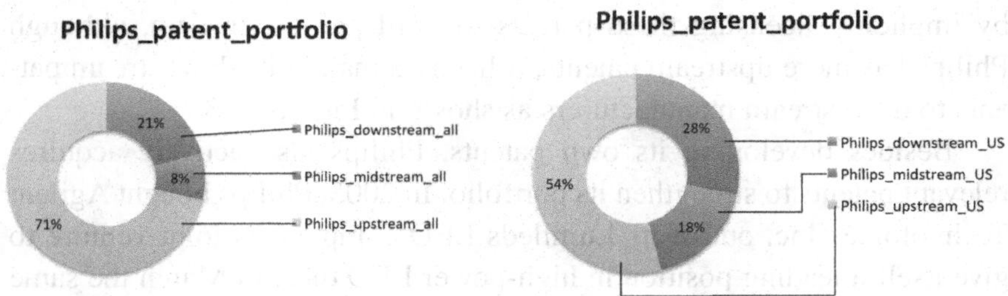

Figure 7.11 Philips' LED patent portfolios distributed along the value chain

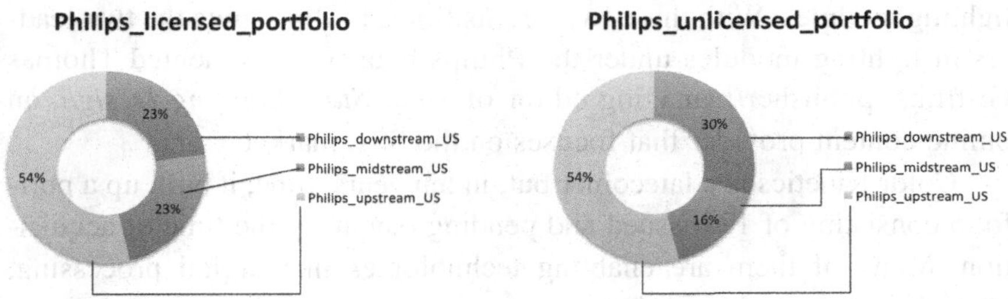

Figure 7.12 Distribution of Philips' LED patents along the value chain in the licensing program

LED luminaries and Retrofit Bulbs Licensing Program, there are patents that can be related to the upstream technologies. Figure 7.12 shows the patents in the program based on the criteria set forth in analyzing patents along the LED value chain. The figure shows that 54% of the patents are upstream, 23% midstream, and 23% are downstream patents. Upstream patents dominate. If a potential licensee designs downstream products that use Philips' patents, they need to license from Philips. However, if the licensee uses midstream products (which include the upstream and midstream patents) from qualified suppliers in their designs or manufacturing, they do not need to pay royalties to Philips. This in turn allows Philips to control the whole upstream, midstream, and downstream to be streamlined to Philips' or its group of qualified suppliers' technologies. If the design house or manufacturer licenses Philips' downstream technology, it is essentially licensing Philips' upstream and midstream technologies. This indicates that Philips tries to cash in from its proprietary technologies by implicitly licensing these patents to third parties. In sum, although Philips has more upstream patents, it licenses mainly its downstream patents to downstream manufacturers as shown in Figure 7.13.

Besides developing its own patents, Philips also actively acquires relevant patents to strengthen its portfolio. In 2005, Philips bought Agilent Technologies Inc. out of its Lumileds LED components joint venture to give itself a leading position in high-power LED dies. In March the same year, Philips purchased Canada's TIR Systems Ltd., which was founded in 1982 and specializes in white-light-producing LED modules. Then, in 2007, Philips acquired Color Kinetics founded in 1997, which is strong in lighting modules. With these two acquisitions, Philips "puts the two leaders in lighting modules under the Philips banner," commented Thomas Griffiths, publisher/managing editor of *Solid State Lighting Design*, an online content provider that focuses on the SSL market.

Color Kinetics is a latecomer but, in ten years' time, it built up a portfolio consisting of 120 issued and pending patents at the time of acquisition. Many of them are enabling technologies like digital processing, control, and networking solutions for specific markets like entertainment, medical, and machine vision. This shows that latecomers in midstream can also develop an enabling patent portfolio for application.

Osram's LED patent portfolios

Like Philips, Osram is also a vertically integrated incumbent in the LED upstream and midstream. However, Osram specializes in lighting and is a world-leading lighting manufacturer. OSRAM was founded in 1919 by the merger of the lighting businesses of Auergesellschaft, Siemens & Halske, and Allgemeine Elektrizitäts-Gesellschaft (AEG). On 5 July

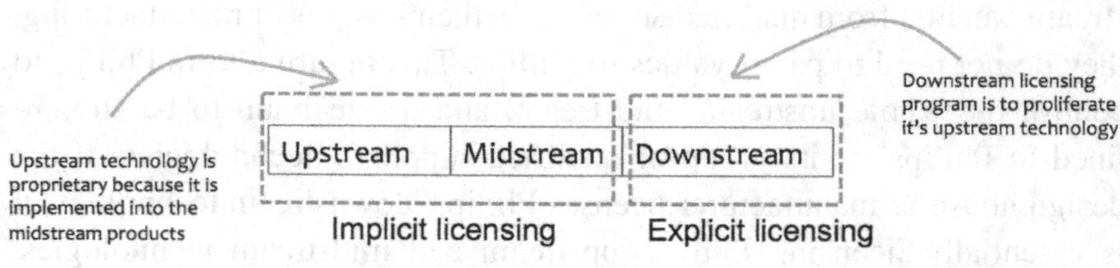

Figure 7.13 Philips' licensing strategy

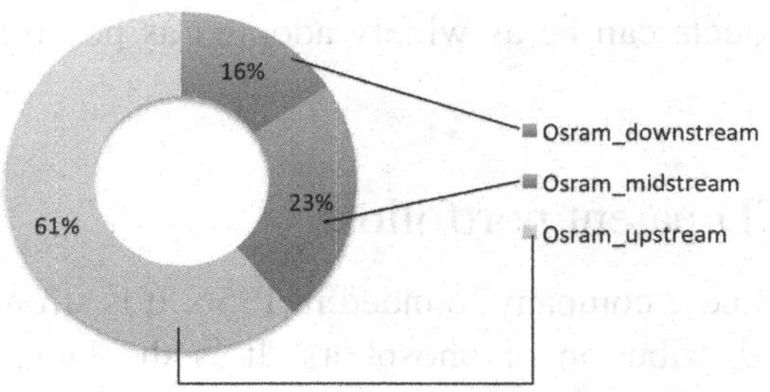

Figure 7.14 Osram's patent portfolio distributed along the value chain

2013, OSRAM was spun-off from Siemens. It is very strong in the upstream. Figure 7.14 shows that 61% of Osram's LED patents are in the upstream.

Osram's licensing program

Unlike Philips, Osram does not have an outright licensing program across the value chain for its LED technology. It offers a licensing program called LEDset for LED control gears and LED modules in the midstream. This set of IP consists of smart electrical interface between LED control gear and modules that are essential to the maturity of SSL components businesses. There is no royalty fee charged for the use of the LEDset 2nd Generation electrical interface (including the LEDset logo's rights of use and specification) by LED modules makers. Its aim is to enable the largest possible adoption. For its LED control gears, a small start-up charge is imposed. Royalty fees apply for this electrical interface by LED control gears makers for LEDset logo's rights of use, rights of use for certain IP, design support, and assistance for compliance to specification in the start-up phase, initiative of standardization process at competent bodies, and joint marketing campaign.[14]

[14] http://www.osram.com.au/osram_au/tools-and-services/services/ledset-licensing-program/ledset---defined-to-team-up/index.jsp (Last accessed 21st November 2016).

Osram's licensing strategy is different from Philips because licensing is not part of its core business. Its aim is to build up the industry so that its products can be as widely adopted as possible as shown in Figure 7.15.

Nichia's LED patent portfolios

Nichia is a Japanese company founded in 1956. It is strong in the manufacturing and distribution of phosphors. It is the largest suppliers of LEDs. Isamu Akasaki, Hiroshi Amano, and Shuji Nakamura, the winners of Nobel Prize for Physics were working for Nichia when they invented the blue LEDs. This invention is a major milestone for today's white LEDs that are fast replacing the conventional light sources. Nichia's patent portfolio is also predominantly in the upstream segment as shown in Figure 7.16.

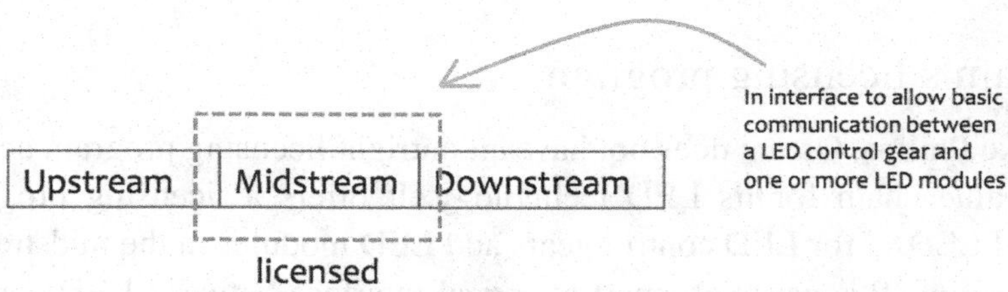

Figure 7.15 Osram's licensing strategy

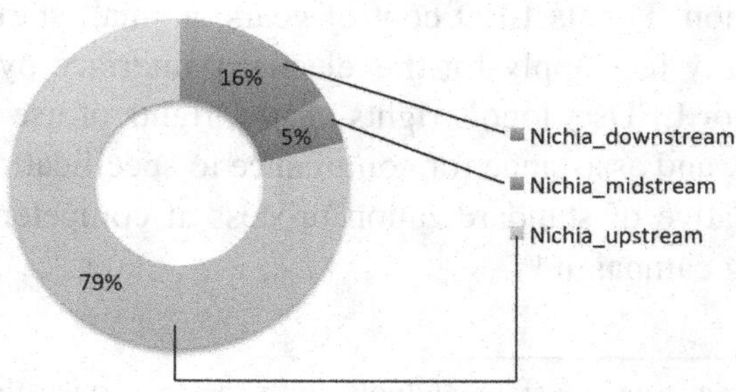

Figure 7.16 Nichia's patent portfolio distributed along the value chain

Nichia's licensing program

Nichia does not have an organized licensing program. Nichia's stand on Intellectual Property[15] is stated on its website, "Income and expenditure solely related to intellectual property are not important, and intellectual property itself should not be a subject of trading." Nichia further mentioned that they "utilize the intellectual property rights system in order to differentiate Nichia from other companies making use of new technologies that we have created, and to prevent illegal imitation." Nichia does not explicitly license out the blue LED technology to anyone. However, Nichia does license its white-LED technology and other light LED technology to some companies who are not direct competitors but make use of LED in their products. For example, in 2002, Nichia licensed out its white LED technology to Citizen Electronics, which makes Watches.

Nichia also cross licenses its technology to LED developers and manufacturers to reduce the threat of patent infringement lawsuits against each other. For example, it signed a cross-licensing agreement in 2002 with Lumileds for LED technology to prevent the two LED giants from filing lawsuits related to LED technology against each other.[16] The ultimate purpose of the cross-licensing deal is to "accelerate the design of more powerful LEDs by enabling each company to incorporate the R&D efforts of the other in new product development, thereby paving the way for more rapid adoption of LEDs." It was mentioned that the LED technologies from these two companies are in fact complementary rather than competing. Therefore, besides avoiding patent infringement lawsuits, cross-licensing also helps to build up each other's capabilities.

Other cross-licensing agreements that Nichia has with other major LED developers, such as Osram and Cree, were the solutions to patent infringement disputes among them. For example, Nichia entered into a patent cross license agreement with Osram covering indium gallium nitride (InGaN) semiconductors and related packaging technology in 2002. That agreement resolved all pending patent disputes between the

[15] http://www.nichia.co.jp/specification/about_nichia/ip/ip_view.pdf

[16] http://www.nichia.co.jp/en/about_nichia/2002/2002_102901.html

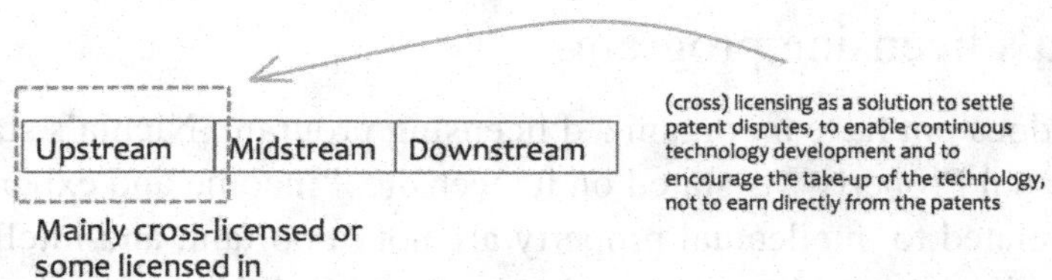

Figure 7.17 Nichia's licensing strategy

two companies at that time. Nichia and Cree also entered into a patent cross license agreement to settle the litigation between the companies concerning gallium nitride-based optoelectronic technology. In fact, this cross-licensing relationship with Cree continued to grow as the two companies signed expanded cross-licensing deals in both 2005[17] and[18] again in 2007.

In addition, Nichia also licenses its LED Technology to manufacturers to facilitate collaboration with LED manufacturers that strengthen Nichia's position as a major LED supplier. Nichia entered into licensing agreement with OPTO Tech in Taiwan in 2004 for the InGaN material.[19] Therefore, licensing is a tool for Nichia to promote its R&D. Therefore, it uses cross licensing that does not earn revenue directly from the licensing deals. Other licensing deals that it adopts enable partnership with manufacturers to help its LED products to proliferate. Nichia's licensing strategy is summed up in Figure 7.17.

Cree's LED patent portfolios

Cree is based in North Carolina, US. It was formed in 1987 by a group of researchers from North Carolina State University. Compared to Philips and Osram, it has a shorter history, but it is a company rooted in research. Figure 7.18 shows that majority of its patents are in the upstream, just as Philips and Osram.

---

[17] http://www.nichia.co.jp/en/about_nichia/2005/2005_021001.html

[18] http://www.nichia.co.jp/en/about_nichia/2007/2007_091702.html

[19] http://www.nichia.co.jp/en/about_nichia/2004/2004_080501.html

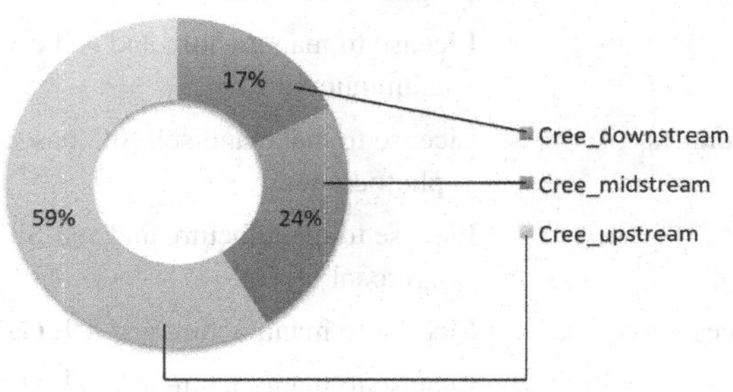

Figure 7.18 Cree's patent portfolio distributed along the value chain

Cree's licensing program

Cree has established licensing programs. Each of the licensing programs is aimed at producing a certain type of LED component. In addition to these generic licensing programs, Cree is also willing to form a customized licensing program with its licensees. Cree monetizes its IP through licensing. The list of licensing programs from Cree is shown in Table 7.1. AIN Substrates, Ultraviolet Photodiodes, and SiC Materials belong to the upstream; GaN Power Devices and Doherty Amplifiers belong to the midstream; Remote Phosphor and Liquid Crystal Displays with LED Backlight belong to the downstream.

From Table 7.1, we see that Cree's licensing program is well spread along the value chain, although there is slightly more focus on the upstream, with three pre-designed programs, compared to two for both mid- and downstream.

Cree does not seem to have a strategic segregation or a deliberate effort to restrict access to certain IP to enable exclusive use for its products (Figure 7.19). According to the statement on its website, its aim is to enable manufacturing for manufacturers. This seems to be aligned with the company's roots, starting off as it did with a group of University researchers.

Table 7.1 Cree's licensing program[20]

Licensing Program	Program Description
AlN Substrates	License to manufacture and sell crystalline aluminum nitride.
Ultraviolet Photodiodes	License to make and sell SiC-based ultraviolet photodiodes.
SiC Materials	License to manufacture and sell SiC wafers and epitaxial layers.
GaN Power Devices	License to manufacture and sell GaN power devices.
Doherty Amplifiers	License to manufacture and sell Doherty-based amplifiers.
Remote Phosphor	License to manufacture and sell remote-phosphor-based LED luminaires and bulbs.
Liquid Crystal Displays with LED Backlight	License to manufacture and sell liquid-crystal displays with an LED backlight.

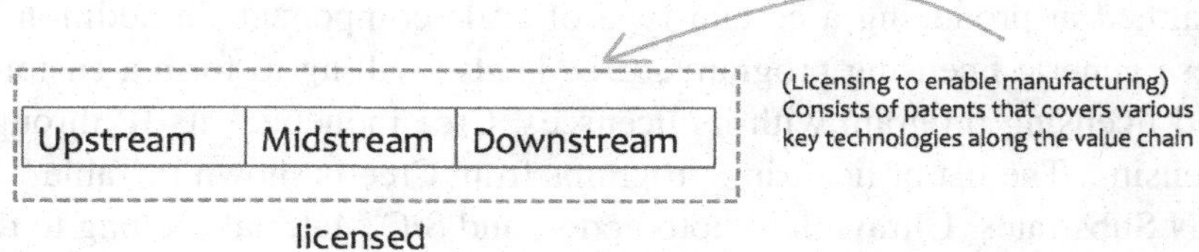

Figure 7.19 Cree's licensing strategy

Epistar's LED patent portfolio

Epistar is the largest LED manufacturer in Taiwan. It was founded in 1996. Epistar's products are primarily upstream based on upstream technology. Epistar's extensive patent portfolio is on information technology outsourcing (ITO) technology, which the founders developed when they were still working at the Industrial Technology Research Institute (ITRI) in Taiwan. A second core technology from Epistar is the bonding technology that can provide flexibility in epi structure substrate selection for LED devices. In addition, Epistar has also developed

[20] http://www.cree.com/About-Cree/Licensing/Licensing-Programs (Retrieved 9th October 2014).

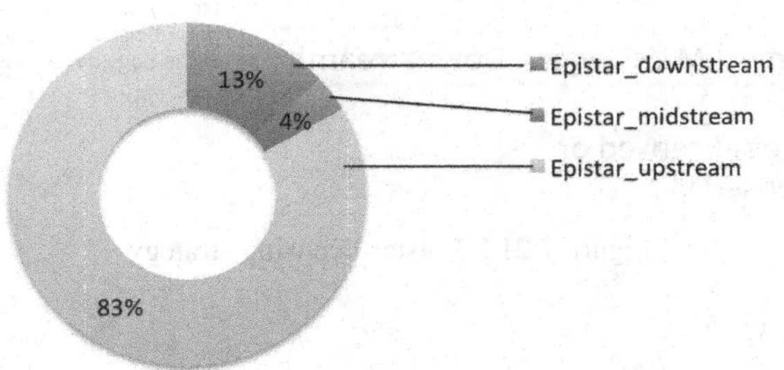

Figure 7.20 Epistar's patent portfolio distributed along the value chain

arrangements for multiple cells on one substrate to be driven by high voltage.[21] Therefore, Epistar's patent portfolio is primarily upstream as shown clearly in Figure 7.20.

Epistar's licensing program

Like Nichia, Epistar does not have an established licensing program for its LED patent portfolio. Most of the licensing deals are cross licenses with companies for strategic reasons to either end patent disputes or to co-develop LED technology. For example, it went into cross licensing with Philips to end their patent infringement cases in courts.[22] In 2010, Epistar signed an agreement with Toyoda Gosei to cross license in order to foster business cooperation. In 2012, Epistar signed a cross-licensing agreement with Toshiba on certain AlGaInP LED technologies.[23]

Recently, in 2014, Epistar and Intermolecular announced a multi-year extension of their existing collaborative development program and royalty bearing IP licensing agreement to reduce the cost and increase the efficiency of Epistar's LED devices.[24] In addition to licensing out and cross

[21] http://www.epistar.com.tw/_english/04_pr/02_detail.php?SID=38

[22] http://patentlyo.com/patent/license

[23] http://www.epistar.com.tw/_english/04_pr/02_detail.php?SID=37

[24] http://semimd.com/blog/2014/04/25/the-week-in-review-april-25-2014/

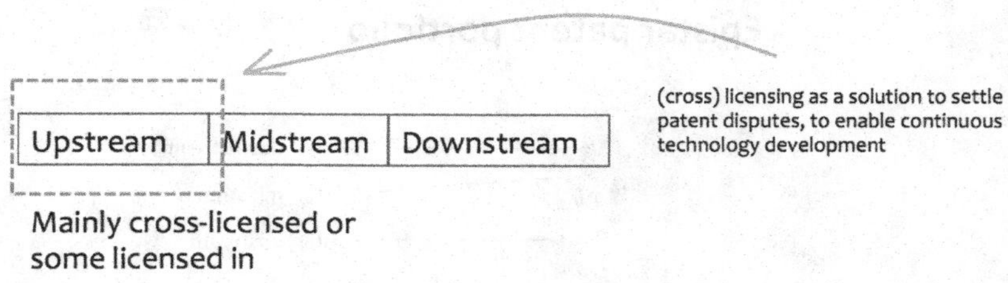

Figure 7.21 Epistar licensing strategy

licensing, Epistar also licensed-in technology to build up its patent portfolio and technology. This is the case for its AC-LED development with ITRI.[25] Therefore, Epistar's licensing strategy is strategic to enable continuous technology development as shown in Figure 7.21.

Zumtobel's LED patent portfolio

Zumtobel is an Austrian company founded in 1950. It is a downstream manufacturer. The company is divided into the component segment and the lighting segment. The component segment is made up of Ledon and Tridonic. Tridonic develops, manufactures, and markets control gear for lighting solutions. It is also an original equipment manufacturer (OEM) supplier. The brand serves luminaire manufacturers worldwide, generating around 80% of its sales outside the Zumtobel Group. Currently Tridonic holds nearly 2,000 patents. The lighting segment is made up of Thorn, which was acquired from Thorn EMI in a leveraged management buy-out. It was completely integrated into Zumtobel in 2000. Thorn Lighting was founded in 1928 by Jules Thorn and Alfred Deutsch. Thorn's products are used in buildings and their surroundings, roads, cityscapes, and sports facilities in more than 100 countries. Figure 7.22 shows Zumtobel's patent portfolio across the value chain. Its patents are primarily in the mid- to downstream categories. However, when Tridonic and Thorn's patents are taken together, it skews towards upstream, as shown in Figure 7.23.

[25] http://www.ledsmagazine.com/articles/2009/03/epistar-expecting-to-launch-ac-led-products-in-2009.htm (Last accessed 21st November 2016).

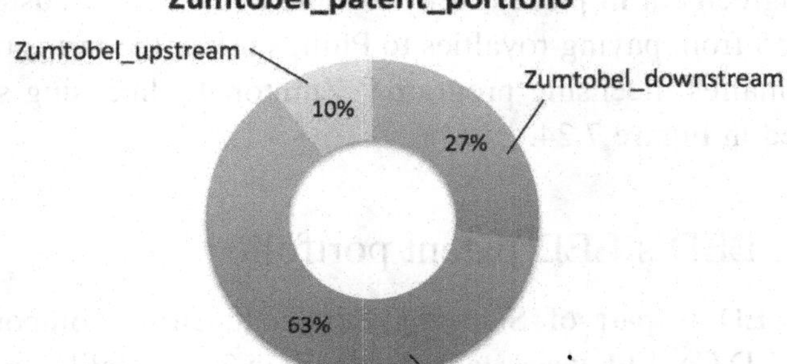

Figure 7.22 Zumtobel patent portfolio distributed along the value chain

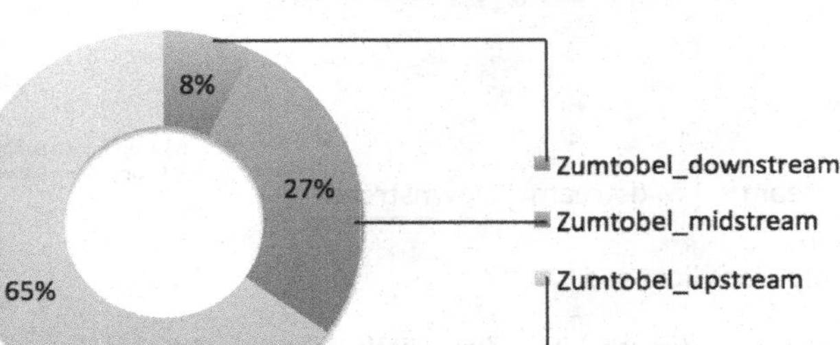

Figure 7.23 Zumtobel patent portfolio with Thorn and Tridonic distributed along the value chain

Zumtobel's licensing program

Zumtobel does not have a comprehensive licensing program. However, it does cross license extensively with other companies, such as Philips.[26] The agreement in 2009 mainly covers driver and control technologies for changing intensity and color of conventional and solid-state lighting systems. These are the upstream to midstream technologies. With that

[26] http://www.newscenter.philips.com/sg_en/standard/about/news/press/archive/2009/20090505_zumtobel.wpd (Last accessed 21st November 2016).

licensing agreement in place, even Tridonic and Ledon's customers can be exempted from paying royalties to Philips under the terms of its LED based luminaires' licensing program.[27] Zumtobel's licensing strategy is summarized in Figure 7.24.

Samsung LED's LED patent portfolio

Samsung LED is part of Samsung Semiconductor's component unit. Samsung LED Co. Ltd. was established only in 2009. Unlike the previous companies analyzed, Samsung LED's patent portfolio is mainly in the downstream segment of the value chain. Many of those patents are related to flip chip packaging, which can be used for other semiconductor products. However, its products do span across the up, mid and downstream. Figure 7.25 shows its patent portfolio distribution along the value chain.

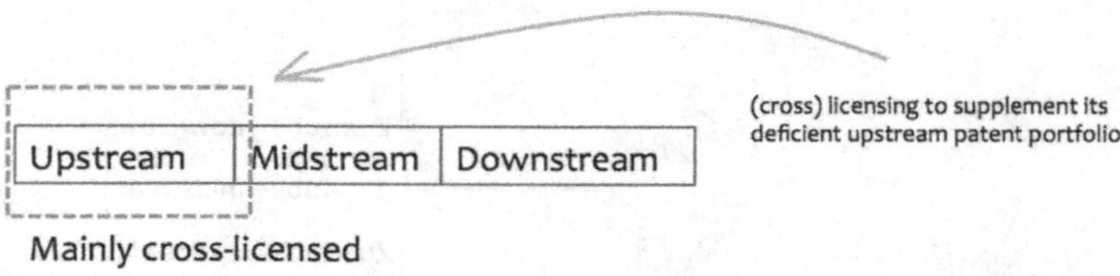

Figure 7.24 Zumtobel's licensing strategy

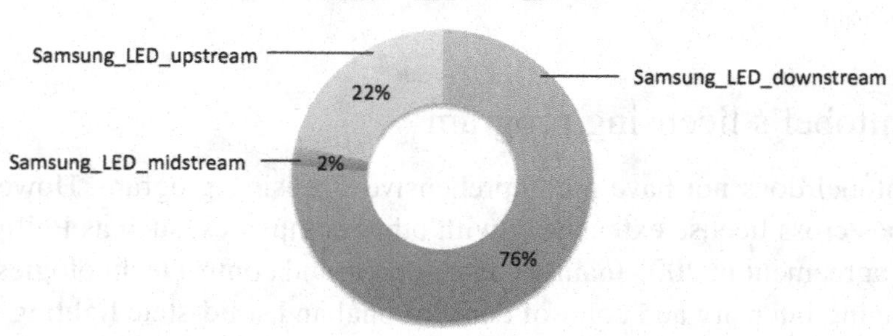

Figure 7.25 Samsung LED's patent portfolio distributed along the value chain

---

[27] http://www.ip.philips.com/licensing/ssl

Samsung LED's licensing program

Samsung LED does not have an open offer to license out its technology. However, it does license-in technology. For example, Samsung entered into a comprehensive patent licensing and purchasing agreement for Evident's quantum dot LED technology. Evident Technologies is a nanotechnology company specializing in the creation of semiconductor quantum dots. This agreement grants Samsung worldwide access to Evident's patent portfolio for all products related to quantum dot LEDs from the manufacturing of the quantum dot nanomaterials to the final LED production.[28]

Besides licensing-in, Samsung also uses licensing to settle patent disputes. Samsung and Osram entered into such an agreement in 2012. The two companies also entered into a separate memorandum to co-develop future LED-based products.[29]

Be it licensing-in or settling the patent disputes, the patents involved are mainly in the upstream technologies. This may be because Samsung LED is not an upstream company and it needed the upstream patents to strengthen its upstream technology. However, it is strong downstream and it has internal sales to Samsung Electronics and external demands from customers in the industry. Samsung LED's licensing strategy is summed up in Figure 7.26.

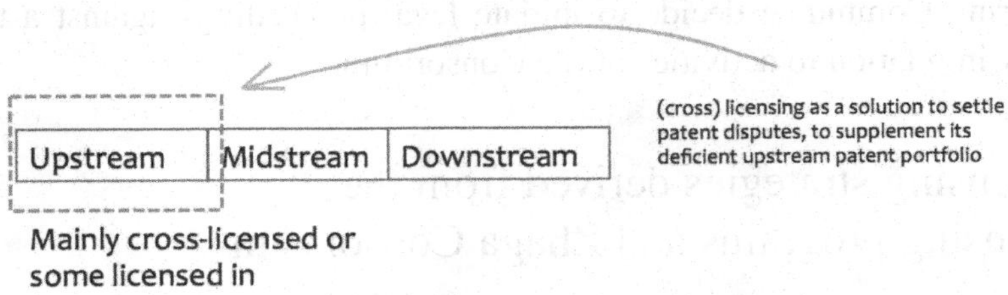

Figure 7.26 Samsung LED's licensing strategy

---

[28] http://electroiq.com/blog/2011/05/samsung-licenses-quantum-dot-led-ip-from-evident/

[29] http://www.samsungvillage.com/blog/2012/08/17/samsung-and-osram-reach-global-settlement-over-led-patent-suits/

7.5.3.3 *LED alliance*

The above licensing programs adopted by the individual companies are the traditional form licensing and cross licensing. In recent years, as the industry is slowly transforming to give more attention to downstream development, a consortium called Zhaga was set up to address these changes and new needs in the LED industry.

The Zhaga Consortium

In 2010, Philips initiated the Zhaga consortium to develop standard specifications for the interfaces of LED light engines. It is stated that Zhaga "will prevent market fragmentation into incompatible products," "increase the confidence to specify and purchase LED products that will be easily replaceable and commercially available" and "foster innovation and competition in the application of LED lighting."[30] Zhaga concerns the mechanical, thermal, electrical, and photometric interfaces of the LED light engine. This allows the LED light engine to be interchangeable. The products that belong to this set of standards are the LED luminaire, LED control gear, LED module, LED lamp holder, and LED light engine. For companies joining the Zhaga program, they agree to promote Zhaga specifications and contribute to new specification developments. They also agree to share costs and benefits in a prorated manner should the Steering Committee decide to initiate legal proceedings against a third party in relation to activities of the Consortium.

Licensing strategies derived from the licensing programs and Zhaga Consortium

From the patent portfolio distribution and licensing program from Philips, one can derive that it uses more co-operative and collaborative approaches to proliferate its dominance into the mid- and downstream segments along the value chain. In 2008, Philips came up with this

[30] http://www.ieee-isto.org/member-programs/zhaga-consortium?page=8

licensing program to license out its technologies related to luminaires. In 2010, the establishment of the Zhaga consortium further provided a platform to direct the development of downstream technologies that would be in compliance with its regular members. In this way, these regular members would be able to shape the direction of downstream technologies development and eliminate many out-of-standard downstream technologies. This makes the downstream less fragmented and eliminates many smaller competitors. From its initial formation to today 2014, the number of licensees to Philips' Luminaires Licensing Program exceeded 400. In fact, the number doubled from 2012 to 2014. The licensing program and the Zhaga consortium created an eco-system for Philips to exert its power into the downstream market, which has been forecasted to be its main profit centre by 2020. Philips' strategy to the change in the LED industry is summarized in Figure 7.27.

From the midstream licensing programs offered by Osram, it encourages and enables proliferation of their technologies to a wider network of manufacturers. On the other hand, it is more competitive in upstream in general. There is much litigation and most companies, like Nichia, use cross licensing to settle these litigations. The cooperative approach

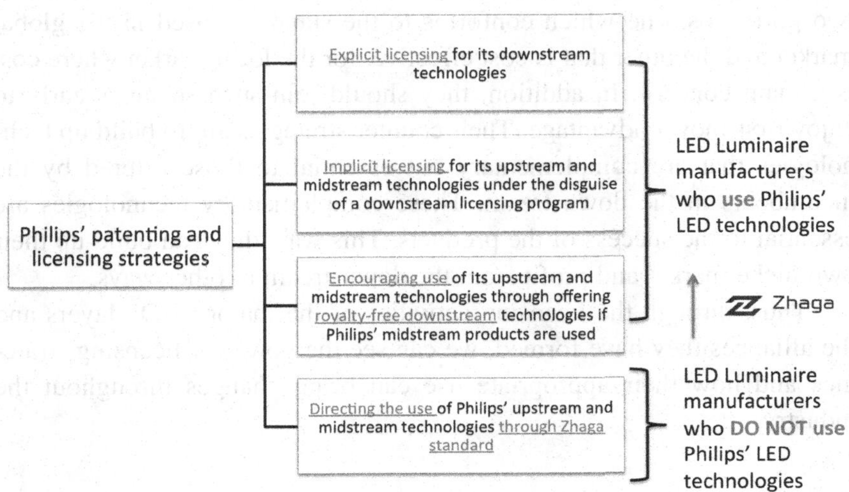

Figure 7.27 Summary of Philips' patenting and licensing strategies

continues for the downstream. Zumtobel is a company made up of a few brands for the midstream and downstream sectors. It cross licensed with Philips and allows the proliferation of its products to be compatible with Philips'. On the other hand, as a latecomer, Samsung LED does not participate in Philips' Luminaires Licensing Program. Samsung has a large patent portfolio in the downstream sector. Many of its products are competitive with that of Philips. However, it did eventually join the Zhaga consortium. Hence, Zhaga is effective in bringing the different downstream players into a standardized format.

Technology latecomers form stronger collaborations, like those in the cross-licensing deals between Epistar and Intermolecular and Color Kinetics that eventually built up a portfolio attractive enough to Philips. In the upstream, these smaller companies tend to either license out their technologies to complement the incumbents' technologies or they license from the incumbents to develop their own technologies further. This is evident from the long list of licensees from Philips' Luminaires Licensing Program. Since the Zhaga program was formed, the number of players joining the Zhaga consortium and signing up with Philips' Licensing Program has soared. In response to the semi-open standard in the midstream, technology latecomers might need to divide their products into two portfolios: one which conforms to the standards used in the global market and the other that is cost effective, for the local market where cost is a main concern. In addition, they should join such schemes early to enjoy first-mover advantage. Their counter strategies are to build up technologies that are complementary but essential to those offered by the incumbents in the downstream. These complementary technologies are essential to the success of the products. This way, they can build up their own niche market and profit from the downstream in other ways.

Thus, through the licensing activities of the major LED players and the alliances they have formed, we can see the power of licensing strategies and how their appropriate use can bring changes throughout the industry.

Bibliography

Berman, B. 2008. *From Assets to Profits: Competing for IP Value and Return.* John Wiley & Sons.

Gilbert, O. G. a. J. L. 1998. Profit pools: A fresh look at strategy. *Harvard Business Review*, article reprint # 98305.

McKinsey & Company. 2012. Lighting the way: Perspectives on the global lighting market, Second edition.

Yole Development. 2012. Status of the LED Industry — market analysis, industry status, players and main applications for LED.

Chapter 8

Valuation

8.1 Overview

Patent valuation is one of the most important aspects of patent management. Patents are assets only if they can generate income for their owners. If a company's patent portfolios cannot be translated into dollars and cents, they are just liabilities. Having knowledge of the value of patents helps to determine whether companies should develop their own proprietary technology or simply license from existing ones. If a company chooses license, an acceptable royalty rate has to be determined. If a company decides to develop its own technology, it may run the risks of being accused of patent infringement. The royalty rate is also important in such patent infringement cases where the damages need to be determined. Increasingly, some patent monetizing companies use the threat of patent infringement as a tool to license out their patent portfolios. Therefore, a lot of effort has been put into deriving methodologies and formulas to value patents. Depending on the purposes of valuation, various methodologies can be used.

One of the most widely researched methods for valuing patents is for the purpose of the accounting. Valuation is not just meant for monetizing patent portfolios; it is also used in financing, taxation, and calculating equity shares. As the monetization of patents occurs at a later stage in the IP life cycle and involves high risks, valuation for these purposes is still at the infancy stage. On the other hand, financing and taxation are more

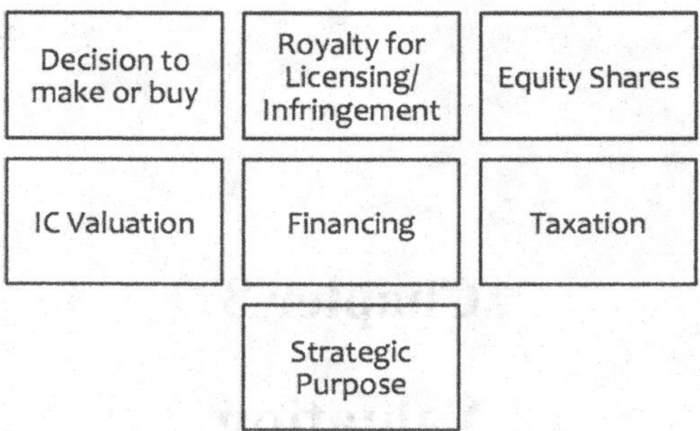

Figure 8.1 Some purposes of patent valuation

commonly encountered and are pressing issues, especially for start-ups. Valuation for financing and taxation receives a lot of attention and much concrete work has been done. There is existing software that helps companies generate a fast estimate of the valuation of their IP. Usually, it involves income calculation. Valuation for patent damages and licensing, on the other hand, is linked to the products. Therefore, depending on the purpose of valuation, the methods for valuation differ. Figure 8.1 summarizes some purposes of patent valuation.

8.2 Principle of Valuation

8.2.1 Exploitation scenarios

Closely related to the purposes of valuation are the scenarios for the exploitation of patents. Different scenarios of exploitation will affect the consideration of complementary assets for the implementation of the technology. Moreover, exploitation of patents by different parties also contributes to different values. When valuing for a potential patent owner, the utility expectations and the availability of the complementary goods are more substantial, thus the valuation result is the utility value of the patents.

On the other hand, if the exploitation of the patents is through a transfer of ownership, the valuation used is a transfer value instead of the direct projected revenue. The consideration for the availability of complementary assets and strategies would be different, in fact, uncertain. Thus, the risks will be higher.

Table 8.1 Examples of different exploitation scenarios

Examples of exploitation scenario	
Offensive	**Defensive**
Cost reduction	Protection of present and future revenues
Licensing, cross-licensing	Protection of promising fields of technology at an early stage
Patent as an asset in company transactions	Prevention of risks of patent infringement and related costs.
Constraint of competitors' activities in distinct fields of technology	

Some of the scenarios for exploitation are summarized in Table 8.1. They can be broadly categorized into offensive and defensive.

Besides the valuation purpose mentioned in section 8.1, we also have to consider other background information that sets the context for valuation.

8.2.2 Background information

Other background information includes defining the valuation object, valuation date and valuation experts. All this information should be present in the valuation report. Valuation object is the unit of valuation. One or more patents can be subjected to patent valuation. When valuing a portfolio of related patents in the same technology, possible synergy effects may arise. The value of a patent portfolio often does not equal the sum of the respective single values of the patents that constitute the portfolio. Very often, a large portfolio may command a high price, which makes the price per patent higher than just a single patent in the same technology. For example, in 2013, Kodak sold and licensed its patent portfolio with 1100 patents in the digital imaging technology for \$527 million. That translates to around \$479K per patent.[1] In 2011, HTC

[1] http://www.kodak.com/ek/US/en/Kodak_Completes_527_Million_Transaction_Related_to_Digital_Imaging_Patents.htm

bought over S3's patent portfolio on Graphics for a price of $300 million.[2] The portfolio has 235 patents. The price per patent is around $1.3 million. It will be hard for a single patent to fetch this high price because it is financially more affordable and less intimidating to challenge one patent than a portfolio of 1100 patents. Therefore, there is a larger negotiation power for the patent owner if he owns a large portfolio of patents in the same technology.

Valuation date determines the cut-off of information to be used for valuation. Influencing factors used to assess risks change over time. For example, in 2011, Google bought over a patent portfolio consisting of 17,000 patents plus some operating business units for a price of $12.5 billion. In 2014, Lenovo took over Motorola Mobility's operation and about 2000 of the patents in the portfolio for a price of $2.91 billion.[3] Although it is impossible to compare the valuation of the patent portfolios alone from these two transactions, it is not difficult to infer that the valuation of the patents changes over time. Another example is the Nortel patent portfolio bought by Rockstar Consortium, which comprises Apple, Microsoft, Sony, Blackberry, and Ericsson. The transaction consisted of 6000 patents valued at $4.5 billion in 2011. In 2014, RPX Corp. took over 4000 patents in the same Nortel patent portfolio from Rockstar Consortium for $900 million. Although 2000 patents in the portfolio have been distributed to the consortium members and are therefore not included in the RPX deal, the value of the patent portfolio has changed substantially with time. It may be argued that the 2000 patents distributed among the consortium members are much more valuable than the 4000 patents purchased by RPX, but the drastic difference in the two prices may also be contributed by the fact that the U.S. courts have started to overturn many huge damages decided by jury. Therefore valuation amount changes with valuation date.

Another crucial factor in the valuation of patent portfolios is the valuation experts. One or a group of experts may carry out the valuation. Not only should the valuation expert understand the theoretical principles of

---

[2] http://www.theverge.com/2012/6/13/3082087/htc-complete-s3-graphics-acquisition-patent-portfolio

[3] http://www.wsj.com/articles/lenovo-completes-motorola-acquisition-1414665138

patent valuation, he should also have practical experience. The theoretical principles that the valuation expert needs to grasp are multi-disciplinary, requiring legal, economic, and technical understanding. He needs to apply his practical knowledge of dealing with and carrying out patent valuations appropriately. He should be able to identify the legal, economic, and technical factors that influence the patent valuation and appropriately assess them in the valuation. Different valuation experts may come up with different valuations because each may consider different factors. Good valuation experts should be able to minimize the discrepancies.

8.2.3 Influencing factors

Many factors influence the valuation of patents. Broadly speaking, they can be grouped into three categories: legal, technical, and economic. For convenience of referencing them in the future, we use the abbreviation "LTE factors" to represent these three categories of factors. These factors are also considered in a German Patent Valuation standard.[4] Of the three, the legal factors bear a great significance because legal strength serves as the first gate to the usefulness of the patents. Without proper legal "power", even patents covering a profitable technology would not be useful, as they cannot be enforced. Therefore, the order of consideration for these factors should be legal, followed by technical and finally economic.

8.2.3.1 *Legal factors*

Many legal factors contribute to the legal strength of a patent and a patent portfolio. Some are quantitative and relatively straight forward to determine. Others are more qualitative and may attract subjective judgment calls. For example, the assessment of the legal status of a patent is not debatable, whereas protectability and enforceability may entail more room for discussion.

[4] Patent valuation — General principles for monetary patent valuation English translation of DIN 77100: 2100-05 by DIN Deutsches Institut für Normung.

Legal status

It involves the assessment of the state of procedure, such as whether the patent is granted or in the process of being examined. Even if it is granted, the remaining life of the patent has to be long enough to be useful. Usefulness of the remaining life can be a relative term. For example, ten years of remaining life is not very long for pharmaceutical technology but considerably long for semiconductor technology. The geographic coverage of the patent family is important too. A patent granted in a country with a very small market is not as valuable as a patent granted in a market where the market size of the covered product is large. In addition, the legal status is also affected by whether there are other IP protecting the same invention as a portfolio. For example, Dolby uses both patents and trademarks to protect the surround sound technology. Trademarks add additional values to the technology. Once these accompanying trademarks have accumulated sufficient recognition, the patents associated with them will be more valuable too.

Protectability

Another legal factor worth evaluating is the protectability of the technology. For most countries, the patents are granted based on the five requirements of patentability: patent eligible subject matter, usefulness, novelty, non-obviousness, and adequate description. The probability of satisfying all these requirements to get a patent granted will affect the value of the patent. Even if the patent is granted, there will always be the possibility that it will be invalidated by challenges to these five requirements in the future. Therefore, protectability must be considered.

Covered products

After establishing the validity of the patent, the covered products have to be identified. It is the revenues from these covered products that will inevitably determine the value of the patent. In recent years, the value of a patent is increasingly capped by the smallest salable unit. This requires the determination of the part of the product that is protected by the patent. In the past few years it has become common practice in the smartphone industry for patent owners to target the smartphone brand owners for patent infringement even though the patented technology might cover just one particular chip inside the smartphone, such as a wireless module. The smartphone brand owners have no involvement in the module except purchasing them and assembling them. Patent owners target the end product producers partly because they want to "try their luck" in claiming the entire market rule (EMR). The EMR will allow a larger base for calculating the reasonable royalties. The possibility of success is diminishing in recent years.

Scope of protection and possibility to circumvent the patent

Extending from the evaluation criteria of covered products is the scope of protection and possibility to circumvent the patent. Even if the patent has a great chance of withstanding invalidation challenges and has a large coverage of potential infringing products, a potential infringer may design around the patent or opt for alternative similar solutions to avoid using the patent. This is the case for many process patents and software algorithm patents. There may be myriad routes that eventually lead to the final outcome. A small alteration at any step will render the patent incapable of covering the product.

Enforceability

A legal factor closely related to the covered products is enforceability. There are a few dimensions to enforceability. First, enforceability relates to a history of prior use of the patent. Usually, a patent or a portfolio of patents is more valuable if they have been successfully enforced before. Besides the actual enforcement, the experience of having gone through a round of invalidation and still being able to hold the patentability affords the patent owner a stronger negotiation power because it has reaffirmed the legal strength of the patent.

Another dimension of enforceability is the traceability and probability of patent infringement. This is known as the evidence-of-use in industry. It entails the construction of claim charts matching each element in each patent claim to the accused product. Usually, at the valuation stage, only preliminary claim charts would be constructed. The claim charts used in the patent infringement case in court would normally be very different from preliminary ones, especially in US patent infringement cases where a discovery process from which proprietary information about the products can be obtained can help the patent owner establish more reliable claim charts. This process is especially useful for process and software patent enforcement.

A third dimension of enforceability is evaluating the influence of different national laws dealing with commercial protection on enforceability. This patent enforcement landscape is global. The smartphone patent war is a great example. Apple and Samsung alone have had patent litigation cases in US, Germany, France, UK, Netherlands, Japan, and South Korea. In particular, the "slide-to-unlock" patent family has been litigated in US, UK, and Germany. In 2012, the patent was found to be invalid by the UK High Court.[5] Recently, in August 2015, the patent has been ruled to be invalid in German courts for not being sophisticated enough to be awarded a patent.[6] These verdicts will have influence over the case in other jurisdiction such as the US. In addition, courts sometimes refer to another jurisdiction for case law. This is especially the case for common law jurisdictions. Therefore, when evaluating the patent value, these legal factors have to be taken into account.

Ability to act and freedom-to-operate

Sometimes, a patent does not have the freedom to be enforced on its own. For example, if the technology hinges upon the use of some background patents. In this case, if the patent owner does not have these background patents, it may result in a lower valuation for licensing or sales, as the use

---

[5] http://www.telegraph.co.uk/technology/apple/9375829/Apple-suffers-High-Court-defeat-over-prize-iPhone-patents.html

[6] http://www.bloomberg.com/news/articles/2015-08-25/apple-loses-german-top-court-case-over-swipe-to-unlock-patent

of that patent stipulates the licensee or the buyer having to pay extra money for the background patents.

Right of disposal and ownership

Besides the above substantial factors to be considered in patent valuation, there are also other procedural factors that require attention. For example, the valuator should check the right of disposal or ownership of the patent, whether the transfer from inventor to the present patent holder has been done properly and whether there are any existing licensing agreements or liens that restrict the use of the patents.

Relevant standards

Other restrictions are the limitations imposed by the standard setting organization for patents that are declared under the standard. If a patent falls under a standard, the value is limited by the FRAND rule. This means that the patent owner does not have the freedom to license at any price as he wishes. The price must be fair, reasonable, and non-discriminatory, thus limiting the value. However, being a standard essential patent does not necessarily mean that the projected revenue is small. More potential licensees may be willing to take a license as the technology is essential. Therefore, even though the negotiated royalty rate may not be high, potentially more licenses can be concluded.

Approval restrictions

There are instances where the exploitation of patent rights is limited by statutory requirements. For example, foreign trade regulations can restrict the export of the covered goods by the patents, thus limiting the revenue. Pharmaceutical patents are sometimes restricted by national policy to ensure that drug prices are not excessive and the drugs do not become out of reach of the average consumers. For example, the UK has a Pharmaceutical Price Regulation Scheme that is intended to ensure that drugs are maintained at "reasonable prices." In Canada, the Patented

Medicine Prices Review Board examines and compares drug pricing with that of seven other countries to determine if a price is "excessive". All these actions put restrictions on the revenue and hence the valuation related patents.

8.2.3.2 *Technical factors*

The legal factors alone are not sufficient to determine patent values because a patent that does not cover a useful technology is not worth much, if anything at all. The technical factors listed below tries to quantify, or at least specify, some criteria to exemplify the meaning of being "useful".

Technical feasibility

As mentioned earlier, a patent can be granted so long as it satisfies the five grounds of patentability: patent eligible subject matter, usefulness, novelty, non-obviousness, and adequate description. However, it does not require experimental results to be presented, nor must the invention be actually realized. For example, there are patents on time traveling machines: "Method of gravity distortion and time displacement" (US 20060073976 A1, "Method of space compression time dilation machine" (WO 2013088425 A2), "Practical Time Machine Using Dynamic Efficient Virtual and Real Robots" (US 20090234788 A1), "Traveling method" (WO 2012046284 A2). Although they have not yet been granted, these patent applications can still be valued for bank loans and applications made for future research funding. The technical feasibility in this case may hinder a hike in the patent values. It is beyond this book to determine the actual technical feasibility of a time machine. However, such question should be raised when valuing patents.

Production-related feasibility (scalability)

The previous examples also touch on the problem of scalability. A technology on time traveling may take a long time to commercialize even though it may eventually be technically feasible. An example on scalability would be something like "Apparatus for facilitating the birth of a child by centrifugal force" (US 3216423 A). The patent describes a technology of strapping the mother-to-be on a turntable that spins fast enough so that the G-force helps to ease the baby out. Although it does make sense scientifically, there may not be a large demand for such technology, as not many mothers-to-be might want to be strapped on such a turntable. There is much less radical patented technology that sounds perfectly feasible, but may not be scalable for large-scale production.

Technology life cycle

As mentioned in our chapter on Patenting Strategies, the stage in which the patent belongs to in the technology life cycle matters. A technology that is at the early stage of the life cycle but with great uncertainty as to whether it will eventually take off may not attract a very high price because there is no guarantee that there will be a market. On the other hand, a technology that is at the end of the technology life cycle may also not be worth much, especially when there is another technology that is going to replace it. For example, in the evolution of wireless communication, the 2G GSM technologies are slowly being replaced. Singapore, for example, is going to phase out the 2G GSM service in 2016. Therefore, the potential market for getting revenue out of the 2G GSM patent portfolios is smaller and so the value would be limited.

Technical field of application

Technical factors to be considered include how widely covered the patent, in particular, a patent portfolio is in terms of application. The wider it covers, the larger the market size and therefore the higher the value of the patent. For example, stem cell technology can be applied in biomedical tools, chemistry and materials, engineering/communication, medical diagnostics, therapeutics/vaccines. Perhaps not a single patent can encompass all these applications. But a patent portfolio that covers all these applications will be worth more than a patent portfolio covering just one application.

Technical substitution

As discussed in the considerations under the legal factors, the possibility to design around affects the value of the patent. For that matter, the design around is primarily in terms of claims construction and a possibility to avoid falling under the scope of the patent claims. Technical substitution means more than just designing around a patent claim, it means there is a competing technology that allows potential users to avoid using the patented technology. An example would be packaging technology in the semiconductor industry. There are many different types of packaging: through-via technology, copper pillar technology, wafer-level packaging, etc. They serve similar package sizes. A chipmaker can choose either one. Therefore, such competitions can potentially affect the value of patents in these technologies.

8.2.3.3 *Economic factors*

Having considered the legal and technical factors that describe the patent portfolio and the technology, the economic factors now bring the valuation criteria closer to the market. The economic factors consider the business aspects surrounding the patent or the patent portfolio.

Market potential of invention

The market potential of a patent portfolio is determined by the revenue generated from the sales of products and the amount of products that can potentially be sold. This factor is considered to be the most relevant in accounting methods of valuing patents, especially the market approach. The market potential determines the forecasted product revenues and thus the patent values.

Availability of complementary goods

When a buyer considers the adoption of a technology, the first question is the cost. He would consider the cost of licensing, technology transfer, and the cost of doing R&D on his own. If the cost of licensing is cheaper than R&D he will opt to license. The cost of licensing, however, is more than just the licensing fee. It includes the technology transfer fee of technical and market know-how. For example, if the technology requires the company to set up new production lines, the cost of setting up such infrastructure will need to be added up to the cost. Therefore, there may be fewer potential licensees who are interested to take up the technology.

Business model

In addition to the market potential, the chosen vehicle to generate the revenue is another important factor for valuation. As mentioned in Chapter one, because of the segmentation of industry, some companies are focused on just licensing out their IP for others to implement. In this case, they rely on patents heavily for earnings. On the other hand, if a company's business model is primarily manufacturing, the patents may not contribute directly to the revenue. These situations need to be evaluated in patent valuation.

Interdependencies

There are many other independent factors that affect the monetization of patents, for example, marketing strategies, and R&D strategies. Sometimes, the failure of the products to generate good sales volumes does not necessarily mean that it is a bad product. It may be due to the fact that it is targeted at the wrong consumer sector. It may also be due to insufficient and inadequate marketing campaigns. There are many factors affecting the success of the products. Sometimes, the market potential for the products can be high, but the company's product may be focusing on a uniqueness that is unfavorable to the consumers. For example, although both are selling smartphones, Samsung is now focusing on curved screens while Apple is focusing on the touch technology, providing different functions with different types of touch. The market share for each company can be very different. When evaluating their smartphone patents, the values obtained may be affected by such differences.

Table 8.2 Influencing factors for determining the values of patents

Legal	Technical	Economic
Legal status (remaining life, structural/procedural claims etc.)	Technical feasibility	Market potential of invention
Patentability (ease to reverse engineering for evidence of use)	Product ion-related feasibility (scalability)	Availability of complementary goods
Covered products (potential infringement possibility)	Technology life cycle	Business model
Scope of protection and possibility to circumvent the patent (prior art, validity challenge)	Technical field of application	Interdependencies
Ability to act, freedom to operate (need to operate in a patent portfolio)	Technical substitution	
Enforceability (jurisdiction, court system)	Complementary technologies	
Right of disposal, ownership (licensing agreement)		
Relevant standards		
Approval restrictions		

Table 8.2 briefly sums up the three categories of factors to be considered in the valuation of patents. Many of these factors are qualitative in nature and do not contribute directly to a mathematics formula that can result in a numeric value for the patents.

8.3 Common Valuation Approaches in Industries

As discussed in the overview of this chapter, the financial and accounting methods of patent valuation are different from that of patent damages. For financial and accounting purposes, the income, market, and cost approaches dominate. There are other practical methods that are commonly used in business transactions and negotiations such as auction, rule of thumb, and other business profiles as summarized in Figure 8.2.

There are other more sophisticated methods of valuation including time based, uncertainty based, flexibility approach, changing risks methods, etc. For example, the time approach takes discounted cash flow into account to allow for the time value of money. In uncertainty methods, the discounted cash flow includes the consideration of fixed risks of cash flow. Such discounted cash flow methods are now incorporated into the income approaches. Thus, the income approach — or some call it the cash flow approach — is the widely used and generally applicable approach for valuation of patents for financial and accounting purposes.

Some highly sophisticated methods of valuation take into account more alternatives. For example, the flexibility approach calculates the discounted cash flow using the Decision Tree Analysis. Others consider changing risks, such as the option pricing theory based methods, the binomial model using discrete time, and the Black-Scholes option-pricing model based on continuous time consideration.

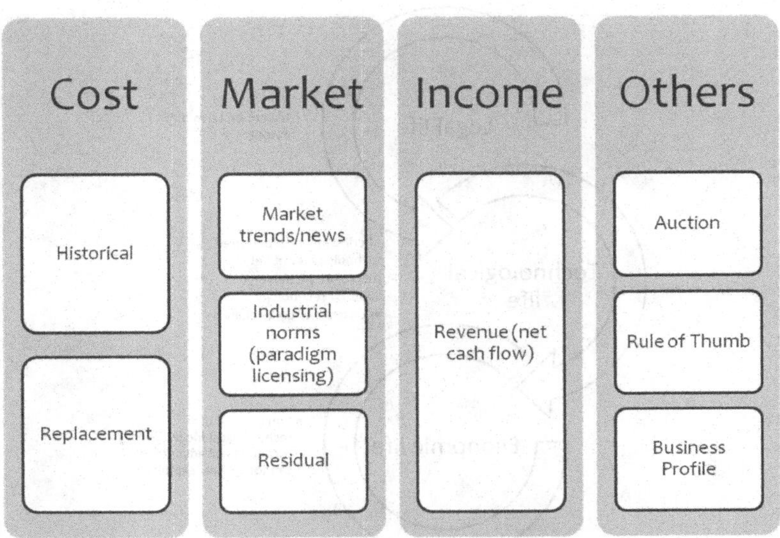

Figure 8.2 General financial and accounting valuation methods

8.3.1 Income approach

The income approach is the most widely adopted approach among the commonly used income, market, and cost methods. Income approach calculates a future payoff using expected future cash flows to be discounted in order to arrive at the present values at the specified valuation date. It is a comprehensive approach as it takes into account all the influencing factors mentioned in Section 8.2 through a step-by-step analysis. The key values to be determined in the income approach are the (1) forecasting period, (2) discount rate, and (3) patent-specific cash flows. The patent-specific cash flow can be determined using the incremental cash flow method as far as possible. It may also be derived from the relief-from royalty method.

To determine the forecasting period, the following process of thoughts that consider the legal, technological, and economic life as shown in Figure 8.3 can be used. The cash flows are calculated up until additional cash flows can be related to the utilization of the patent.

The discount rate can be determined by various methods as discussed in section 8.2. Some general considerations take into account inflation,

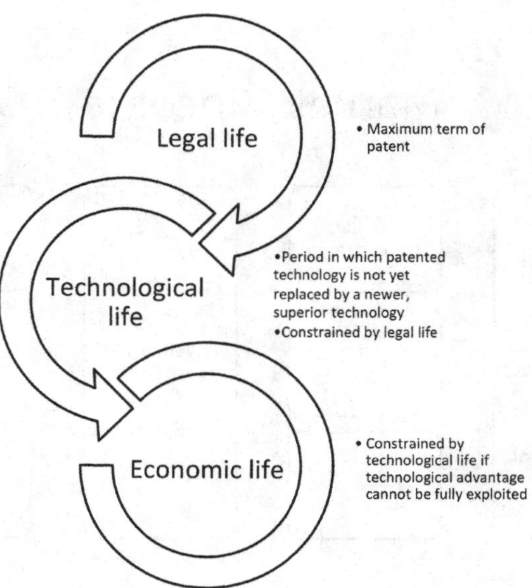

Figure 8.3 Cash flow valuation method

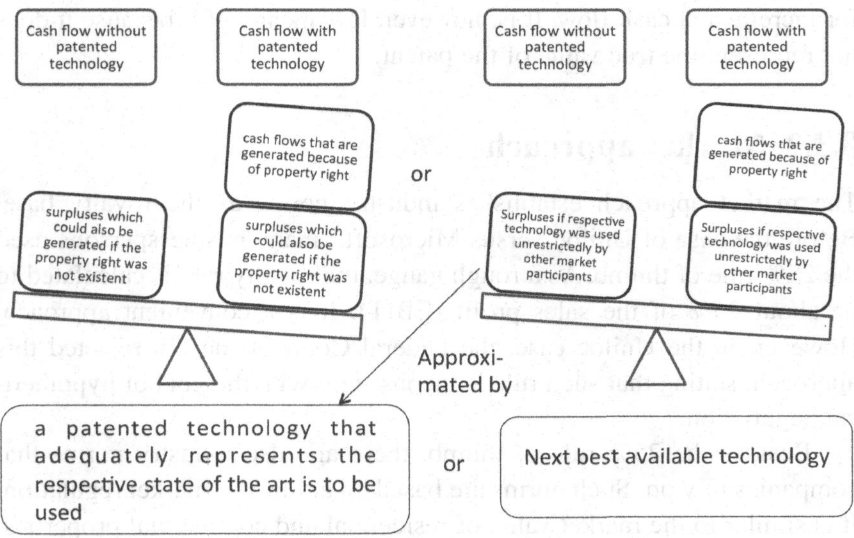

Figure 8.4 Determination of the patent value using the incremental cash flow method

interest rate or capital market and some fixed expected risks. Many books on financial valuation usually cover such formation and they are not treated here.[7]

For determining the patent-specific cash flow, a basic approach uses the historical data as reference. It determines the market share and cost reduction, taking into account the exploitation scenarios. Alternatively, the cash flow can also be determined using the incremental cash flow method by comparing the cash flow when the patented technology is used and when the patented technology is not used. Usually, it is very difficult to isolate the situation, so an alternate technology that can represent the state of the art is considered. The process can be illustrated in Figure 8.4. Another approach to determine the patent-specific cash flow is the relief from royalty method. It is more useful when information is not available

[7]An example of a comprehensive reference for intellectual property valuation is: Smith, Gordon V., and Russell L. Parr. Valuation of intellectual property and intangible assets. Vol. 13. Wiley, 2000.

for incremental cash flow. It is, however, less meaningful because it does not represent the true value of the patent.

8.3.2 Market approach

The market approach establishes industry norms as the royalty base. Before the case of Uniloc versus Microsoft,[8] many businesspersons used the 25% rule of thumb. As a rough gauge, the royalty rate is calculated to be about 25% of the sales profit (EBIT). It is a convenient approach. However, in the Uniloc case, the Federal Court of the US rejected this approach, stating that such rule is inconsistent with the goal of hypothetical negotiation.

Besides the 25% rule of thumb, there are also industry norms that companies rely on. Such norms are based on automatic market regulation. It is similar to the market value of residential and commercial properties. The market regulates the price of the property according to supply and demand. For example, in the electronics industry, 50% of the licensing deals were concluded with a royalty rate between 2–5%, another 45% between 5–10% and only around 5% of the licensing deals fetched between 10–15% royalty rates. On the other hand, in the telecoms industry, most licensing deals can reach between 10–15% royalty rates.[9] Such industrial norms are often used as a convenient starting point and basis for further negotiation.

The downside of this approach is that it does not take into account the uniqueness of inventions and there is no discounting of patent-specific cash flows. It is difficult to identify patents with the same utility and in the same market for meaningful comparisons.

8.3.3 Cost approach

The cost approach also calculates the present value of patents by summing up the positive and negative cash flow and equates them with the value of

[8] Uniloc USA versus Microsoft Corp., 10-1035, US Court of Appeals for the Federal Circuit (Washington).

[9] Richard Razgaitis, Valuation & Pricing of Technology-Based Intellectual Property.

the patents. For example, it sums up the positive costs of product revenues, revenues through licensing or sales, saved costs and indirect patent revenues. There are also some negative costs such as property rights, maintenance costs, costs of inventor's remuneration, taxes, and license payments because of some other dependencies. The cost approach then adds up all these positive and negative costs to derive a value for the patents.

The disadvantage of using the cost approach is that it may overestimate patents with low economic values. On the other hand, it may underestimate the patent with great economic value. The commonly cited example for this is the 3M post-it invention. It was an invention accidentally discovered by a 3M employee.[10] There was no budget and there was no problem to be solved when it was invented. So the cost can be minimal if the cost approach is used. However, as it turns out, the post-it notes generate a USD50 billion market each year.

8.3.4 Other approaches

Other sophisticated approaches include a real option approach, which is binomial in nature. A simplification is shown in Figure 8.5.

As there are always uncertainties in life, such as in the case of a transfer mode where the transfer value is computed, the uncertainties need to be taken into account. This is shown in Figure 8.6.

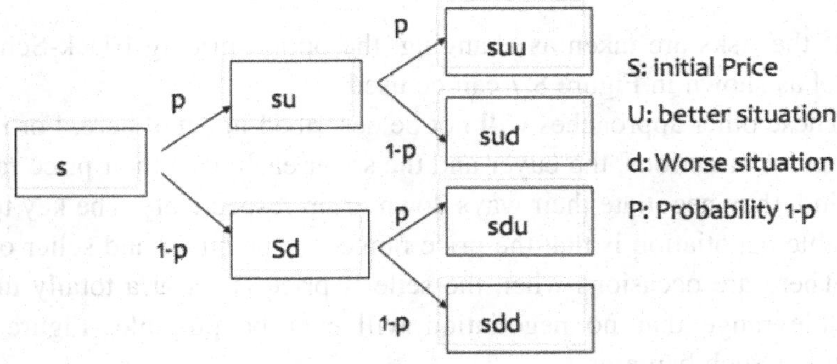

Figure 8.5 Real option approach — binomial mode

[10] http://edition.cnn.com/2013/04/04/tech/post-it-note-history/

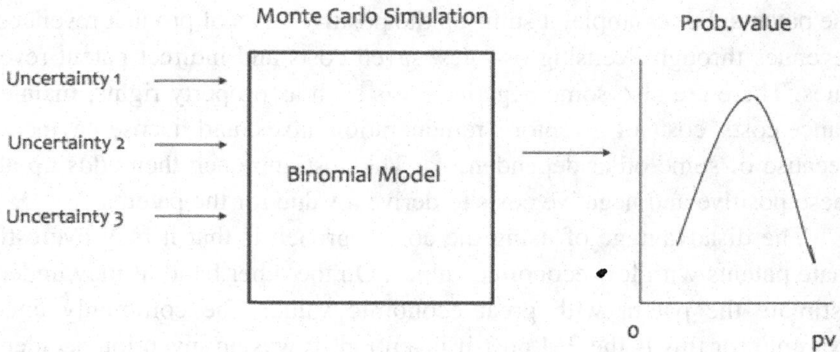

Figure 8.6 Real option — binomial mode with uncertainty

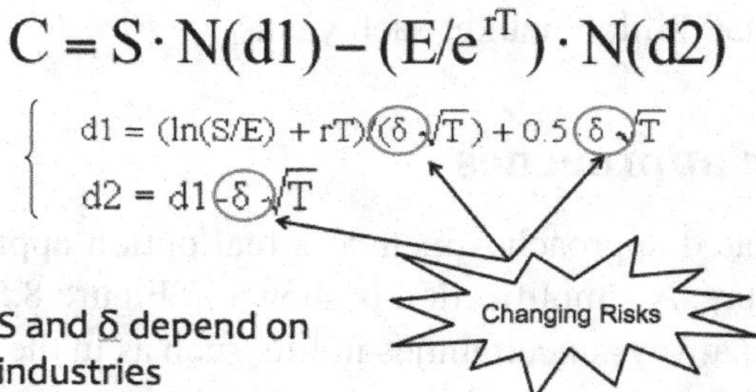

Figure 8.7 Option pricing — Black–Scholes model

If the risks are taken as changing, the option pricing Black-Scholes Model as shown in Figure 8.7 can be used.

These other approaches will not be described in detail here. For most business transactions, the buyer and the seller each have their price range in mind, they negotiate their ways down or up respectively. The key to an operable negotiation is that the price ranges of the buyer and seller overlap. There are occasions when the seller's price is set at a totally unacceptable range that no negotiation will ever be possible. Figure 8.8 illustrates such bargains.

Similarly, in auctions, there is a process to reach the final price. However, in this case, only the potential buyers call the shots and the price will only go up from the initial price. The buyer cannot negotiate a lower price. This is illustrated in Figure 8.9.

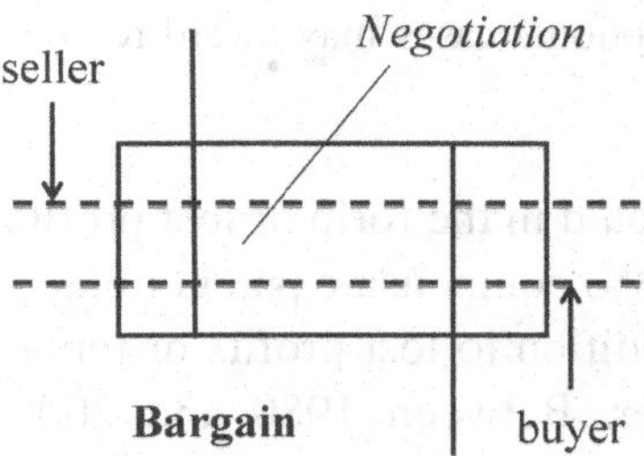

Figure 8.8 Negotiation

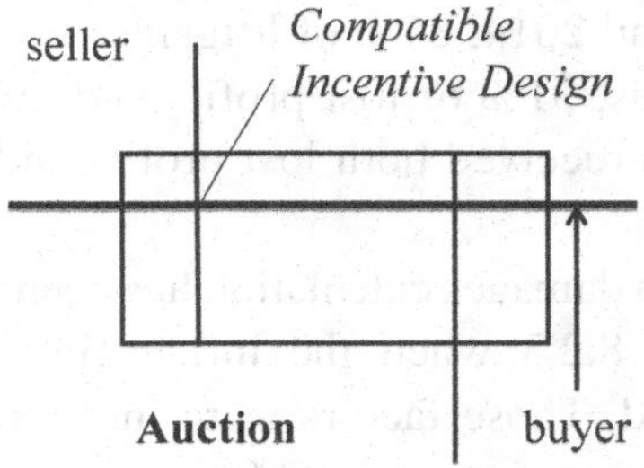

Figure 8.9 Auction

8.4 Patent Damages

In patent infringement disputes, once patent validity and infringement have been confirmed, the final step would be to determine damages to be paid by the patent infringer. Under 35 U.S.C. §284,

> "upon finding for the claimant the court shall award the claimant damages adequate to compensate for the infringement, but in no event less than a reasonable royalty for the use made of the invention by the infringer, together with interest and costs as fixed by the court.
>
> When the damages are not found by a jury, the court shall assess them. In either event the court may increase the damages up to three times the amount found or assessed.
>
> The court may receive expert testimony as an aid to the determination of damages or of what royalty would be reasonable under the circumstances."

The additional sections related to the award of damages are 35 U.S.C. §285 on Attorney fees:

"The court in exceptional cases may award reasonable attorney fees to the prevailing party."

Damages can be paid in the form of lost profits. In the event that lost profits are inadequate to compensate patent holders, reasonable royalties can be awarded in addition to lost profits or replacing compensation by lost profits altogether. Between 1980 and 2000, 83% of the patent infringement cases used lost profits as the basis to award damages to patent holders. Since 2005, more than 80% of the patent infringement cases have used reasonable royalties to calculate awarded damages. In fact, between 2005 and 2014, 81% of litigants received damages awards of reasonable royalties, 31% of lost profits and 2% based on price erosion.[11] Some litigants received both lost profits and reasonable royalties as damages awards.

An introduction to damages calculation has been briefly and informally discussed in Section 8.2.3 when the influencing factors for valuation were being introduced. Those factors were introduced in the vacuum of any scenarios and are pure factors that affect mostly the intrinsic values of the patents. Patent damages calculations used in many of the US patent infringement cases, however, are considered in context. In the case of lost profits, for example, the court will take into account the relevance of the highly related sales to determine whether it is appropriate to use the EMR. In determining reasonable royalties, it is all the more scenario-based, as it is determined under a hypothetical negotiation scenario.

In general, the principles of patent damage calculation are based on the "but for" principle that simulates, as closely as possible, the market place in absence of infringement. There are four principles that require adherence:

1) A patent's economic and commercial value derives largely from the market power it confers to the patent owner; therefore, in estimating damages from patent infringement, the market power conferred by the patent must be taken into account;

[11] https://www.pwc.com/us/en/forensic-services/publications/assets/2015-pwc-patent-litigation-study.pdf.

2) When the price of a good increases, consumption of the good declines, and vice versa (law of demand);
3) Only costs incurred through extra sales should be charged against extra sales revenues; therefore, incremental costing is the proper approach. Both the technology and the size of the output increment determine which costs are relevant;
4) Royalties are determined in hypothetical negotiations in which both the market power flowing from the patent and the relative bargaining power of the negotiators influence the outcome.

In order to establish damages, the court first considers all relevant evidence as to how much the patent was worth and the damages to the patent owner from the infringement.

This can be assessed based on market demand for the patented product, the existence and availability of non-infringing substitutes, and the patent owner's manufacturing and marketing capability. Second, if the patent owner cannot establish within a reasonable probability the amount of profit it would have made but for the infringement, those factors may be considered in setting a reasonable royalty. Third, the total recovery must be adjusted to approximate damages adequate to compensate for the infringement. These are the general guidelines for establishing damages. In the following section, we look at the two main modes of damage awards: lost profits and reasonable royalties.

8.4.1 Lost profits

Lost profits simply mean the amount of money the patent owner lost as a result of the patent infringement. Therefore, the patent owner must prove that there is a causal relationship between the infringement and the lost profits. If the patent owner cannot produce such proof, reasonable royalty damages are the next available remedy. A patent owner may recover a mixed or split award of lost profits and reasonable royalties. The patent owner, however, cannot recover the infringer's profits except for design patent cases, for which the infringer's profits are still recoverable (35 U.S.C. §289).

8.4.1.1 *The Panduit test*

The causation between the infringement and the lost profits is often referred to as the "but for" test. In general, any types of evidence can be used to establish the "but for" causal linkage. The Sixth Circuit, in Panduit Corp. versus Stahlin Bros. Fibre Works, Inc. (575 F.2d 1152, 197 U.S.P.Q. 726 (6th Cir. 1978)) established the widely adopted test for determining "but for" causation. The four factors set forth are:

1) demand for the patented product,
2) absence of acceptable non-infringing substitutes,
3) the patent owner's manufacturing and marketing capability to exploit the demand, and
4) the amount of the profit that the patent owner would have made.

The first three *Panduit* factors are directed towards establishing the market for the patented item and assessing the ability of the infringer and the patent owner to meet that demand. The fourth factor assesses the calculation of such lost profits identified from the first three factors. This way, the *Panduit* factors help to establish a 'but for' connection between the infringer's acts and the patent owner's losses.

The first factor on the demand for the patented invention is often not contested. It can usually be satisfied by proof of substantial sales of products with the patented invention. Otherwise, it is subsumed within the second factor. The third factor may sometimes be difficult for some companies to prove. The patent owner must show that it has capacity to exploit the demand for the patented product such as by showing its excess manufacturing capacity, ability to obtain financing to support the demand, and ability to market these additional units of the product. The fourth element, which is related to the amount of profit the patent owner would have made absent the infringement, is recognized by the courts to include not only that not only should the price at which the patent owner would have made these sales, but also any additional costs he would have incurred in connection with these sales. The "incremental income" approach is usually used to determine such costs.

Most disputes, however, center upon the application of the second factor, which is related to the presence or absence of adequate non-infringing substitutes. In a two-supplier market, proof of damages can be easily established because there is a clear demand for the patented product by the infringer's act of selling the patented product. There are also no non-infringing substitutes because there are no other competitors in the market. The patentee can use its existing facilities or expand the facilities to meet the demand. Therefore, "but for" the infringement, the patentee would have made the sales otherwise made by the infringer.

In a market with several participants, a market share analysis can be used to determine the appropriate measure of a lost profits award. For example, in State Industries, Inc. versus Mor-Flo Industries, Inc. (883 F.2d at 1573, 12 U.S.P.Q.2d) the patent owner's product competed with several products in the market, some of which were infringing substitutes. Even though the patent owner was not able to satisfy the second requirement of the Panduit test, which is the absence of non-infringing substitute, the court nonetheless awarded lost profits to the patent owner because his market share remained relatively stable at 40%. The district court inferred that "but for" the infringement, the patent owner would have made 40% of the infringer's sales. Therefore, so long as the patent owner had the "sufficient marketing and manufacturing capabilities to meet its market share of the demand," such an inference was reasonable.

Notwithstanding the above, the second factor of the *Panduit* requirement that there be an "absence of non-infringing substitutes" typically means that there are no other products in the market that compete with the patented product so that if not for the infringer's sales, those would have been made by the patent owner. (Zygo Corp. versus Wyko Corp., 79 F.3d 1563, 1571, 38 U.S.P.Q.2d 1281, 1287 (Fed. Cir. 1996)) Not all competing products, however, can be considered as "acceptable" non-infringing substitutes. The competing product must have "all the beneficial characteristics of the patented device." (TWM Mfg. Co. versus Dura Corp., 789 F.2d 895, 901, 229 U.S.P.Q. 525, 529 (Fed. Cir. 1986)). On the other hand, the non-infringing alternatives do not have to be actually sold (185 F.3d 1341, 51 U.S.P.Q.2d 1556 (Fed. Cir. 1999)).

The patent owner bears the burden of proof in this case to show with a reasonable probability that it would have made additional profits but for the infringement. The patent owner also bears the burden of proof in showing the amount of lost profits.

When a patent owner exploits its patent by making, using, or selling the patented product, the *Panduit* "but for" test can usually be satisfied. However, the law is still unclear as to whether or not the patentee *must* make the patented product in order to be entitled to an award of lost profits.

In some circumstances, however, the patent owner may be able to obtain lost profits even where the patent owner does not sell the patented product or where there is only potential competition between the patent owner and the infringer. For example, if the patent owner does not manufacture or sell the patented product but does sell an unpatented product, the patent owner may be able to demonstrate that the infringement caused the patent owner to lose profits on the unpatented product. Rite-Hite Corp. versus Kelley Co., 56 F.3d 1538 (Fed. Cir.), cert. denied, 516 U.S. 867 (1995). In addition, patent owners with only a small share of the relevant market may nevertheless be awarded lost profits, at least in proportion to their market share. And in some cases where the patent owner does not have a competing product at all, it may still obtain lost profits damages if it can prove it "would have made" a competing product absent the infringement. See Wechsler versus Macke Int'l Trade, Inc., 486 F.3d 1286 (Fed. Circ. 2007). The only limitations are that the infringement must cause the loss and that the loss must have been reasonably foreseeable.

Lost profits damages frequently bring the patent owner much more than royalty awards. This has caused patent owners to seek lost profits in nearly every case in which the patent owner manufactures or sells something that could reasonably be interpreted as competing with the infringer's product.

8.4.1.2 *Compensable losses*

After determining if an award of lost profits can be granted to the patent owner, the court must decide the amount of lost profits that the patent owner is entitled. There are, broadly speaking, six categories of lost profits that the patent owner may be entitled to recover:

1) Patented Products
2) Unpatented Products
3) Unpatented Components and the Entire Market Value Rule
4) Price Erosion
5) Future Lost Profits
6) Lost Profits for Pre-infringement Conduct

Patented products

Lost profits from sales of patented products are the classic and most common type of lost profits damages. Such lost sales constitute sales that the patent owner failed to make as a result of the infringement, as well as sales the infringer made that the patent owner would have made but for the infringement. One common method for determining the amount of lost profits is the incremental income approach. The approach has two main types of costs: fixed and variable, for any amount of sales. The fixed costs do not change with increased volume, while the variable costs do. Lost profits are then calculated using the difference between the incremental revenue that the patent owner would have made if it had sold its product in lieu of the infringer's sales, and the variable costs attributable to that incremental sales volume.

Unpatented products

In addition to patented products, in Rite-Hite Corp. versus Kelley Co. (56 F.3d 1538, 35 U.S.P.Q.2d (Fed. Cir. 1995) (en banc)), the Federal Circuit made it clear that the patentee can also recover lost sales of unpatented products so long as those lost sales "w[ere] or should have been reasonably foreseeable by an infringing competitor in the relevant market." In that case, the patentee sold two products in the same market: a less expensive one, which is covered by the asserted patent and a more expensive product, which is not covered by the asserted patent. The infringing product, however, was designed to compete with the patent owner's more expensive, but non-patented product. The district court found that "but for" the infringement, the patentee would have sold 80 more units of the less expensive, patented product and 3243 more units of its more expensive, but non-patented product. The Federal Circuit affirmed the award of lost profits on both products because both of these products competed in the same market and the lost sales of these products should have been reasonably foreseeable to the infringer.

Unpatented components and the entire market value rule

The patent owner can also recover damages based on the entire market value of the whole product that consists of both patented and unpatented components so long as the patented feature is the basis of consumer's demand for the whole product. The federal court has made this clear in State Indus., Inc. versus Mar-Flo Indus., Inc., 883 F.2d 1573, 1580, 12 U.S.P.Q.2d 1026, 1031 (Fed. Cir. 1989). In that case, the asserted patent covered a method for insulating water heaters using foam. The court affirmed an award of lost profits based on the sales of the whole water heater under the entire market value rule instead of limiting the award to the foam-insulating component of the heater.

There are, however, restrictions on the applicability of the entire market value rule. In *Rite-Hite* (56 F.3d at 1549-51, 35 U.S.P.Q.2d), the federal court asserted that the unpatented components must function together with the patented component to produce a desired end product or result. All the components together must be analogous to components of a single assembly or be parts of a complete machine, or they must constitute a functional unit.

In Rite-Hite, the Convoyed Product was, in fact, a separate product. Although it was often sold together with the patented product in a bundle for marketing convenience, there was no evidence that the Convoyed Product functioned together with the patented product or that the Convoyed Product was part of a single assembly with the patented product. Therefore, the court held that Rite-Hite was not entitled to such a recovery because it was under the entire market value rule.

Price erosion

Price erosion damages arise where the patent owner was forced to lower its prices or offer discounts to counter the infringer's competition. It may also result from the patent owner's inability to raise prices due to the infringement. Generally, lost sales and price erosion damages both depend on how the patent owner and infringer interact in the market. Lost sales and price erosion are normally evaluated separately, but they should not be analyzed in isolation to prevent inconsistent results. If the infringer's conduct held down prices in the relevant market, it may be difficult for the patent owner to prove that he would have made that much of the sales.

Future lost profits

Future lost profits are losses that the patent owner expects to incur in the future due to the infringement. If the patent owner can project substantial losses far into the future, the potential rewards be large. However, future lost profits can be highly speculative. As a result, the courts are circumspect about awarding future lost profits and will not do so unless compelled to. Such unpredictability can be used by the infringer to his advantage.

Lost profits for pre-infringement conduct

In addition to past lost profits or for profits that would have made for products placed on the market, the patent owner is also entitled to lost profits as a result of infringer announcing a future infringing product. The patent owner may be entitled to recover damages for lost sales prior to the first sales of the infringing products.

8.4.2 Reasonable royalties

The CAFC uses two methods to calculate reasonable royalties: the analytical approach and hypothetical negotiation approach. The analytical approach calculates damages based on internal profit projections of the infringing item at the time the infringement began. It then apportions the projected profit between the parties as a percentage of sales to determine the reasonable royalty damages. In the hypothetical negotiation approach, reasonable royalty is defined as the amount which would have been set in a hypothetical negotiation between a willing licensor and a willing licensee in the infringer's position when the infringement began and both parties assumed the patent was valid and enforceable. As the analytical approach relies on getting internal financial documents from the patent infringer, which are usually difficult to obtain, the hypothetical negotiation approach is used more often in courts. This approach will be further analyzed in the next section.

8.4.2.1 *Georgia-Pacific factors*

The seminal case for the hypothetical approach is Georgia-Pacific Corp. versus United States Plywood Corp., 318 F. Supp. 1116 (S.D.N.Y. 1970), mod. and aff'd, 446 F.2d 295 (2d Cir. 1971), cert. denied, 404 U.S. 870 (1971). The hypothetical approach is a fictional "willing licensor-willing licensee" negotiation analyzed as of the date the infringement began. The negotiation requires that the royalty rate be determined on the assumption that the patent was valid and infringed. The courts may, however, consider evidence of events subsequent to the onset of infringement, in order to compensate for the difficulties and uncertainties in recreating the hypothetical negotiations. In this case, the court has put forward 15 factors for the determination of reasonable royalties as provided in Table 8.3. The factors are coded for easy reference later.

Not all the 15 factors may be applicable in any given case. In using the factors to determine the reasonable royalty, each factor will be examined. Some factors act to lower the royalty damages while others neutralize or increase it. The court, however, did not explain how these factors should be applied, explaining that "there is no formula by which . . . [they] can be rated precisely in the order of their relative importance or by which their economic significance can be automatically transduced into their pecuniary equivalent". Instead, the court would exercise "judicial discretion" to consider "all pertinent factors" based on the evidence.

As the patent litigation landscape evolves, applying the Georgia-Pacific factors, however, poses many problems. Most important of all, many patent damages are now tried before a jury, which has less time and

Table 8.3 Georgia-Pacific factors

Code	Code name	Code explanation (1970)
GF1	Established royalty	The royalties received by Georgia-Pacific for licensing the patent, proving or tending to prove an established royalty.
GF2	Rates for similar products	The rates paid by the licensee for the use of other similar patents.
GF3	Nature and scope of license	The nature and scope of the license, such as whether it is exclusive or non-exclusive, restricted or non-restricted in terms of territory or customers.
GF4	Patent monopoly power of licensor	Georgia-Pacific's policy of maintaining its patent monopoly by licensing the use of the invention only under special conditions designed to preserve the monopoly.
GF5	Commercial relationship between licensor and licensee	The commercial relationship between Georgia-Pacific and licensees, such as whether they are competitors in the same territory in the same line of business or whether they are inventor and promoter.
GF6	Sales generation power of patent	The effect of selling the patented specialty in promoting sales of other Georgia-Pacific products; the existing value of the invention to Georgia-Pacific as a generator of sales of non-patented items; and the extent of such derivative or "convoyed" sales.
GF7	Licensing terms	The duration of the patent and the term of the license.
GF8	Commercial success of patented product	The established profitability of the patented product, its commercial success and its current popularity.
GF9	Utility and advantage of patent property	The utility and advantages of the patent property over any old modes or devices that had been used.
GF10	Nature and character of patent invention	The nature of the patented invention, its character in the commercial embodiment owned and produced by the licensor, and the benefits to those who used it.

(*Continued*)

Table 8.3 (*Continued*)

Code	Code name	Code explanation (1970)
GF11	Benefits of patent to infringer	The extent to which the infringer used the invention and any evidence probative of the value of that use.
GF12	Industrial norms for products' profits	The portion of the profit or selling price that is customary in the particular business or in comparable businesses.
GF13	Profits attributed to the patent	The portion of the realizable profit that should be credited to the invention as distinguished from any non-patented elements, manufacturing process, business risks or significant features or improvements added by the infringer.
GF14	Expert opinions	The opinion testimony of qualified experts.
GF15	Hypothetical agreed royalty	The amount that Georgia-Pacific and a licensee would have agreed upon at the time the infringement began if they had reasonably and voluntarily tried to reach an agreement

expertise than a judge to decide the amount of damages. The jury is also not required to make a detailed written summary on the derivation of the damages amount for post-trial review. For example, in February 2007, Lucent was awarded $1.53 billion against Microsoft as a reasonable royalty for infringement of two patents used in the MP3 audio compression format (Lucent Techs., Inc. v. Gateway, Inc., 509 F. Supp. 2d 912 (S.D. Cal. 2007), *aff'd on other grounds*, 543 F.3d 710 (Fed. Cir. 2008). In October 2010, Mirror Worlds was awarded a total of $625.5 million as a reasonable royalty against Apple for infringement of three patents — $208.5 million per patent — by Apple's computers and mobile devices (Verdict Form, Mirror Worlds, LLC versus Apple, Inc., No. 6:08-CV-88 (E.D. Tex. Oct. 1, 2010)). The huge amount of damages increases the likelihood of an appeal case to the higher court to seek reversal to the jury's decision. The appeal raises the cost of legal fees even higher. All these add pressure for a desire to have a more structured way of finding reasonable royalties for awarding damages.

8.4.2.2 *Standard of evidence*

Factor 14 of the Georgia-Pacific factors states that expert testimony has to be considered. This expert testimony on the royalty rate proposed is subject to standards of evidence. Daubert versus Merell Dow Pharmaceuticals, Inc., 509 U.S. 579 (1993) set the standard for expert testimony to be admitted.

In Daubert, the Supreme Court ruled that the trial judges must ensure that expert testimony is both relevant to the case and is supported by a "reliable foundation." The Court provided a non-definitive list of factors it deemed relevant in determining whether an expert's methodology is "scientifically valid." These factors included whether the theory could be empirically tested, whether the theory has been subject to peer review, what the known or potential error rate is, the "existence and maintenance of standards controlling the technique's operation," and "general acceptance" of the theory.

The challenges in asserting the reliability of expert testimony typically center around the expert's qualifications and the quality of an expert's analysis. A court usually looks into an expert's education and experience to determine his or her qualifications. The reliability of an expert's analysis is determined by the acceptance of the methodology. Some common issues with the reliability of expert testimony may include misusing the Georgia-Pacific factors and adopting an incorrect hypothetical negotiation date. Testimony that fails the Daubert standard is inadmissible.

8.4.2.3 *Entire market value rule and apportionment in reasonable royalties*

Entire market value rule (EMVR)

EVMR was originally designed for the lost profit context. However, in Rite-Hite Corp. versus Kelley Co., Inc., it was established that a royalty award may be based on the entire unit if (1) the infringing component forms the basis for consumer demand for the entire product, (2) the infringing and non-infringing components are parts of a complete machine, or single assembly of parts, and (3) the infringing and non-infringing components are analogous to a single functioning unit. This is in effect the Entire Market Value Rule.

In 2012, the Federal Circuit, however, limited the application of EMVR to "narrow" circumstances in LaserDynamics, Inc. versus Quanta Computer, Inc., 694 F.3d 51, 67 (Fed. Cir. 2012). LaserDynamics claimed infringement to a patent describing "a method of optical disc discrimination" that allows optical disc drive to determine the type of disc inserted, for example, a CD or a DVD. Quanta used LaserDynamics' patent in manufacturing their laptops. The Court found that LaserDynamics failed to show the patent "drove demand for the laptop computers," the court denied application of EMVR and set a high evidentiary hurdle for plaintiffs in the future.

In general, the EMVR increases the royalty base, thereby increasing the reasonable royalty. It may be inappropriate to apply EMVR to reasonable royalties because patent owners seeking reasonable royalty awards are unable to make the sale that captures the entire market value of the product. Even if the EMVR can be applied in reasonable royalty damages, it is not the same as in the case of lost profits. EMVR for reasonable royalty merely expands the royalty base (Interactive Pictures Corp. versus Infinite Pictures, Inc., 274 F.3d 1371, 1384-86 (Fed. Cir. 2001)) to the entire product whereas a true application of the EMVR in the case of lost profits would award all profits from an infringing multi-component product to the patentee.

There are, however, some instances when the royalty rate can be partially increased. This is the scenario when Georgia Pacific factor 6, convoyed sales, "the effect of selling the patented specialty in promoting sales of other products of the licensee; that existing value of the invention to the licensor as a generator of sales of his non-patented items; and the extent of such derivative or convoyed sales" is to be considered. In Interactive Pictures, the Federal Circuit found no error by the district court's inclusion of the unpatented items in the royalty base and together with factoring the convoyed sales into the royalty rate. Moreover, in the context of the royalty rate, there appears to be no explicit requirement for a "functional unit". The patent owner may argue that the existence of convoyed sales by the infringer increases the reasonable royalty. On the other hand, the infringer could argue that the absence of convoyed sales decreases the royalty rate. Both do not need to prove that the unpatented and patented items form a functional unit or are part of a single assembly.

Apportionment

Apportionment seeks to limit a patentee's damages to the contributed value of the patent. Its origin dates back to Seymour versus McCormick 57 U.S. 480 (1854). The Supreme Court rejected a jury instruction that would have allowed a patent for an improvement to recover the same damages as a patent for the entire device. The first basic rule came about in Garretson versus Clark, 111 U.S. 120, 121 (1884), the court stated:

> "When a patent is for an improvement and not for an entirely new machine or contrivance, the patentee must show in what particulars his improvement has added to the usefulness of the machine or contrivance. He must separate its results distinctly from those of the other parts, so that the benefits derived from it may be distinctly seen and appreciated. ... The patentee ... must in every case give evidence tending to separate or apportion the defendant's profits and the patentee's damages between the patented feature and the unpatented features, and such evidence must be reliable and tangible, and not conjectural or speculative; or he must show, by equally reliable and satisfactory evidence, that the profits and damages are to be calculated on the whole machine, for the reason that the entire value of the whole machine, as a marketable article, is properly and legally attributable to the patented feature."

In fact, the concept of apportionment in reasonable royalty affects both the royalty base and the royalty rate. In consideration of the royalty base, it is most often reflected in taking the smallest saleable unit into account, instead of the entire product. In a way, this is similar to applying the EMVR in reasonable royalty damage awards. For example, in Lucent Technologies, Inc. versus Gateway, Inc. Lucent, 580 F.3d at 1336, the CAFC discussed the entire market value rule by stating that, in order to use the entire market value of the accused product as the royalty base and avoid apportionment, "the patentee must prove that the patent-related feature is the basis for customer demand… but [there] is nothing inherently wrong with using the market value of the entire product, especially when there is no established market value for the infringing component or feature, so long as the multiplier accounts for the proportion of the base represented by the infringing component or feature."

Similarly, in LaserDynamics Inc. versus Quanta Computer Inc., 694 F.3d 51, 67–68 (Fed. Cir. 2012), the court stated that "we reaffirm that in any case involving multi-component products, patentees may not calculate damages based on sales of the entire product, as opposed to the smallest salable patent-practicing unit, without showing that the demand for the entire product is attributable to the patented feature." All these cases show that appointment affects the royalty base.

In addition to affecting the royalty base, apportionment can also affect the royalty rate. This can be seen in the Federal Court's opinion in Ericsson, Inc. versus D-Link Systems, Inc., Nos. 13-1625, -1631, -1632, -1633 (Fed. Cir. Dec. 4, 2014). The court reiterated the decision in "VirnetX, Inc. versus Cisco Systems, Inc., 767 F.3d 1308 (Fed. Cir. 2014), where multicomponent products are involved, the governing rule is that the ultimate combination of royalty base and royalty rate must reflect the value attributable to the infringing features of the product, and no more." From an economic perspective, apportionment can occur via the royalty rate, the royalty base, or a combination that sufficiently reflects the contribution of the patented features to the accused products. The court mentioned in Ericsson, "a jury must ultimately apportion the defendant's profits and the patentee's damages between the patented feature and the unpatented features" using "reliable and tangible" evidence. This can be achieved by careful selection of the royalty base to reflect the value added by the patented feature, so far as differentiation is possible. It may also be realized by adjusting the royalty rate to discount the value of a product's non-patented features. A combination of both is possible too.

The court did, however, provide potential constraints on permissible base and rate combinations that may seem to be theoretically sound from an economic perspective but can be confusing to jurors. For example, the court mentioned that "It is not that an appropriately apportioned royalty award could never be fashioned by starting with the entire market value of a multi-component product — by, for instance, dramatically reducing the royalty rate to be applied in those cases — it is that reliance on the entire market value might mislead the jury, who may be less equipped to understand the extent to which the royalty rate would need to do the work in such instances". It also restated LaserDynamics versus Quanta that "barring the use of too high royalty base" — even if mathematically offset by a "low enough royalty rate" — because such a base "carries a considerable risk" of misleading a jury into overcompensating, stating that such a base "cannot help but skew the damages horizon for the jury" and "make a patentee's proffered damages amount appear modest by comparison." The court stated that "in each case, district courts must assess the extent to which the proffered testimony, evidence, and arguments would skew unfairly the jury's ability to apportion the damages to account only for the value attributable to the infringing features".

8.4.3 Principle of valuation and reasonable royalty

In Section 8.2.3, we introduced the influencing factors for valuing patents. Putting these factors into the context of determining reasonable royalties, the legal factors should still be first considered in the valuation of the patents. These factors establish whether there is a case for a valuable patent portfolio. Some examples of legal factors are legal status, protectability, enforceability, right of disposal, ownership, and approval restrictions. Some legal factors as covered products, scope of protection, some dimensions of enforceability, freedom to operate and relevant standards may add some intrinsic values to the patent portfolio during the valuation.

The technical factors primarily affect the royalty rate of the valuation. Some factors such as the technical and production-related feasibilities determine whether there is a case for valuation, meaning whether there is a need to consider further the rest of the technical factors and economic factors. They consider the inherent factors of the technology itself. Other factors consider the external technical factors. Factors such as technology life cycle and technical substitution will primarily determine the royalty rate. Technical field of applications will also affect the royalty base as more fields will result in more infringement products.

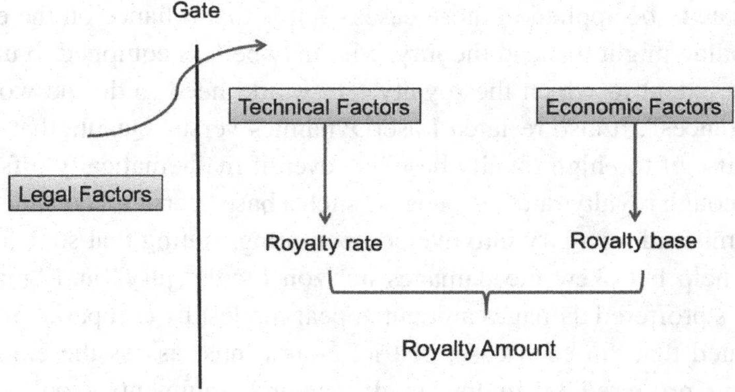

Figure 8.10 Relationship between LTE and reasonable royalty

Most economic factors determine the royalty base. The method of damages awards based on reasonable royalties is primarily based on the formula:

Damage amounts = royalty rate × royalty base.

The economic factors may help to determine whether the EMR or the Smallest Salable Units (SSU) shall be used for the total amount due. EMR and SSU are usually the most important factors to consider in damage calculation for patent litigation. Market potential and availability of complementary goods will directly affect the royalty base. The business models and interdependencies may also affect the royalty rate. An overview of the relationship between these factors and how they affect the valuation can be found in Figures 8.10 and 8.11.

8.4.4 Principles of valuation and Georgia-Pacific factors

Our discussion in Sections 8.4.2 and 8.4.3 shows that both Georgia-Pacific factors and the principle factors related to the LTE considerations are applicable for calculating the reasonable royalty. An important question that follows is what linkage there is between the LTE factors with the

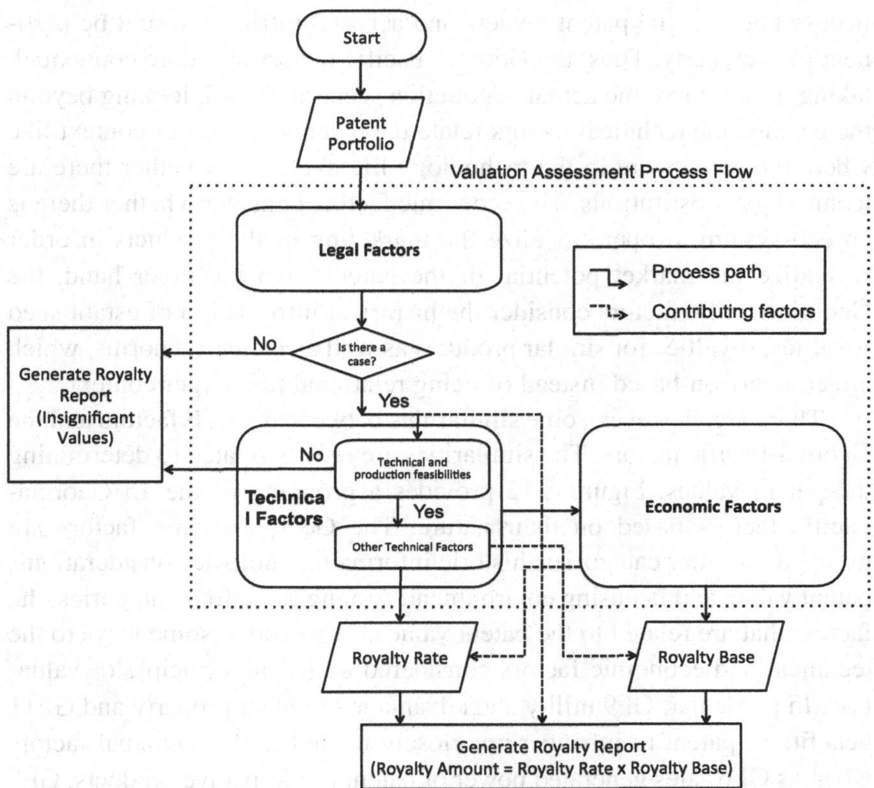

Figure 8.11 An overview of the fundamental process flow of determining reasonable royalty from the legal, technical and economic perspectives

Georgia-Pacific factors. Which of these are to be used? Are there conflicts in applying these two different sets of factors? What are the differences?

First, the LTE factors discussed under the principles of valuation are designed for the overall valuation of the patent portfolio. The amount of reasonable royalties obtained from each accused defendant is only a portion of this overall valuation. Second, the considerations of the LTE factors are purely between the patent and the technology and market, devoid of any relationship that the patents hold with the negotiating parties. The Georgia-Pacific factors provide many factors that guide the negotiation process by considering the licensing environment and how the particular license between the patent owners and accused infringer would be pertinent to each party. Thus, the Georgia-Pacific factors are more contextual, taking into account the actual negotiation scenario. Third, looking beyond the patents, the technical factors relate the patents to a larger context like where the patents are in the technology life cycle and whether there are technology substitutions. The economic factors consider whether there is an eco-system to operationalize the marketing of the products in order to realize the market potential of the patents. On the other hand, the Georgia-Pacific factors consider the historical information of established royalties, royalties for similar products as well as industrial norms, which are comparison-based instead of being relational to a larger context.

There are, however, some similarities between the LTE factors and the Georgia-Pacific factors. The similarities are mostly related to determining the patent values. Figure 8.12 provides a grouping of the 15 Georgia-Pacific factors based on their nature. The Georgia-Pacific factors are grouped into four categories: historic information, holistic considerations, patent value, and licensing environment. Among these four categories, the factors that are related to the patent value correspond in some ways to the technical and economic factors considered under the principle of valuation. In particular, GF9 utility and advantage of patent property and GF11 benefits of patent to infringer are closely related to the technical factors whereas GF6 sales generated power of patent for derivative products, GF8 commercial success of patented products and GF13 profits attributed purely by the patent are closely linked to the economic factors. GF10 nature and character of patent invention contribute both to the technical and economic factors.

From the figure, it can be seen that LTE factors and Georgia-Pacific factors complement each other for providing a valuation under different scenarios. LTE factors may be more useful for general financial valuation. Georgia-Pacific factors are meant for negotiation purposes. However, it should be noted that the two sets of factors are not meant for mutually exclusive scenarios and considerations. This is especially the case when the valuation is done for a business model for licensing, where negotiation viability applies. Thus, the Georgia-Pacific factors such as the industrial norms and established royalties should be considered. On the other hand, some of the LTE factors such as the technology cycle that the invention is

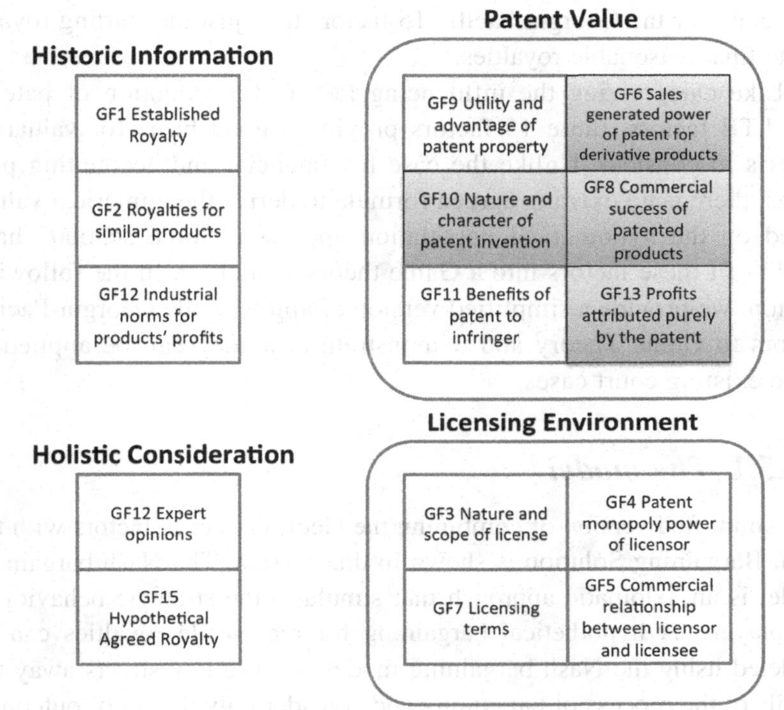

Figure 8.12 Grouping of the GF factors based on their nature

in, the business model might be able to help in determining the royalty rate and base.

8.4.5 Georgia-Pacific factors and Game Theory

In determining a reasonable royalty, the court will first determine the royalty base, starting royalty and then use the Georgia-Pacific factors to adjust the final reasonable royalty. In the first step, the court would check through the claims in the patent to determine whether the royalty base should be based on the entire product or just an element in the product. In the second step, the court will determine the starting royalty by considering similar established licenses, as well as the benefits of the patent to the patentee and licensee, respectively. In the third step, the court would then consider the Georgia-Pacific 15 factors to adjust the starting royalty to the final reasonable royalties.

Like categorizing the influencing factors for valuation of patents into LTE factors, these 15 factors provide a good basis for valuation experts to consider. Unlike the case for financial and accounting purposes, there is no existing agreed formula to derive the numerical values based on the hypothetical negotiation approach. Some scholars have tried to fit these factors into a Game theory model[12,13]. In the following section, we provide a simplified version of applying the Georgia-Pacific factors to Game Theory and demonstrate how they can be applied to some existing court cases.

8.4.5.1 *The model*

One simplified version of combining the Georgia-Pacific factors with the Nash Bargaining Solution is shown in this section. The Nash bargaining model is an axiomatic approach that simulates the strategic behavior of the players. A hypothetical bargaining for reasonable royalties can be modeled using the Nash bargaining model because it abstracts away the details of the process of bargaining and consider only the set of outcomes or agreements that satisfy "reasonable" properties. For obtaining player 1's and 2's payoff according to the Nash bargaining solution, let Π denote the total expected payoff if the negotiations are successful.[14] If the players decide to bargain over dividing the total expected payoff, they first agree to give each their respective disagreement payoffs and then they split the remaining payoff according to their negotiating power, α.

This can be represented using the Nash bargaining model with unequal bargaining power (Zimmeck, 2012)

---

[12]Zimmeck, S. 2012. A game-theoretic model for reasonable royalty calculation. *Alb. LJ Sci. & Tech.*, 22: 357–433.

[13]Choi, W., & Weinstein, R. 2001. Analytical solution to reasonable royalty rate calculations, an idea, 41: 49.

[14]William Choi and Roy Weinstein provide an example of this. Choi & Weinstein, *supra*note 30, at 54–55.

the payoff for player 1, the licensor is given by:

$$\pi_1 = d_1 + \alpha\,(\Pi - d_1 - d_2)$$

the payoff for player 2, the licensee is given by:

$$\pi_2 = d_2 + (1-\alpha)\,(\Pi - d_1 - d_2)$$

π_1, π_2 : payoffs for player 1 and 2, respectively
Π: total expected payoff
d_1: patent holder's disagreement payoff
d_2: licensee's disagreement payoff
α: bargaining power

In calculating the reasonable royalty, player 1 should get back the portion of payoff that is attributed only to the value of the patents. Therefore, the payoff for player 2 should be the profit margin that he gets from the product sales minus the value attributed to the value of the patent. If the margin is calculated per number of units and per unit time, e.g., one year, then another equation can be formed.

$$\pi_2 = (\mathrm{m} - \nu)\,\mathrm{Xt}$$

m: margins
v: profits attributed to patents
X: number of units sold
t: duration of hypothetical license

Therefore, reasonable royalty, s can be calculated as:

$$\text{reasonable royalty, s} = \pi_1 = d_1 + \alpha\left(\frac{\pi_2 - d_2}{1-\alpha}\right)$$

The corresponding Georgia-Pacific factors that are involved in calculating these terms are shown in Figure 8.13.

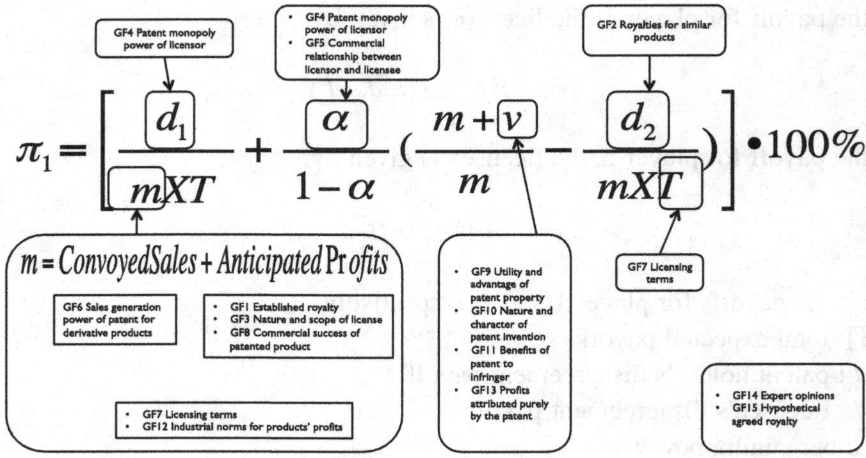

Figure 8.13 Correspondence between Georgia Pacific factors and Nash Bargaining solution

8.4.5.2 *Some examples using the Georgia-Pacific factors with Game Theory*

Using LexisNexus, the cases where judges have referenced the Georgia-Pacific case since 1995 have been identified. There are 96 cases cited. After some manual sorting, those cases where these factors have been discussed (35 cases out of 96, i.e., 36%) were singled out and included in the study. The criteria used to select those cases are the mention of the initial and final royalty, the calculation basis and the use of the Georgia-Pacific 15 factors to determine the final royalty. Only 10 cases out of these 35 cases fulfill these criteria. Based on this completeness of financial information, the data was applied to the Nash bargaining solutions to give a quantified analysis based on the Georgia Pacific factors. With sufficient financial information provided, the corresponding reasonable royalty rates can be calculated.

Figure 8.14 shows the results of the 10 cases that provided relevant information for this research. For example, in the case Procter & Gamble Co. versus Paragon Trade Brands (1997) (989 F. Supp. 547), the court decided the royalty to be 8.0%. With the Nash bargaining

Cases	Court assigned royalties (%)	Royalty calculated based on Nash bargaining solution (%)	% difference
I4i v Microsoft	19.6	4.02	79.5
P&G v Paragon	8	8.01	- 0.1
Revolution v Aspex	5	4.99	0.2
Presidio v ATC	12	12.51	- 4.25
Ball v Limited Brand	20	20.55	- 2.75
Boss v JBL	7	6.93	1
Finjan v Secure Computing	8	7.86	1.75
Fresenius v Baxter	3.4	3.27	3.8
Paymaster v US	3.5	3.70	- 5.7
Wright v US	4.5 with upfront	5.43	- 20.7

Figure 8.14 Comparison between court assigned royalties and those calculated from Nash Bargaining solution

solution described above, the calculated reasonable royalty was 8.01%. In another case Revolution Eyewear versus Aspex Eyewear (2008) 2008 WL 6873809 (C.D.Cal.), the court decided reasonable royalty was 5%. After considering all the Georgia-Pacific factors and fitting into the Nash Bargaining solution, the calculated reasonable royalty was 4.99%.

However, among the ten cases, two gave rise to inconsistencies between the court-decided reasonable royalties and the Nash Bargaining solution. They are i4i versus Microsoft (2009) (670 F. Supp. 2d 568 (E.D. Tex. 2009), aff'd, 598 F.3d 831 (Fed. Cir. 2010), cert. granted, 79 U.S.L.W. 3128 (U.S. Nov. 29, 2010) (No.10-290)) and Wright versus US (2002) (53 Fed. Cl. 466 (2002)). In i4i versus Microsoft, the court calculated the reasonable royalty rate to be 19.6%, whereas using the Nash Bargaining solution the calculated rate was 4.02%. The percentage difference between them is 79.5%. In Wright versus US, the court calculated the reasonable royalty rate to be 4.5%, whereas the Nash Bargaining solution gave 5.43. The percentage difference between them is –20.7%. These discrepancies are discussed in the following section.

Discrepancies

Among the ten cases analyzed, eight of them are within the 5% difference between the court determined reasonable royalties and the reasonable royalties calculated by the Nash Bargaining solution. Two out of the 10 cases resulted in 79.5% and −20.7% differences. Looking into the judgments from the court, it is found out that in the case of i4i versus Microsoft (2009), the judge clearly stated that Microsoft's failure to file a pre-verdict JMOL prevented the court from using the necessary information in the damage calculations. If Microsoft had filed this pre-verdict JMOL, the results might have been different. In the results obtained from the Nash Bargaining solution, all the market information provided in the judgment was used to arrive at the calculated results.

In the case of Wright versus US (2002), the reasonable royalties given by the court were with an upfront payment. Therefore, the reasonable royalties should have been higher if this upfront payment was to be converted into a running royalty rate. In the results calculated using the Nash Bargaining solution, only the running royalty rate is calculated and this is higher than the amount given by the court. Therefore, it is consistent with this argument.

From this analysis, we notice that GF 4, Patent monopoly power of licensor and GF5 Commercial relationship between licensor and licensee affect the calculated reasonable royalties significantly. Therefore, even if this simple pairing between the Nash Bargaining Solution and the 15 Georgia-Pacific factors is simplistic in nature, we can still conclude that qualitatively, these two factors will determine the overall trend of the negotiation outcome. Thus, buyers and sellers should consider their commercial relationship and monopoly power when preparing for negotiation.

8.5 Standard Essential Patents

8.5.1 Modified Georgia-Pacific factors

The Georgia-Pacific factors are useful in most licensing scenarios. However, in the case of standard essential patents, some adjustments are needed. This has recently been addressed in the FRAND case Microsoft Corp. versus Motorola Inc. (No. 2:10-cv-01823-JLR (W.D. Wash. April 25, 2013). This judgment was later appealed by Motorola to the Federal Circuit. Microsoft managed to move the case to the Ninth Circuit. The decision was finally handed down in July 2015. The Ninth Circuit affirmed the decision by the district court on the FRAND calculation.

The case started in early October 2010 when Microsoft accused Motorola of patent infringement of smartphone related patents in both the US International Trade Commission (ITC) and W.D. Washington district court. Motorola responded by sending two letters to Microsoft offering a license for Motorola's patents, which were claimed to be essential to the IEEE 802.11 WiFi standard and the ITU-T H.264 video encoding standard. Motorola sought a royalty of 2.25% of the price of Microsoft's end products using that technology. These products included the XBox 360 game consoles, surface tablets, or Windows with video encoding capability. Under the rules of ITU and IEEE, royalties for patents covering H.264 and 802.11 must comply with FRAND requirements. According to Microsoft, Motorola's royalty demands were anything but "reasonable" and would have resulted in royalty payments in excess of $4 billion per year. Microsoft responded by seeking a declaratory judgment that Motorola had breached its FRAND licensing obligations. The judgment on FRAND royalties came about because Motorola then sued Microsoft in W.D. Wisconsin district court seeking to stop Microsoft from using the H.264 patents. At the same time Motorola sued Microsoft in the ITC seeking to exclude importation of Microsoft's Xbox products. The district court cases were then consolidated before Judge Robart in W.D. Washington district court.

In November 2012, Judge Robart held a bench trial to determine what would be a range of reasonable FRAND royalty rate and what would be the specific FRAND royalty rate to apply for this case between Microsoft and Motorola. Eventually, on April 25, 2013, Judge Robart issued the long anticipated ruling to set a FRAND royalty for the Motorola 802.11 and H.264 patents in application to Microsoft's alleged infringing products. He found a FRAND royalty rate of 0.555 cents per unit (from a reasonable FRAND range from 0.555 to 16.389 cents per unit) for Motorola's H.264 video encoding patents and a FRAND royalty rate of 3.471 cents per unit (in a range from 0.8 to 19.5 cents per unit) for Motorola's 802.11 WiFi patents. Both of these rates were far below the 2.25% of the end-unit selling price (which translates into about $4.50 per $199 Xbox) that Motorola requested in its initial offer letters to Microsoft.

Judge Robart's legal framework for resolving FRAND was premised on a modified *Georgia-Pacific* royalty rate with adjustments made to take into account the FRAND commitment. According to Judge Robart, SEPs are valued separately from the value associated with the incorporation of the patented technology into the standard. However, SEPs should be valued in light of the contribution of the patented technology to the capabilities of the standard, and how that standard adds values to the licensee and its products. The valuation should also consider the alternatives that could have been incorporated into the standard instead of the patented technology. In taking license agreements into consideration, they should not be those that resulted from settling SEPs disputes or those that were concluded after imminent litigation. Instead, the royalty rate should be relative to the overall licensing landscape relating to the standard and the licensee's products.

The modified Georgia-Pacific factors are summarized in Table 8.4.

8.5.2 Implications of the Microsoft-Motorola ruling

Many practitioners argued that the framework used by Judge Robart to determine a FRAND royalty rate is bad news for patent holders that rely on license fees for essential technology. The guideline provided by Robart presented a methodology for technology implementers to negotiate patent holders' licensing demands downwards. If the negotiation stalls, they can seek recourse from the court. This shifts the balance of power away from patent holders. In the past, there was a lot of uncertainty about the FRAND rate and patent holders' threats to demand injunctions pushed the implementers to a corner when faced with SEPs. Implementers may eventually settle on a rate that is not fair.

Table 8.4 Modified GF for FRAND royalty calculation

Code	Code explanation (1970)	Judge Robart's modification (2013)
GF1	The royalties received by Georgia-Pacific for licensing the patent, proving or tending to prove an established royalty.	"In the FRAND context, such licensing royalties for a given patent(s) must be comparable to FRAND licensing circumstances. In other words, to prove an established royalty rate for an SEP, the past royalty rates for a patent must be negotiated under the FRAND obligation or a comparable negotiation. Thus, license agreements where the parties clearly understood the FRAND obligation, and as discussed below, patent pools, will be relevant to a hypothetical negotiation for SEPs."
GF2	The rates paid by the licensee for the use of other similar patents.	No modification.
GF3	The nature and scope of the license, such as whether it is exclusive or non-exclusive, restricted or non-restricted in terms of territory or customers.	No modification.
GF4	Georgia-Pacific's policy of maintaining its patent monopoly by licensing the use of the invention only under special conditions designed to preserve the monopoly.	"This factor is inapplicable in the FRAND context because the licensor has made a commitment to license on FRAND terms and may no longer maintain a patent monopoly by not licensing to others. In fact, as the court has found in this case, the FRAND commitment requires the SEP owner to grant licenses on FRAND terms to all implementers of the standard."

(*Continued*)

Table 8.4 (*Continued*)

Code	Code explanation (1970)	Judge Robart's modification (2013)
GF5	The commercial relationship between Georgia-Pacific and licensees, such as whether they are competitors in the same territory in the same line of business or whether they are inventor and promoter.	"Similar to factor 4, this factor does not apply in the FRAND context. This is because having committed to license on FRAND terms, the patentee no longer may discriminate against its competitors in terms of licensing agreements. Instead, as explained, the patent owner is obligated to license all implementers on reasonable terms."
GF6	The effect of selling the patented specialty in promoting sales of other Georgia-Pacific products; the existing value of the invention to Georgia-Pacific as a generator of sales of non-patented items; and the extent of such derivative or "convoyed" sales.	"Although these factors [6 and 8] are relevant to a reasonable royalty in the FRAND context, it is important to focus the analysis of both of these factors on the value of the patented technology apart from the value associated with incorporation of the patented technology into the standard. With respect to Factors 6 and 8, a reasonable royalty would not take into account the value to the licensee created by the existence of the standard itself, but would instead consider the contribution of the patent to the technical capabilities of the standard and also the contribution of those relevant technological capabilities to the implementer and the implemented products."
GF7	The duration of the patent and the term of the license.	"The analysis concerning Factor 7 is greatly simplified in the context of a dispute over a reasonable royalty for a FRAND-committed patent because the term of the license would equate to the duration of the patent. In many circumstances, this factor will have little influence on what constitutes a reasonable royalty under the FRAND commitment."

GF8	The established profitability of the patented product, its commercial success and its current popularity.	As mentioned in GF6.
GF9	The utility and advantages of the patent property over any old modes or devices that had been used.	"Through this factor, the parties to a hypothetical negotiation under a FRAND commitment would consider alternatives that could have been written into the standard instead of the patented technology. The focus is on the period before the standard was adopted and implemented (i.e., *ex ante*). Thus, through factor 9, Microsoft's incremental approach to determination of a FRAND royalty rate is realized, in part."
GF10	The nature of the patented invention, its character in the commercial embodiment owned and produced by the licensor, and the benefits to those who used it.	"In the FRAND context, both of these factors [10 and 11] focus the hypothetical negotiation on the contribution of the patent to the technical capabilities of the standard and also the contribution of those relevant technical capabilities to the implementer and the implementer's products. Again, in such an analysis, however, it is important to separate the patented technology from the value associated with incorporation of the patented technology into the standard. Nevertheless, evidence of the benefit and value of the patent to the owner and implementer is relevant to the contribution of the patent to the certain capabilities of the standard, as well as the contribution of the standard's capabilities to the implementer."

(*Continued*)

Table 8.4 (*Continued*)

Code	Code explanation (1970)	Judge Robart's modification (2013)
GF11	The extent to which the infringer used the invention and any evidence probative of the value of that use.	As mentioned in GF10.
GF12	The portion of the profit or selling price that is customary in the particular business or in comparable businesses.	"This factor must be viewed through the lens of business practices involving FRAND commitments. In other words, licensing fees for non-FRAND committed patents customary in a business industry cannot form the basis for comparison. Instead, factor 12 must look to customary practices of businesses licensing FRAND-committed patents."
GF13	The portion of the realizable profit that should be credited to the invention as distinguished from any non-patented elements, manufacturing process, business risks or significant features or improvements added by the infringer.	"As with many of the other factors, in the FRAND context, it is critical to consider the contribution of the patented technology apart from the value of the patent as the result of its incorporation into the standard, the latter of which would improperly reward the SEP owner for the value of the standard itself. Rewarding the SEP owner with any of the value of the standard itself would constitute hold-up value and be contrary to the purpose behind the FRAND commitment."
GF14	The opinion testimony of qualified experts.	No modification.

GF15	The amount that Georgia-Pacific and a licensee would have agreed upon at the time the infringement began if they had reasonably and voluntarily tried to reach an agreement.	"The SEP owner and the implementer would consider the FRAND commitment and its purposes in their efforts to reach a license agreement. In trying to reach an agreement, the SEP owner would have been obligated to license its SEPs on FRAND terms which necessarily must abide by the purpose of the FRAND commitment of widespread adoption of the standard through avoidance of holdup and stacking." "With respect to hold-up, the parties would examine a reasonable royalty rate under the FRAND commitment based on the contribution of the patented technology to the capabilities of the standard, and in turn, the contribution of those capabilities of the standard to the implementer and the implementer's products." "With respect to stacking concerns, the parties attempting to reach an agreement would consider the overall licensing landscape in existence vis-a-vis the standard and the implementer's products. In other words, a FRAND negotiation would not be conducted in a vacuum. The parties would instead consider other SEP holders and the royalty rate that each of these patent holders might seek from the implementer based the importance of these other patents to the standard and to the implementer's products."

Robart's decision was based on hypothetical bilateral negotiation. He analyzed the relative significance of Motorola's patents to the two standard-essential technologies at issue in the case. The conclusion was that Motorola's role in both was very minor. There were thousands of patents on each technology. Motorola was responsible for 16 patents related to the video compression standard and 24 to the standard wireless communications technology. None of these was at the core of either standard nor were they at the core of any of Microsoft's products. In fact, Motorola's video compression patents involved technology that was increasingly irrelevant in the marketplace. The 11 Motorola wireless communications patents incorporated in Microsoft's products were only minimally important. This implies that each patent has to be evaluated individually on its own contribution. Being a SEP does not mean the right ticket to extort high royalty rates.

Faced with the problem of royalty stacking, Robart agreed that patent pool rates could be useful considerations, though they typically charge less than individual patent holders. This can be good news for technology implementers like Microsoft and for consumers. However, for this may discourage SEPs owners from participating in a standard-setting process or from contributing relevant patents to the standard if they cannot charge sufficient licensing fees to recoup their investments in developing the SEPs. In the end, the standard might not incorporate the best available technology. Only time will show the effects of this ruling. But for now, a framework for determining the reasonable royalty rate for FRAND has finally been established.

8.6 Royalty Contracts, Terms and Conditions

8.6.1 Types of royalties

Finally, to operationalize the collection of royalty fees, the latter have to be included in the terms and conditions of a contract. There are several common types of royalties that the patent owner can collect by licensing out the technology. The traditional royalty fees are collected as licenses for the use of the technology. Alternatively, an advanced payment is a popular type of royalty collection for a patent owner to continue the development of technology. This is increasingly popular in recent years with the current economy that segments the supply chain. More companies are involved in just the R&D portion of the production. Many of these companies do not have the pool of resources enjoyed by the R&D departments in large companies in the past. The advanced payments provide funding for these entrepreneurs for the next stage of research. With all the policies to suppress the negative impact of NPEs, many smaller NPEs are switching investments to developing seed patents. They license out the seed patents at relatively lower royalty rates but with an upfront or advanced payment. The R&D Company can then fund the next stage of research. In the process, more patents can be generated and these patents can be further licensed out at a slightly higher rate because the patent portfolio becomes larger and there are lesser risks compared to the initial stage.

There are also scenarios where the technologies have already been fully developed but not taken up yet. In order for the technology to be successfully transferred and applied at the licensees' premises, the patent owner can provide a technology transfer service to ensure that the production lines are properly set up and the quality of products from that technology is guaranteed. For this assurance, the patent owner charges a technology transfer fee.

8.6.2 Basis for royalty calculation

The income approach, cost approach, market approach, Georgia-Pacific factors, and Game Theory are methodologies that have been carefully designed for professionals in the field to calculate the values of patents. These methods, however, can be intimidating for the C-suites who are down in the field negotiating licensing deals. Therefore, there is a need for some general guidelines to help them reach a quick decision whether a counter offer is acceptable and whether the company should develop their own technology instead. Usually, the value of the technology is calculated based on:

- The cost of technology development;
- The cost of continual technology development;

- The profits received from the products using that technology;
- The real needs by the potential licensee.

Besides the nature of benefits from the technology, licensing parties may consider other dimensions of licensing scope for negotiation. For example,

- The length of license;
- The field of application for the technology;
- The geographic coverage of the license.

With these basic guidelines, the royalty rate can be calculated as the product of the sales volume and the royalty rate. Usually, the net sales volumes are used because that resembles a hypothetical negotiation between the two parties where they share the gains from the use of the technology. Technology implementers would be at a disadvantage if the gross sales volume are used. Their earnings would be much less after deducting taxes, insurance, transportation, and other costs. Licensing agreements can never be concluded if the licensee loses money as a result of paying for the licensing fees. In negotiating a license, the items to be deducted from gross sales should be specified with no ambiguity. As mentioned, some examples of such deductions are company tax, import tax, excise, transportation, insurance, sales commission, sales return, etc. Only when there are no products involved in the licensing of technology will the gross sales be used.

The above method of deriving the royalty amount can be useful in licensing contract negotiations and should be used with the carefully designed methodologies for patent valuation.

8.6.3 Modes of collecting royalties

8.6.3.1 *Lump sum payment*

There are a lot of flexibilities and innovative solutions targeted at the collection of royalty fees, depending on the needs of the two parties. Settlement fees resulting from litigation cases or imminent litigation threats are very often collected as a lump sum payment. This is also the case when the potential licensees have already been using the technology for some time and there is no technology transfer involved.

8.6.3.2 *Upfront payment*

For new adoptions of technology, especially when the technology provider is pushing the technology to be adopted by technology implementers, the royalty fee to be collected is usually in the form of an upfront payment with subsequent quarterly or annual installments. The upfront payment is crucial for many start-ups and SMEs who do not have much cash to circulate. The initial payment funds them so that they can further develop the technology or use it to start the next wave of technology development. In collecting running royalties, companies need to specify how the quantity produced should be reported on a regular basis. Most importantly, for the running royalty system to operate efficiently, there should be a dedicated professional to follow up on the reporting. External auditing firms should be engaged biannually or annually to carry out royalty audits. If not done properly, the company will suffer from inadequate collection of running royalties. Many start-ups and SMEs, in particular, suffer from the failure to collect running royalties simply because they do not have the work force to monitor the process.

8.6.3.3 *Advanced payment*

Another type of payment mode similar to the lump sum payment is the advanced payment. The total sum to be collected in the case of an advanced payment is less than an upfront payment, if the royalty rate is the same. The licensee pays, in advance, one lump sum, such as $50,000. Subsequent running royalties are deducted from the $50,000 progressively until this amount runs out, the next $50,000 will then be due. There may also be adjustments to the royalty rate when the first advanced payment is due. The advantages of collecting advanced payments are that there are less administrative difficulties in the collection of royalties. The licensors will also gain from the boost to their cash flow.

8.6.3.4 *Milestone payment*

When the licensing agreement involves a technology transfer, they may be collected in milestone payments. This provides an opportunity for the licensee to monitor the progress of the technology transfer. For example, one milestone can be set at the completion of setting up the production line. The second milestone can be the successful production of sample run, while the third milestone can be the first production run. Such arrangements provide incentives for the licensor to solve any problems encountered during the technology transfer. It also provides a form of insurance for the licensee.

Besides the attractiveness to the licensee, the licensor can also use the milestone payments to incentivize the licensee to increase the production volume. If the quantity produced has reached a certain amount, e.g., 10,000 pieces, the royalty rate for the next 10,000 pieces would be reduced by 20%. Such arrangements encourage the licensee to push for the use of the technology, thus benefiting both licensor and licensee.

8.7 Conclusion

In this chapter, we have provided an overview of the various methods of patent valuation. The principle of valuation laid out the guiding factors for awarding values to patents whereas the valuation approaches commonly used in the financial industry provided ways to include the intangible assets into the accounting books.

Patent damages is a topic that we have dwelt on extensively. From the lost profits to reasonable royalties calculation, we explored ways that the U.S. judicial courts have used to award values to patents. The analytical approach for awarding damages in patent infringement cases bears resemblance to the accounting approaches used in the industry. Reasonable royalties calculation draws information from the LTE factors described in the principle of valuation. For example, the legal factors determine the validity of the patents; the technical factors contribute to the royalty rate, and the economic factors affect the royalty base of calculation.

Reasonable royalty calculation based on the Georgia-Pacific factors is another area of patent valuation that cannot be ignored. Like the

LTE factors, the Georgia-Pacific factors can be grouped into categories. Those factors related to patent value are similar to the technical and economic factors. As Georgia-Pacific factors are designed for negotiation between two parties, the historical information, holistic considerations and licensing environment factors provide the context for valuation. When valuation is required for a business using licensing as the business model, the Georgia-Pacific factors can complement the general principle of valuation.

Valuation is a complex process and requires extensive research on the background information in addition to the know-how for determining the appropriate methods for valuation. The methods of patent valuation are still evolving and will continue to be an exciting and demanding research area.

Bibliography

Zimmeck, S. 2012. A Game-Theoretic Model for Reasonable Royalty Calculation. *Alb. LJ Sci. & Tech.*, 22, 357–433.

Index

N

O

P

Printed in the United States
By Bookmasters